Advance Praise for

Enough Blood Shed

Practical, possible and   inspiration,
motivation, exam   n leave
this worl

So many of   t.
Ashford'
and spec

Enough Blood Shed   of peace
and enforcing the   ity at the
crossroads of glob   e, where
ordinary people, b   to bring
about peaceful   ar and
preparations fo   s lend
themselves to h   so that

— Dr. Ron McCoy,   uclear War
and member of   eapons

Mary-Wynne Ashford makes a loving, soul-filled argument that lawful, peaceful world culture is possible and already on the way. Take heart, she demands: Find your place in the global parade of civil conscience. She shares an astonishing array of inspiring examples from all over the world to prove it can be done and how to do it. The message is clear: love life, live with hope, and seek common ground in conflict. I thought I was a seasoned peacemaker. I'm in awe of all that she has opened my eyes to see and my heart to know about staying the course of non-violent peacemaking.

— David Hall, author of *Stop Arguing and Start Understanding: Eight Steps to Solving Family Conflicts*

Exciting. Creative. Concrete. It would be hard to over-praise *Enough Blood Shed;* I have never seen a better format for the presentation of peace themes in such a vivid and compelling style. Ashford and Dauncey have scored a hit.

— Canadian Senator Emeritus Douglas Roche, O.C.

This book is for all of us who feel fear and despair about the future of our violent world, and who care deeply about what is ahead for the children and all the other cohabitant species of the planet. Mary-Wynne Ashford tells us scores of things we can get up and do. Her joy and faith in humanity illuminate each page.

— Joanna Santa Barbara, Centre for Peace Studies, McMaster University; past-president of Physicians for Global Survival, past-vice-president of International Physicians for Prevention of Nuclear War

Enough Blood Shed is a timely and thoughtful reminder to us all that enough lives have been lost through senseless violence in our times. It provides a roadmap for peace advocates in diverse settings, exploring ways to address differences in less conflictive ways and identifying practical measures for those who aspire to build a future that is different from the past. It is must reading for policy makers and activists alike who wish to reframe the struggle against terrorism, and build a peace that is both just and durable.

— Prof. Ed Garcia, Senior Policy Advisor, International Alert, U.K. and author, *A Journey of Hope*

MARY-WYNNE ASHFORD with GUY DAUNCEY

Foreword by ARUN GANDHI

ENOUGH BLOOD SHED

101 SOLUTIONS TO VIOLENCE, TERROR AND WAR

NEW SOCIETY PUBLISHERS

Cataloging in Publication Data:

A catalog record for this publication is available from the National Library of Canada.

Cover design by Diane McIntosh. Images: Melina Mara/*Kitsap Sun*; Getty Images, Brand X Pictures.

Printed in Canada.
First printing May 2006.

New Society Publishers acknowledges the support of the Government of Canada through the Book Publishing Industry Development Program (BPIDP) for our publishing activities.

Paperback ISBN 13: 978- 0-86571-527-1
Paperback ISBN 10: 0-86571-527-0

Inquiries regarding requests to reprint all or part of *Enough Blood Shed* should be addressed to New Society Publishers at the address below.

To order directly from the publishers, please call toll-free (North America) 1-800-567-6772, or order online at www.newsociety.com

Any other inquiries can be directed by mail to:
New Society Publishers
P.O. Box 189, Gabriola Island, BC V0R 1X0, Canada
1-800-567-6772

New Society Publishers' mission is to publish books that contribute in fundamental ways to building an ecologically sustainable and just society, and to do so with the least possible impact on the environment, in a manner that models this vision. We are committed to doing this not just through education, but through action. We are acting on our commitment to the world's remaining ancient forests by phasing out our paper supply from ancient forests worldwide. This book is one step toward ending global deforestation and climate change. It is printed on acid-free paper that is **100% old growth forest-free** (100% post-consumer recycled), processed chlorine free, and printed with vegetable-based, low-VOC inks. For further information, or to browse our full list of books and purchase securely, visit our website at: www.newsociety.com

NEW SOCIETY PUBLISHERS   www.newsociety.com

Contents

Author's Preface

by Guy Dauncey

This is a book about war, and the end of war.

For those who have been fortunate enough to avoid war, its horrors should be learnt by a careful reading of history. For those who have lived through war, or participated in one, its horrors are hard to describe.

The fear, the explosions, the knives, the bullets, the bombs. The limbs torn off; the bellies torn apart. The rapes; the babies smashed against walls for the perverted pleasure of the killers. The generals in their bunkers who give the orders. The cities that are obliterated. The soldiers in uniform who kill and die. The civilians whose homes are destroyed, who may be massacred or taken into slavery. The guerillas, freedom fighters, terrorists, and suicide bombers who believe they are making the world a better place. The engineers who devote their careers to designing better weapons. The priests who bless them.

It is all so crazy, and ours is the generation that can end it.

Mankind must put an end to war, or war will put an end to mankind. John F. Kennedy

Many animal species fight on Planet Earth. They fight for food, space, sex, power, and sometimes just because they are irritated or their hormones are raging. Fighting is one of the methods that many species use to survive.

Successful fighting allows a species to pass on more of its genes, rewarding the habit of aggression. Unsuccessful fighting teaches the wisdom of withdrawal and submission. In this way, evolution rewards both aggression and submission. What ants, caribou, and flies lack in fangs, they make up in numbers.

For humans, warfare has become established deep within our psyches. Boys play with guns and go "Bang! Bang!" We have often celebrated victories and glorified war, forgetting those who were maimed or who never came home to say what it was really like.

But humans have a choice. However, if we imagine we have some biological imperative to fight, we are surrendering our free will. We can sit up and ask ourselves, "Is this an intelligent thing to do?"

And here's the interesting thing. We have fought for our clans, tribes, and nations, both defensively and aggressively. But we have also pursued a different dream: a quest to know what lay beyond the furthest horizon, what lay behind the mysteries of nature, what it would take to achieve a lasting peace or justice for all humanity.

Who knows where this other dream comes from? One day, maybe, we will discover its source. As a result of this quest, however, we have gradually widened the boundaries of our consciousness. We used to think "I am a member of the High Rock Clan; those other people are my enemies." Then, after generations of conflict, trade, victory, defeat, and intermarriage, we thought "I am a member of the North Nation; those other nations are my enemies." Generation by generation, we mustered our way towards unity.

When the Prophet Mohammed became inspired with the insights that gave birth to the Muslim religion, he did so in order to create unity among the warring chiefs and factions who all worshipped their own local gods. When he had achieved his victories, the peace, science, and wisdom of the Muslim civilization stretched from Cordoba in Spain to the frontiers of India.

Today we stand on the threshold of one last step into a single global civilization that will bring peace to all. With a few minor exceptions, and one major one, the people of this planet increasingly think "I am a member of the Earth people; I have no enemies." When we sing "Let there be peace on Earth, and let it begin with me," this is what we are saying: that we should contribute to peace in our personal lives, in our families, in our schools and communities, between the nations, and in the world.

The exceptions are those who still think in limited terms, whose primary identity still rests with a limited clan, religion, or nation, and not with the whole of humankind, and who think "We are better than you, so we deserve to dominate you." This generates conflicts, but if we attempt to solve them with more conflict, in a world that contains 30,000 nuclear warheads, we risk global suicide. We must therefore learn how to act on the nonviolent belief that "peace is the way." The solutions in this book are aimed at these exceptions, which represent the final hurdles to a world without war.

This book is the work and inspiration of Mary-Wynne Ashford; I have been just a small voice of encouragement and support. The vision that underlies her book says "Enough blood has been shed. Now is the time to engage in the peaceful, assertive, nonviolent resolution of our remaining conflicts."

This is a challenge that we cannot afford to refuse, and why should we refuse it, for the prize is the greatest of all: to put an end to war. In the words of folksinger Ed McCurdy:

Last night I had the strangest dream
I'd ever dreamed before
I dreamed the world had all agreed
To put an end to war
I dreamed I saw a mighty room
Filled with women and men
And the paper they were signing said
They'd never fight again
And when the paper was all signed
And a million copies made
They all joined hands and bowed their heads
And grateful pray'rs were prayed
And the people in the streets below
Were dancing `round and `round
While swords and guns and uniforms
Were scattered on the ground
Last night I had the strangest dream
I'd never dreamed before
I dreamed the world had all agreed
To put an end to war.

— TRO ©1950,1951 & 1955
Almanac Music, Inc. New York, NY

Author's Preface

by Mary-Wynne Ashford

Twenty-five years ago, when I began working with International Physicians for the Prevention of Nuclear War, I recognized that disarmament was only one dimension of our work. We would also have to examine the roots of war and try to understand why, for over 5,000 years, human groups have repeatedly chosen to use violence to dominate others. And perhaps more importantly, we must investigate what makes some societies choose *not* to use violence to dominate others.

For my doctoral research into the roots of war and genocide, I studied societies that plunged into wars that were characterized by unrelieved depravity and brutality. These stories demonstrated that, again and again, individuals gave up their moral inhibitions and assumed a group ethos of savagery.

At the same time, the research revealed extraordinary acts of courage and compassion by individuals and groups who rose to great heights of heroism in their resistance to the call to war. Those stories have sustained me through many dark times when, despite enormous efforts by civil society, nations have yet again chosen to go to war.

As I began writing this book, I found hundreds of stories of successful nonviolent actions, including many that were breathtaking in their audacity and power. It gradually dawned on me that these were not simply isolated stories. They represent a global revolution in our thinking about power and domination. Wherever I looked, people were taking a stand, putting their lives on the line in service of a greater good. I have tried to give a flavor of the scope of actions taking place around the world, and I have listed the websites where more information is available.

In my speeches I often tell the stories of those who have stood against the storms of hatemongering, and succeeded in preventing or ending violence. Many of the stories involve women, particularly women in countries where they don't even have the right to vote. People have often told me years later how much it meant to hear those stories and to know that what seem to be simple actions can often have a profound effect in moving a society towards peace.

In this book I have tried to convey some of these heroic stories and some that are more prosaic but are nonetheless important in laying the groundwork for a nonviolent society. Some are solutions; others are successes, partial successes, temporary successes, and promising ideas. They are not intended as templates, but rather as examples to encourage people to take risks and apply their own creative energy to finding new ways to manage and resolve conflicts.

Some of the successful actions I describe may have fallen apart by the time this book is in circulation; others may have blossomed. This is because we are human, and we must constantly renew our commitment to nonviolence. Our actions contribute to the advancement of a global culture of peace because each is a step forward, and our actions often influence many people, even when a step forward is followed by a half-step backward.

I hope that many who read this book will contribute new examples of nonviolent successes and promising ideas to the website of *Enough Blood Shed* (www.enoughbloodshed.ca). I will share them when I speak, and I hope that the result of your efforts and mine will be an expanding series of ripples from our different communities, bringing us closer to the world we want.

— Mary-Wynne Ashford
February 23, 2006

Acknowledgments

Thanks to Chris and Judith Plant of New Society Publishers for asking me to join Guy Dauncey's Solutions Project and encouraging me through false starts and dry spells.

Working with Guy Dauncey has been a great pleasure because he is not just a problem solver, he is a problem seeker. He loves finding an issue that needs to be turned on its head and addressed in a new way. I thank him for his creative and thoughtful discussions as I worked through the ideas in this book.

Ingrid Witvoet and Audrey McClellan, my meticulous and sensitive editors, guided me through the writing process. Audrey not only improved the flow of words, she pushed me to clarify my thinking and in doing so led me to some new conclusions. Ingrid's endless patience and good humor kept me going through the inevitable frustrations of writing.

My husband Russell drew the wonderful portraits that enliven these pages. He has also listened to me, commented on various drafts, cooked dinner, and maintained his incredible patience. Russell's daughters Gillian and KatyAnn, who are both professional photographers, shot many of the beautiful photos that illustrate the stories.

The rest of our blended family and their partners: Karen, Richard, Graham, Theresa, Patrick, Leah, Victoria, Daryl, and Emma enriched my thinking about child raising strategies, spirituality and meaning in life.

When I began to search for photos I wrote to people all over the world and was completely astonished by the generosity of strangers. Many wrote back enthusiastic letters about the project, corrections to the text, and collections of their photos. I am delighted to have included as many of them as I could. I thank everyone who went out of their way to provide the images, but particularly I want to thank A.H. Westing, Anne Wright, Anna Schori, Vicki Smith, Dan Sikorskyi, Gabriela Diaz, Dave and Anne Hall, Kazuo Matsui, Sachiyo Oki, Nicola Kaatsch, Khursh Ahmed, Michael Joseph, Kate Dewes, Bob Dalton, Rama Singh, Raj S. Chandola, Xanthe Hall, Julie-anne Wilce, and Yair Gill. They gave so much time and energy to finding these photos for me I must give them special thanks. Gerri Haynes, Phil Esmonde, and Geoff Spriggs inspired me by their courageous contributions to peacebuilding, as well as their photos.

Several children were photographed as they played and gardened. They were: Aidan Ashford and Miles Fuller on pages 88 and 93; Matthew Robertson, Ryan McNeil, and Justin Jubinville-Mah on page 105; Thiabaud Engelbrecht, Graham and Gavin Ashford on page 68: and Darren Simons on page 24.

Thanks to friends and colleagues who kept encouraging me in the writing, and have sent me news clippings and ideas to follow up. Joanna Santa Barbara, Metta Spencer, and Phil Esmonde were kind enough to read first drafts and send me their valuable comments. I have very much appreciated the enthusiastic support of Elinor Powell, Ben Hoffman, Neil Arya, Phil and Christa Rossner, Scilla Elworthy, Heather McAndrew, and David Springbett.

I hope that I have accurately portrayed the organizations and stories in this book, but if I have not, the fault is entirely mine. I hope that readers will send any corrections and updates to www.enoughbloodshed.ca so that I can post them. I also look forward to receiving stories from those working for peace around the world.

Finally, I thank those thousands of people who are in these stories and stories I have not included. Their actions and words have inspired me and given me new energy to join with them.

Foreword

Enough blood shed! is a cry on the lips of every citizen in every country of the world. There is hardly a country that is not wracked by violence or war. Yet everyone wants peace and many of us work hard to attain it but peace remains as elusive as ever. Some have even begun to feel that peace is impossible to achieve. Are human beings really incapable of living in peace? I think the reason why we have not been able to attain peace is because we really don't know what peace actually means. We commonly think that peace is the absence of war and violence, whereas it is really about relationships, compassion and understanding.

This well-researched book gives us a cogent blueprint to work for peace. It will be useful to remember that the tools provided in this book must be seen as the basic medication in a doctor's dispensary — they provide some means, not all means, to work for peace. To understand the holistic concept of peace it must be remembered that we humans commit more kinds of violence than just physical fighting. In fact we commit more "passive" or non-physical violence which adds up and then culminates into physical violence and even wars. In other words it is passive violence that fuels the fire of physical violence so, logically, if we wish to put out the fire of physical violence we must cut off the fuel supply. It means that every individual must honestly assess one's own behavior and relationships and examine how one practices passive violence.

Allow me to place before you a conundrum. Imagine a building on fire and the fire department arrives with two tankers — one filled with water and the other with gas. What do you think would happen if one fireman pumps water into the fire and another fireman intermittently pumps gas into the same fire? One does not have to be a rocket scientist to realize that the fire is unlikely to be completely doused. This, unfortunately, is the reality of the world today. Every time peace is achieved in one conflict area, fighting breaks out in another so that sometimes it feels like we are constantly "putting out fires."

It was not until my grandfather, Mohandas K. Gandhi, initiated me into the daily practice of self-introspection that I became aware of the extent and depth of violence I was committing consciously and unconsciously. Every evening I had to analyze the day's experiences and categorize them into two groups — passive violence and physical violence. Passive violence being the kind of violence where no physical force is used yet what we do or don't do causes hurt to someone, somewhere. And, physical is, of course, the kind of violence that hurts immensely and therefore, obsesses us the most.

Tragically, human societies everywhere are built on greed and selfishness. Consequently, every human being, to a lesser or larger extent, indulges in exploiting. This represents the gas we pour into the fire. The result is that we trust no one; in fact, we are imbued with negative thoughts and attitudes so that our relationships with each other are based on self-interest. For the most part we are good to each other only as long as we can milk each other for what we need. With relationships that lack respect and understanding, we set the stage for conflict.

My exercise in introspection revealed to me the mind-blowing extent to which we practice "passive" or non-physical violence every day. This, my grandfather explained, drives the victim to anger and, since justice in a culture of violence has come to mean revenge, the victim resorts to violence to destroy the perceived exploiter. Since all of us contribute the fuel that ignites the fire of discontent and dissension, Gandhi said: "We must become the change we wish to see in the world." Peace begins in our hearts and only then can pervade all aspects of human society.

Let me not detract from the importance of this book and the lessons contained in it. I believe one can use available tools effectively only when one has an understanding of the larger picture. A carpenter would be better able to use his tools if he has a comprehensive idea of what he wants to build. Without a holistic concept, the best of carpenters with the best of tools would flounder. I am sure the book will serve the purpose it is intended to and take humanity a few steps closer to understanding and working for peace. I recommend it wholeheartedly to all those who value peace and are eager to leave behind for future generations a world that values harmony more than conflict.

— Arun Gandhi, May 2006

Arun Gandhi, President of the M. K. Gandhi Institute for Nonviolence, Memphis, TN, is the fifth grandson of Mohandas K. Gandhi. He lived for 18 months with his grandfather and for 24 years with his parents, Manilal and Sushila Gandhi, who taught him all the rudiments of the nonviolent way of life.

Dedication:

For my grandchildren and the world they inherit

Sam, Lucy, Aidan, Gavin, Quinn, Lauren, Brandon, Connor, and Natalie

Part I

What We're Facing

1

Two Superpowers: The United States and World Public Opinion

> The fracturing of the Western alliance over Iraq and the huge antiwar demonstrations around the world this weekend are reminders that there may still be two superpowers on the planet: the United States and world public opinion.
> — **Patrick E. Tyler**, *New York Times*, **February 17, 2003**

In the months before the bombing of Iraq, while the leaders of the United States and the United Kingdom were piecing together their justification for war, public opinion around the world rose up against them. The media said that war was inevitable, but on February 15, 2003, people from Melbourne to Milan and from Vancouver to Tokyo took their protests to the streets. Some 15 million people marched — the largest mobilization of civil society in history to oppose a war before it began.

As I read the comment quoted above, I wondered if the *New York Times* was aware that we are at the beginning of a global social revolution. This revolution is the rise of civil society, bringing conscience to guide the behavior of governments and financial institutions.

For over 20 years I have spent every spare minute working on nuclear disarmament, and I have been watching the parallel growth of militarism and civil society. One force is moving us toward destruction, the other toward peace. In the 1980s, at the same time that nuclear arsenals were increasing astronomically, the active involvement of people on both sides of the Iron Curtain was growing at an equal rate. People were not just opposing the bomb; they were fighting pollution, human rights violations, corruption, and violence against women.

The growth of civil society is a response to the failure of governments, both capitalist and communist, to address the concerns of humanity. Now that the communist model has been discredited, we can see more clearly democracy's vulnerability to corruption, as well as the shortcomings of the free market economy. The new superpower is more than just public opinion; it is public engagement in decision making.

This idea of two superpowers captures the essence of our current situation: one power is based on military domination and control of people by force; the other power is based on cooperation and the rule of law. The future is far from clear. The second superpower will flourish only if the huge number of people who want an end to violence, terror, and war continue to demand to be heard.

Civil society includes organizations as well as individuals who are acting to bring the values and conscience of humanity to the global issues we face. Women, youth, indigenous peoples, trade unions, faith groups, and academics are some of the diverse voices of civil society.

All three pillars of society — government, economy, and culture — are essential and must interact to benefit society, but one sector must not take over the role of another.[1] Throughout history, people — alone and in groups — have

Anti-war demonstration in Seattle, USA.

DAVID SILVER

- CIVICUS (World Alliance for Citizen Participation): www.civicus.org
- UBUNTU (World Forum of Civil Society Networks): www.ubuntu.org

constrained the attempts by rulers and the wealthy to assume unbridled power. Today there is an imbalance because governments and huge multinational corporations have become enmeshed. The result is that fundamental needs of society are not being met — especially the need to ensure a sustainable environment.

Furthermore, the disproportionate influence of militarization is distorting democracy. The military-industrial lobby influences decision makers to choose and fund military solutions to conflict instead of diplomatic alternatives. They see the military as the only way to combat terrorism. In fact, precise intelligence and police actions to arrest and charge terrorists are more effective ways to protect the public than military attacks that affect whole populations. Police actions must comply with laws that protect the innocent from arbitrary arrest or injury resulting from mistaken identity. Military actions do not. The Carnegie Commission reports that today, for every soldier who dies in war, ten civilians die, about half of them children.[2] Targeting the innocent is now a deliberate strategy, whether the attack is carried out by the state or by a terrorist, and whether people are killed by a suicide bomber or by a bomb dropped from 35,000 feet, they are just as dead.

Civil society calls for a different response to terrorism, one that applies the dictum of medicine: "Above all, do no harm." Ordinary people recognize that the barbarity of modern warfare is

Civil Society Values

- Human security above national security
- Compassion above profit
- Environmental restoration
- Human rights
- Participatory democracy
- International law
- Nonviolent conflict resolution
- Social justice
- Equity for the disadvantaged

not acceptable. That is why millions of people hit the streets in 2003.

The stories of civil society are rarely on the front pages, but they inspire actions by others, and their stories are spread in vast networks worldwide. Some of them are in this book.

Anti-war demonstrations in London, UK.

DOUGLAS CAPE DOUGLAS@z360.COM

2

Two Possible Futures

The most significant democratic transformations in our lifetime, from South Africa to the break up of the Soviet Union and its gulag, were essentially peaceful transformations led by citizens of those nations given courage by international solidarity, but making change from the bottom up. Brave advocates faced violence, and many died. But in the end, these revolutions overwhelmed repressive governments not by the force of arms, not by outside intervention, but by the amassed power of people and ideas.

— Gara La Marche, Open Society Institute

We are at a crossroads and must choose one of two paths into the future. On one path we follow the law of force, which means might makes right. On the other path we follow the force of law, which means we agree to comply with laws we have developed jointly that apply to all nations.

Consequences of the Law of Force

The law of force threatens the death penalty for all because there are enough nuclear weapons to kill everyone on Earth many times over. The law of force inspires terrorists to take desperate action because they see no alternative to bring about change.

The law of force is often used by unscrupulous leaders who seek to gain personal power and wealth by inciting others to fight, often using money-laundering schemes to buy weapons with funds from the illegal drug or diamond trades.

War brings injuries, death, and economic and social disruption that plunges both winners and losers into poverty. Refugees flee their homeland and bring stress to adjoining countries that can ill afford more demands on their resources. Military conflicts increase domestic violence, rape, and the spread of disease, especially HIV/AIDS.

War devastates the natural environment and often contaminates it with radioactive waste, chemical pollutants, and landmines left behind after the end of hostilities. The use of depleted uranium (DU) munitions is just the most recent example of weaponry that leaves long-lasting human and environmental devastation.

The trauma of war is suffered by the victorious forces as well as by the defeated. Large numbers of US troops have returned from the Gulf Wars with lifelong severe disabilities, post-traumatic stress disorder, or Gulf War Syndrome. They suffer high rates of depression, alcoholism, and suicide.

Consequences of the Force of Law

The force of law, on the other hand, means building a world based on cooperation, with support for treaties and international law, the UN, the Declaration of Human Rights, and international norms of behavior. It means a world where all have a right to participate fully in civic life and governance; where women and minorities can vote and run for office; where everyone has a right to education, health care, shelter, and work; and where parents can put their children to bed at night without fearing an attack.

GERRI HAYNES

UNICEF poster warning of danger of unexploded ordnance in Iraq.

- Carnegie Commission on Preventing Deadly Conflict: www.ccpdc.org
- Institute for Energy and Environmental Research: www.ieer.org
- Oxford Research Group: www.oxfordresearchgroup.org.uk
- Transcend: www.transcend.org

The force of law is designed to apply evenly to all states and all people. With the recent establishment of the International Criminal Court (see Solution 78), leaders who commit war crimes or crimes against humanity can now be held personally accountable to the law.

The nonviolent resolution of conflict is possible through the rule of law because we have expertise and skills that were just emerging a decade ago. We know how to recognize the early signs of an escalation of conflict in time to stop it. We know more about the root causes of war and terrorism than ever before, and we know many strategies that can successfully prevent them.

We also know much more about the resolution of conflict. In Northern Ireland, after several previous agreements had broken down, the governments of Northern Ireland and the United Kingdom acknowledged that those who were at the table were not those who were fighting. At that point they chose to include the political wing of the Irish Republican Army in the negotiations, and real changes began to occur. The IRA gave up its armed struggle, and in 2005 it turned over its massive arsenal for destruction under the supervision of international weapons inspectors.

The world has learned much from the mistakes of the past, and civil society has also learned from nonviolent successes over many years. We are inspired to continue our work because we know what is needed and what is at stake.

The World of Violence

Domination by force
Dictatorships tolerated
Huge military budgets
Male-dominated societies
Competition
Win-lose philosophy
Large gap between rich and poor
Racism and sexism common
Injustice tolerated on religious, racial, or ethnic grounds
Disregard for treaties and international law
Social and environmental concerns trumped by military
Social services sacrificed for military budget
Punitive justice system with many in prison
People committed to defeating "the enemy"

The World We Want

Cooperation and collaboration
Elected, accountable governments
Small military budget or none
Gender partnership society
Minimal competition
Win-win philosophy
Large middle class, little inequity
Tolerance of diversity
Injustice not tolerated
Support for UN and international law
Social and environmental concerns given high priority
Social safety net
Restorative justice and rehabilitation of prisoners
People committed to peace and justice

3

What Is at Stake?

> Auschwitz showed what
> man is capable of, and
> Hiroshima showed what is
> at stake.
>
> — Victor Frankl

The stakes could not be higher, nor the choices clearer. Human survival and the survival of our natural world are at risk if we continue on the present path of military domination. The UN and international law cannot coexist with military empires and warlords.

Human Survival

Nuclear war is the only thing that could end life on Earth by accident — in an afternoon. The United States and Russia each maintain about 2,000 missiles on high alert. If one side fired a missile, whether by accident or intent, the other side would retaliate by launching thousands of missiles before the first one even exploded.

We have narrowly escaped nuclear holocaust on several occasions when a computer error or a misreading of a radar screen appeared to show an incoming missile. In 1995, a weather rocket launched from Norway was mistakenly identified by the Russians as an incoming American missile. With only minutes remaining before President Yeltsin had to decide whether to launch Russian missiles, the error was discovered and the emergency ended. Had Yeltsin launched Russian missiles, the United States might have launched thousands of missiles in response, and human life on Earth would have ended.

The astronomer Carl Sagan concluded that if cities were targeted, a war involving only 100 megatons (in 1,000 100-kiloton bursts over 100 or more major cities) could trigger nuclear winter.[1] Massive amounts of smoke and debris rising into the atmosphere would block out the sunlight, causing the temperature of the Earth to drop and crops to fail in

Mangrove forest in Gia Dinh Province, South Viet Nam, destroyed in 1970 by the USA during the Second Indochina War via a single attack with an anti-plant chemical warfare agent, probably Agent Orange.

A.H. WESTING

- Global Security Institute: www.gsinstitute.org
- International Physicians for the Prevention of Nuclear War: www.ippnw.org
- Lawyers Committee on Nuclear Policy (USA): www.lcnp.org
- Middle Powers Initiative: www.middlepowers.org
- Physicians for Social Responsibility USA: www.psr.org
- Western States Legal Foundation: www.wslfweb.org

both the northern and southern hemispheres. Nuclear winter would mean the end of human life.

The Natural World

Even without the use of weapons of mass destruction, modern warfare is enormously destructive of the environment. During the Vietnam War, some 19 million gallons of herbicides, including the defoliant Agent Orange were sprayed over 35 percent of South Vietnam to kill vegetation that hid enemy troops.[2] The defoliant contained dioxin, a highly toxic and carcinogenic chemical that persists today in the soil, food, wildlife, human breast milk, and fat tissues of the Vietnamese people. Many US veterans have died of various cancers and other illnesses thought to be caused by their exposure to Agent Orange, as have tens of thousands of Vietnamese people. Children born to people who were exposed to the agent often have severe deformities and mental retardation, and many have died of cancer.

Veterans of the wars in the Balkans, Afghanistan, and Iraq were exposed to a range of toxic substances including depleted uranium, nerve gas (released when a chemical weapons factory was bombed), vaccines, and other chemicals. More than 25,000 American veterans have developed symptoms known as Gulf War Syndrome since serving in these areas.[3] Iraqi doctors have reported widespread cancer and birth deformities around Basra, where DU munitions were used. Where DU contaminates soil

and drinking water, populations may be exposed to its radioactive and toxic effects for generations to come.

Ruth Leger Sivard, author of *World Social and Military Expenditures*, reported in 1991 that the world's armed forces are the single largest polluter on Earth; in the United States they produce more toxic products annually than the top five chemical companies combined.[4]

Landmines also leave vast tracts of land unusable for decades after a war; in malarial areas, mosquitoes breed where the craters from landmine explosions have filled with water.

The United Nations and International Law

The decisions being made by the US administration under George W. Bush have serious consequences for the world because they undermine international law and the authority of the UN. In 2005, the Pentagon released a nuclear planning document that includes the possible preemptive use of nuclear weapons.

White House decisions are also undermining the Geneva Conventions on the rights of prisoners and the prohibition of torture. The accused's loss of the rights to have a lawyer, to not be held without charge, and to have a fair and open trial sets the law back hundreds of years, to 1215, when the Magna Carta was signed in Britain.

4

A World Awash in Armaments

The world cannot continue to wage war like physical giants and to seek peace like intellectual pygmies.

— Basil O'Connor

This is the most sobering part of the story. The arms that are available today are ever more deadly and ever more widespread. They are a measure of our alienation from each other, from the Earth that nurtures us, and from our deepest selves.

Nuclear Weapons

The declared nuclear weapons states are the United States, United Kingdom, Russia, France, China, India, and Pakistan. Israel is assumed to have 200 nuclear weapons (undeclared), and North Korea now claims to have nuclear weapons as well.

There are 30,000 nuclear weapons held mostly by the United States and Russia, of which some 4,000 are set for "launch on warning." The United States has declared that nuclear weapons will be central to its defense for the foreseeable future. It has withdrawn from the Anti-Ballistic Missile Treaty and blocked progress at the Nuclear Non-Proliferation Treaty Review Conference in 2005.

In 2004 the United States Congress cut funding for development of a Robust Nuclear Earth Penetrator, which was designed to destroy enemy underground bunkers with a nuclear bomb. The plan was widely discredited by several organizations including the US Academy of Sciences, which showed that even a one-megaton bomb could not destroy a deep bunker and that such a bomb would release a huge radioactive cloud. Nonetheless, funds were requested again in the 2006 budget.

The risk of nuclear terrorism is extremely serious because Al Qaeda is reported to be seeking fissile materials. Terrorists might gain access to a small nuclear bomb, but it is more likely that they could make a "dirty bomb" using fissile materials blown up by conventional explosives. The third nightmare scenario would be if they caused a nuclear meltdown by flying a 747 into a nuclear power plant.

Chemical and Biological Weapons

Several countries, including Britain, Germany, Japan, the United States, and Iraq, have used both chemical and biological weapons in the 20th century. The Aum Shinrikyo cult used nerve gas in a terrorist attack on a Japanese subway in 1995. These weapons have major disadvantages including the danger to one's own troops, the long-lasting contamination of the environment, their uncontrollable nature, and their uncertain effectiveness. If used as a terrorist weapon, however, spread in air or water, they could inflict major damage on a population, and a relatively small act would produce a high level of fear. Many countries in the Middle East have stockpiles of chemical weapons in response to Israel's nuclear weapons program.

Landmines

At the time the treaty banning landmines was signed, the UN estimated there were 120 million mines in the ground in over 60 countries. Since the signing, the use of landmines has decreased and millions of landmines have been removed from the ground and from stockpiles and destroyed. At least 140,000 antipersonnel mines, 50,000 antivehicle mines, and some 3 million items of unexploded ordnance were destroyed

- Coalition to Ban Depleted Uranium Weapons: www.bandepleteduranium.org
- International Campaign to Ban Landmines: www.clearlandmines.com
- International Physicians for Prevention of Nuclear War: www.ippnw.org
- Iraq Body Count: www.iraqbodycount.net
- Physicians for Social Responsibility: www.psr.org

during clearance operations in 2004.[1] However, many remain in the ground, and new landmines continue to be laid by guerrilla groups and by countries that have not signed the 1997 treaty (see Solution 30). There are currently 154 signatories, although the United States, China, and Russia have not yet signed.

Landmines kill or maim between 15,000 and 20,000 people each year. About half the victims die. Mines are a favorite weapon because they are so cheap — as little as $3 each. Tragically, they last for decades after hostilities have ended and can be triggered indiscriminately by a child, a farmer, or an animal.

Small Arms and Light Weapons

According to Project Ploughshares, about 500,000 people die every year from wounds caused by small arms — 300,000 in conflict, and 200,000 from homicide, crime, suicide, and accidents. The numbers are numbing, but the result is one death every minute worldwide. There are 639 million military-style arms in the world, with manufacturers making profits of about $4 billion per year and illegal traders making profits of under $1 billion per year.[2]

Physicians for Social Responsibility/USA reports that 32,000 people are killed by guns annually, including ten children each day. The United States has 190 to 250 million handguns.

Conventional Weapons

Precision bombing supposedly spares civilians, but by destroying civil infrastructure it is, in effect, a war on public health. Civilians are left without safe water, sewage disposal, hospitals, immunization, medicines, shelter, or nutritious food. The result is that the weakest in society die — infants and children, the sick and the elderly. The bombing of Iraq has resulted in between 25,000 and 100,000 Iraqi deaths between 2003 and 2005.[3]

Depleted Uranium Munitions

Munitions tipped with radioactive waste are hard enough and heavy enough to penetrate tanks and armored vehicles.[4] DU is weakly radioactive — a dose of radiation from DU would be only about 60 percent of the dose from the same mass of purified natural uranium.[5] DU has a half-life of 4.5 billion years. It is toxic if ingested because it is a heavy metal. DU burns on impact and forms an aerosol that can be inhaled. Particles lodged in lungs can spread through the blood and lymphatic systems and can cause cancer.

Iraqis scavenge for food and other items behind a military dump truck.

9

5

Thirty Thousand Nuclear Weapons

The nuclear bomb is the most anti-demo-cratic, anti-human, outright evil thing that man has ever made .... This world of ours is four thousand, six hundred million years old. It could end in an afternoon.

— Arundhati Roy, Incian author and activist

Nuclear weapons are the greatest threat to human survival today, yet they are at the center of the world's power structure. The Big Five (the United States, United Kingdom, France, Russia, and China) are the permanent members of the UN Security Council because they have nuclear weapons. Unfortunately, when India and Pakistan tested their nuclear weapons, they gained prestige as well as condemnation. Israel bases its security on having nuclear weapons to deter its enemies. North Korea has declared that it also has nuclear weapons and will not give them up without a security guarantee that the United States will not attack it.

Worldwide public opinion consistently demands the elimination of nuclear weapons. In fact, in opposition to their government, a poll in 2005 found that 66 percent of Americans say no nation should have nuclear weapons, including the United States.[1] The threat of terrorists gaining access to a nuclear bomb has raised public concerns about nuclear weapons again after a decade of thinking that the danger had disappeared with the collapse of the Soviet Union.

- Atomic Archive: www.atomicarchive.com
- International Physicians for the Prevention of Nuclear War: www.ippnw.org
- Nuclear Age Peace Foundation: www.napf.org
- Physicians for Global Survival (Canada): www.pgs.org
- Pugwash Conferences on Science and World Affairs: www.pugwash.org

The Need for Education

Many young people who have grown up since the end of the Cold War in 1992 were not taught about nuclear weapons in school and have not been exposed to the dread that was pervasive in the previous decades. Students often believe some of the following myths:

- That nuclear weapons are necessary, at least for their country.
- That their country would never use nuclear weapons.
- That mini-nukes are not really dangerous.
- That you can survive a nuclear explosion if you are prepared.

It is clear that education about nuclear weapons is once more a matter of life and death.

Doctors in India are very active in the antinu-clear movement. They report that Indian medical students are almost unanimously in favor of nuclear weapons until they learn about the med-ical consequences of a nuclear explosion and the high risk of accidental launches. Then they join their professors in protesting against India's bomb.

Medical Consequences of a Nuclear Explosion

International Physicians for the Prevention of Nuclear War (IPPNW) won the Nobel Peace Prize in 1985 for its efforts to bring together doctors from the United States and the Soviet Union to raise public awareness of the threat of nuclear war.

When the 15-kiloton atomic bomb exploded above Hiroshima in 1945, the blast caused a flash of light brighter than the sun. The ground temperature at the hypocenter reached 7,000°C, and everything close to the center was vaporized. The only sign that people had been there was the shadows left on the stone pavement. Everything within 8.1 miles (13 kilometers) of the center was reduced to ashes.[2]

The blast blew with hurricane force, hurling people and chunks of buildings outward from the center. Then the wind reversed to feed air to the huge firestorm. Black radioactive rain fell for seven hours afterward. Survivors staggered toward the Ota river, begging for water. Their skin was burned and hanging down in sheets.

Most of the doctors and nurses were killed, and the hospitals were destroyed. The few doctors who survived were overwhelmed by the scale of the disaster. They described themselves as acting like automatons, cleaning and swabbing burns, even though they knew their patients were dying. They couldn't think clearly, could not stop to rest or sleep, and were numbed by knowing their efforts were almost useless. Many of them succumbed to radiation and died.

Radiation sickness in a population was unknown to the world. People began vomiting, their hair fell out, their gums bled, and many died within a few days. Many others showed signs of bone marrow failure and died of internal bleeding. Later, leukemia and other cancers appeared. Burn victims who survived developed grotesque scar tissue, called keloid, and required multiple plastic surgeries to repair their skin.

Today's nuclear weapons are many times more powerful than the Hiroshima bomb. A typical 150-kiloton bomb, exploded on a major city, would cause between 730,000 and 8,660,000 deaths depending on the population density of the city.[3] There would be no hospitals, no electricity, no sterile bandages or IV solutions, no antibiotics or morphine available. Nearby cities, if they were not also hit, would be overwhelmed by the number of patients needing emergency treatment. Those going to the aid of victims could be exposed to lethal radiation. IPPNW studies conclude that there is nothing meaningful that doctors can do in the event of a nuclear war. Prevention is the only solution.

Hiroshima after the atomic bomb of August 6, 1945.

PHOTOGRAPHED BY YOSHITO MATSUSHIGE. COLLECTION OF CHUGOKU SHIMBUN.

11

6

The Roots of War

> All violence consists in some people forcing others, under threat of suffering or death, to do what they do not want to do.
>
> — Leo Tolstoy

At the peak of the Cold War, the threat of a nuclear holocaust led to a huge global movement to ban the bomb. Privately, I worried that we might get rid of nuclear weapons and find the superpowers had simply moved on to another genocidal weapon. Or that we might get a treaty banning tests of all nuclear weapons and find the superpowers had already developed ways to test the weapons by computer simulation. In some ways, both concerns have been borne out.

As important as the weapons are, if we are going to prevent war, we have to explore the root causes of war. Above all, we must be aware of who benefits from war. News reports often state that a war is the result of ethnic or religious conflict, without noting the underlying competition for resources or the interests of the great powers in the region. The justifications given by the combatants have often been stirred up by leaders who use the conflict to gain power. Differences in religion, ethnicity, or ideology are exploited to fuel anger between groups so that they will fight and kill each other.

When we look deeper, we find that corporations make billions of dollars by destroying and then rebuilding a country. We find arms traders, drug runners, and money launderers. Power and greed fuel and prolong war.

What Are the Roots of War?

Competition over resources: Competition for land, water, and control of resources like oil, diamonds, timber, gold, and coltan (a mineral needed to make cell phones) fuel armed conflict. Third parties often contribute to the conflict by selling arms to combatants and profiting from the illegal sale of resources such as protected timber or stolen diamonds.

Historical grievances: Disputes over nationalism, ethnocentrism, religion, ideology, and sovereign rights to territory or historical monuments provoke emotional responses. Present injustices are seen as resulting from differences that can only be resolved violently.

Weapons: Arms manufacturers from outside a country often supply weapons to both sides in a conflict and profit by fueling discontent. After a war ends, it is essential to remove weapons from the society in order to sustain peace.

Injustice: When a religious or ethnic minority is prevented from sharing the wealth of a country or from participating in its governance, anger and resentment build up, setting one group against another. Easy access to weaponry makes war more likely, especially if

NEIL ARYA

Old grievances are set in concrete with Israel's wall closing out Palestinians.

- Carnegie Commission on Preventing Deadly Conflict: www.wilsoncenter.org/subsites/ccpdc/index.htm
- Project for a New American Century: www.newamericancentury.org
- US Space Command's *Vision for 2020*: www.fas.org/spp/military/docops/usspac/visbook.pdf

there are large numbers of unemployed young males. In a healthy society, young men marry and settle down to raise a family. They work and contribute to a stable community. Without work they cannot support a family and often become isolated and angry that they face an empty future. Their frustration makes them susceptible to those who encourage armed conflict.

Lust for power: The lust for power and status is legendary, and the ability of the unscrupulous to convince others to fight on their behalf is dumbfounding. By offering followers land, money, and position, leaders build a force that becomes self-perpetuating. Often the original grievance is forgotten in the overwhelming unity of battle.

Profits: Weapons manufacturers, military suppliers, companies that build bases or provide food and housing, those who reconstruct after a war, and those who gain access to valuable resources all have a vested interest in starting and prolonging war.

Empire: When colonial empires were disbanded in the last 50 years of the 20th century, it seemed that the era of empires was over. Now, with the George W. Bush administration in the United States, it is clear that one nation's drive to control the world has risen once again.

In 1999, the conservative Project for a New American Century (PNAC) laid out a plan for the United States to dominate the world economically, politically, and culturally for the next century. PNAC is not a fringe think tank. Its statement of principles is signed by, among others, Jeb Bush, the president's brother; Dick

Cheney, the vice president; Donald Rumsfeld, the Secretary of Defense; and Paul Wolfowitz, now president of the World Bank. PNAC advocates ballistic missile defense and the weaponization of space to give the United States freedom from attack and freedom to attack. The US Space Command's *Vision for 2020* calls for "full spectrum military domination" of the planet from outer space in order to protect US interests and investments.

PNAC plans must be taken seriously because many parts of the strategy have already been implemented. The war on Iraq was planned before Bush took office. The events of September 11, 2001 simply provided convenient justification for attacking both Afghanistan and Iraq. A document prepared by PNAC in 2000 states: "The United States has for decades sought to play a more permanent role in Gulf regional security. While the unresolved conflict with Iraq provides the immediate justification, the need for a substantial American force presence in the Gulf transcends the issue of the regime of Saddam Hussein."

Preventing war when faced with an imperial agenda of global domination by force is a daunting task for governments, the UN, and civil society. The scale of US military domination is far beyond anything the world has seen before. Terrorism, especially suicide bombing, is a response to this asymmetry of power by people who are angry and who feel powerless to bring about change without the most extreme actions. For many terrorists, the anger is rooted in humiliation.

7

War As a Disease

May we learn from the barbaric and bloody deeds of the 20th century and bestow the gift of peace to the next millennium. Perhaps in that way we shall redeem some measure of respect from generations yet to come.

— Dr. Bernard Lown, IPPNW, Nobel Peace Prize acceptance speech, 1985

Wars killed 110 to 188 million people in the 20th century.[1] Probably twice as many or more suffered permanent emotional or physical disability as a result of war. War can be studied as a disease that has afflicted humanity for millennia. We know a great deal about its causes and the factors that contribute to death and injury. And, like other diseases, it can be prevented.

Epidemiology

In medicine, we apply a standard paradigm to the analysis of a disease beginning with how many cases there are right now, how many cases occur per year, how many people are dying, and how many people are injured. The same paradigm applies to war as a disease.

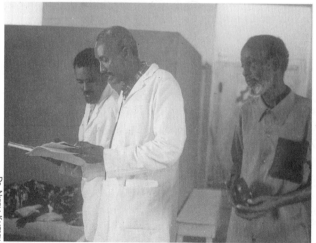

Dr. Nicola Katsch

Doctors Without Borders at Kismayu Hospital in Somalia, 1992.

Etiology (causes)

Doctors look at the causes of a disease at several levels. For example, if we are studying tuberculosis, we know that the disease is caused by a mycobacterium, but we ask why this particular patient has TB, and why now? Those questions bring out the social conditions of poverty, overcrowding, and HIV/AIDS as factors that contribute to the spread of the disease. At an even deeper level, we ask why Africa, for example, does not have the drugs needed to stop the spread of HIV/AIDS or TB.

Likewise, with war we must search for the immediate causes and ask why this group, and why now? Armed conflict is often blamed on longstanding ethnic discord or religious differences, but underlying those tensions there are almost always economic or power inequities that discriminate against one group. Beneath that level there are frequently the influences of third parties who have interests in resources like oil and minerals. The role of a power-hungry leader or old grievances must also be considered.

Treatment

The treatment must address each of the war's causes or it is likely to recur. The immediate response must be to stop people dying. Health workers in groups like Doctors Without Borders intervene to provide emergency medical care to the wounded and to organize clinics in the chaos of a war zone. Other outside groups meet with the combatants to bring about a ceasefire and negotiate peace terms and agreements. This step requires sensitivity to ethnic or cultural triggers and awareness that deeper injustices must be addressed and reconstruction planned. Finally, there is the important but difficult task of exposing the role of other countries in prolonging the conflict. So far, we do poorly at stopping third-party interference.

Prevention

In medicine, prevention occurs at several levels. The healthy population must be protected from getting the disease by means of education, inoculation, isolation, nutrition, and so on. Where the disease already exists, efforts must be made to limit its spread and the harm it causes. Those who have the disease must be treated, rehabilitated, and protected against recurrence of the disease.

The parallel in preventing war is that first we must build the resistance to war and armed conflict in the healthy population. That is where peace education, support for traditions of conflict resolution, tolerance, and respect must be fostered. This is what UNESCO calls building the "culture of peace."

Where conflict has already broken out, action can be taken while it is still possible to stop the violence. At this level, mediation, confidence-building measures, peacekeeping, outside observers, financial restrictions on leaders, and arms embargoes are some of the interventions used.

If a genocide is occurring, and the government is unable or unwilling to protect all civilians, that responsibility falls to the outside world. Armed intervention may be authorized under the UN (see Solution 98). Post-conflict reconstruction of societies must include reconciliation and restoration of justice between the groups.

The advantage of applying the medical paradigm to armed conflict is that it emphasizes planning for prevention, treatment, and rehabilitation to address all the root causes. Unless the multilevel causes of a conflict are recognized and addressed, a recurrence is likely.

Medical Ethics

A further advantage of applying a medical perspective to armed conflict is that medicine has an ethical foundation that brings conscience to bear on prevention and treatment.

- Prevention is the most important step.

- Above all, do no harm.

- Use the smallest and least invasive intervention first, before considering actions that may be more harmful.

- Remember that everything you do must be for the good of the patient, not for your own benefit.

- Peace Through Health: www.humanities.mcmaster.ca/peace-health

- Physicians for Global Survival (Canada): www.pgs.ca

- Responsibility to Care: www.r2care.org

- UNESCO (UN Educational, Scientific, and Cultural Organization): www3.unesco.org/iycp

8

Empires and War

The hidden hand of the market will never work without a hidden fist. McDonald's cannot flourish without McDonnell Douglas, the builder of the F-15. And the hidden fist that keeps the world safe for Silicon Valley's technologies is called the United States Army, Air Force, Navy and Marine Corps.

— Thomas Friedman, *New York Times*, 1999

Empires are not compatible with a world order based on cooperation and peace. The Project for a New American Century (PNAC) appears at first glance to be a plan for the US government to dominate the planet for the next century, but closer examination shows it is more than that. Its purpose is to protect American interests and investments, not to protect American citizens, their health, or well-being. PNAC is really a strategy for US-based multinational corporations to dominate the planet by military force. Such an empire will be as destructive of American life as it will be of lives in the rest of the world.

A healthy society is based on three pillars: good government, a sound economy, and a culture expressed by a strong civil society. When government is enmeshed with big business, it distorts the relationship that government must have with the people and leaves civil society out in the cold, just when its conscience is most needed.

The war on terror provides an excuse for governments to advance the agenda of multinational corporations and the World Trade Organization through the departments of defense, trade, and foreign affairs. By limiting civil liberties, the war on terror also limits dissent by social justice groups. Empire is expanded by free-trade agreements that overrule governments' ability to protect social, environmental, and human rights. The corporate empire integrates more and more countries through trade and security agreements.

John Perkins, in his book *Confessions of an Economic Hit Man*, describes from the inside the deliberate steps he took to trap countries into crippling debt.[1] He would arrange for developing countries to borrow

Global Network Against Weapons & Nuclear Power in Space.

billions of dollars for the construction of infrastructure projects like dams. The contract for construction would go to a US firm — usually Halliburton or Bechtel. The money stayed in the United States, while the developing countries, now saddled with huge debts, came under the control of the United States government, the World Bank, and other agencies that dictated repayment terms. If a country resisted such programs, Perkins reports that the CIA organized threats and assassinations. If that failed, the US military attacked. Perkins' book is a chilling exposé of the ruthless system that condemns millions of people to servitude and starvation in order to benefit massively wealthy corporations.

Corruption is one of the problems behind the poverty in Africa, but corruption is not limited to developing countries. Corporate corruption scandals in North America and Europe repeatedly show the callous disregard of the very rich for those they victimize. The last two US elections have been characterized by irregularities in voter registration, voting procedures, ballot counting, and final reporting.

Many Americans are outraged that democracy in their own country is threatened, and there are widespread campaigns for reform.

When a few corporations control the media, access to information is limited. Corporations promote consumerism, tax breaks for the rich, and minimal government regulation in health or environmental protection. They glorify violence in news, sports, and entertainment because it attracts viewers. Corporate media promote war, and justify the loss of civil liberties and the flouting of international law as necessary in the interests of security.

An empire with a war economy needs military industries to enforce domination of other countries and to provide jobs at home. It needs an enemy in order to justify the war economy. PNAC's plans describe the need to win several wars on different fronts simultaneously.

When the expanding corporate empire is no longer under the control of government, the consequence for civil society is loss of the rule of law and loss of hope for a world without war. It is crucial for civil society to transform the environment that allows corporate domination.

- David Korten (Author of books on corporations and civil society): www.davidkorten.org
- Project for a New American Century: www.newamericancentury.org

9

Corporations and War

The modern conservative is engaged in one of man's oldest exercises in moral philosophy: that is the search for a superior moral justification for selfishness.
— John Kenneth Galbraith

If we are diagnosing the causes of war in order to seek a remedy, we must focus our attention on one of the causes that contains a difficult and uncomfortable truth: Many wars have been supported and financed by business corporations. Some have been fought for no other reason than to protect the interests of a corporation or to expand its realm of power.

The roots of this unseemly marriage go back deep and far. When the Vikings made war on

Filmmakers Mark Achbar, Joel Bakan and Jennifer Abbott analyze the inner workings of the modern business corporation.

various parts of Europe, it was often to seek commercial and trading advantages. When the Spanish sent warriors to conquer the Mayan and Aztec tribes of Mexico and Incas of South America, it was to bring back gold to the financiers who paid for their expeditions. When the British used violence to maintain their control over India, it was in part to break India's thriving cotton industry and guarantee the East India Company's monopoly.

The tradition continued in the 19th century, when Cecil Rhodes led his British South Africa Company to war in southern Africa in pursuit of gold and seized control of the lands of the Mashona (today's Zimbabwe), and in the 20th century, when American governments intervened militarily in countries such as Honduras (1903), Mexico (1914), and the Dominican Republic (1916) to safeguard them for American fruit, oil, and sugar companies.

Today, US corporations such as Lockheed Martin and Halliburton are deeply embedded in the war machine. Their directors provide campaign finances to politicians, who repay the favor by voting for bigger Pentagon budgets and more military activity. Who controls the game? At some stage, war becomes a racket, promoted for the sake of the revenues it will provide.

If we are to remove this contributing cause of war, we must address something very fundamental in the legal nature of a corporation.

The modern corporation evolved from its origins in the merchant guilds of England in the 12th century. The early "corporations" were groups of wealthy individuals who were given a charter that allowed them to raise money and build an institution for the public good, such as a hospital or university.

Corporate powers grew further in 1886, when the US Supreme Court recognized the corporation as a "natural person" under law, allowing the 14th Amendment ("No state shall deprive any person of life, liberty or property.") to be used to strike down regulations that might limit a corporation's powers.

Today, a corporation's directors are required by law "to act in the best interests of the corporation." The courts have interpreted this to mean that a corporation's only legal goal is to maximize its shareholders' profits above all else. The writers of the film *The Corporation* concluded that recognizing the corporation as a person who can only act for profit makes the corporation behave like a psychopath, utterly untouched by the suffering and death that may be caused by its actions.

There are three developing solutions to this problem. First, there is a global movement by the corporations toward corporate social responsibility, in which companies voluntarily commit to do good works and refrain from evil.

Second, there is a growing activism, exemplified by the Rainforest Action Network, which is successfully shaming large corporations such as Home Depot,

Citigroup, and Bank of America to change their ways in order to avoid the negative publicity arising from activist campaigning and hostile shareholder resolutions.

And third, there is a growing movement to redefine the legal rights of a corporation. This is best expressed in the work of corporate lawyer Robert Hinkley, who is building a movement to add 28 words to corporate law, creating a Code for Corporate Citizenship: "The duty of directors henceforth shall be to make money for shareholders *but not at the expense of the environment, human rights, public health and safety, dignity of employees, and the welfare of the communities in which the company operates.*"[1]

Something has to change. Our world cannot afford to have powerful corporations fomenting pain, suffering, and war for the benefit of their own bottom line. Something has to change.

- Aurora Institute: www.aurora.ca
- *The Corporation*: www.thecorporation.com
- Corporate Watch: www.corpwatch.org
- Global Compact: www.unglobalcompact.org
- Robert Hinkley: www.thesunmagazine.org/345_Hinkley.pdf
- David Korten: www.davidkorten.org
- Program on Corporations, Law and Democracy: www.poclad.org
- Rainforest Action Network: www.ran.org
- *YES! Magazine*: www.yesmagazine.org

10

Oil and War

Our children and grandchildren are going to be mad at us for burning all this oil. It took the Earth 500 million years to create the stuff we're burning in 200 years. Renewable energy sources are where we need to be headed.

— Jack Edwards, Professor of Geology, University of Colorado

Without oil, economies crumble and nations fall. One of Germany's prime goals in World War II was to gain access to Russia's oil fields to fuel its quest for global dominance. Similarly, Japan lusted after Indonesia's oil fields when it invaded large areas of east Asia. Neither Germany or Japan has any oil supplies of its own.

A country with aspirations to be a military power must have oil: an F-16 jet on a training mission lasting less than an hour uses twice as much fuel as the average motorist uses in a year.[1] Worldwide, almost a quarter of all jet fuel is used for military purposes. A modern army tank has a fuel efficiency of just half a mile per gallon.

Popular wisdom has it that Iraq would not have been bombed and occupied if its main export had been coconuts. As soon as they were in Baghdad, the Americans took great care to protect the oil ministry, while allowing everything else to be looted.

The journalist Gwynne Dyer says "You don't have to occupy oil-producing countries militarily at vast expense to get oil from them. You just write them a check."[2]

Life in the oil lane is not as simple as that, however. The United States is heavily dependent on oil from Saudi Arabia, and there are concerns that if the Saudi monarchy falls to Shiite fundamentalists, they might use their control over the oil to hold the US economy to ransom, much as OPEC did in 1973 when it launched the Arab oil embargo, pushing oil prices to record levels and flattening the US economy. If you are a neo-conservative who believes that the United States should dominate the world, gaining control over the Middle East's second-largest oil reserves (in Iraq) becomes essential, since the United States imports 60 percent of its daily oil needs (17 percent from Canada, the rest from overseas). According to Linda

Wind turbines in Denmark.

KURT S. HANSEN, TECHNICAL UNIVERSITY OF DENMARK

McQuaig, "Seizing Arab oilfields was too risky as long as the Soviet Union existed. The Soviet collapse in 1991 opened up new possibilities."[3]

And then there's "peak oil," the reality that the world seems to be hitting the halfway mark in its consumption of the global oil reserves. This means that for the next 30 years, or until most of the remaining oil is gone, the tension over who gains control of the world's remaining oil will increase. The underlying cause of the war in southern Sudan is the desire of the northern Sudanese to control the oil reserves in the south, which they did by redrawing the map and assuming control of the oil fields.

Unless there is a clear global initiative to make an orderly transition to a world based on sustainable energy, there will be further conflicts and wars in the Middle East, central Asia, west Africa, Angola, and Russia. Since the use of oil and other fossil fuels is also the primary cause of climate change, which threatens more global instabilities, the need for such a transition is imperative.

In Colorado, the Rocky Mountain Institute has produced a plan called *Winning the Oil Endgame: Innovation for Profits, Jobs, and Security*, which shows how the United States could completely phase out the use of oil while saving $70 billion a year.

In the San Diego/Tijuana area, Jim Bell has written *Creating a Sustainable Economy and Future On Our Planet*, which shows how the region could become self-sufficient in energy.

In Sweden, the government has made a national policy commitment that it will seek to end Sweden's dependence on oil by the year 2020.

The solutions call for far greater energy efficiency; the use of solar, wind, and other renewable energy sources; electric, hybrid, biofuel (and maybe hydrogen) vehicles; cycling, walking, car sharing, rail, and public transit; organic agriculture; strong local economies that reduce the need for trade; and lifestyle changes in which we stop wasting, stop buying goods we don't need, eat local food grown organically, and live more simply.

The solutions also call for global treaties in which all nations participate, both to tackle global climate change and to share out the remaining oil supply equitably so that we can cooperate to make a just and orderly transition out of oil, instead of fighting.

- Jim Bell: www.jimbell.com
- Peak Oil: www.peakoil.net
- *The Party's Over: Oil, War and the Fate of Industrialized Societies* by Richard Heinberg, New Society Publishers, 2003.
- *Powerdown: Options and Actions for a Post Carbon Future* by Richard Heinberg, New Society Publishers, 2004.
- *Petrodollar Warfare: Oil, War and the Future of the Dollar* by William Clark, New Society Publishers, 2004
- *Stormy Weather: 101 Solutions to Global Climate Change* by Guy Dauncey with Patrick Mazza: www.earthfuture.com/stormyweather
- *Winning the Oil Endgame*: www.oilendgame.com

11

Addressing Terrorism

Terrorism is what we call the violence of the weak, and we condemn it; *war* is what we call the violence of the strong, and we glorify it.

— Sydney J. Harris

The first step in preventing armed violence is to recognize that the deliberate infliction of terror, injury, suffering, and death on a population for political or economic gain is wrong whether it is done by an individual or a state. Nothing can justify suicide bombers purposely killing innocent people in order to make a political point, but nothing can justify the carnage of warfare, either.

Understanding why people become suicide bombers does not justify their actions, but it is the first logical step to prevention. Terrorism creates enormous fear because it is unexpected, indiscriminate, horrific, and because its victims are often children. We must equally abhor the dropping of cluster bombs on a civilian population. We must remember that civilian deaths are not unintended "collateral damage" in present-day wars; they are the predictable result of bombing populated areas and civil infrastructure — water purification plants, electricity grids, sewage disposal plants, and food distribution systems.

Terrorists like those who attacked the World Trade Center and the Spanish and British transportation systems are a minority in the countries they attacked. They operate in cells, connected in networks, but there is little popular support for their cause and no significant group ready to protect or hide them. The task of finding and arresting the people in such cells properly falls to the police, not the military. The task involves tracking people down, cutting supplies of weapons and explosives, and stopping the flow of money. Military action does not reduce the number of terrorists. In fact, as Mary Kaldor, the director of the Center for the Study of Global Governance at the London School of Economics, writes, "To use military means against an assortment of criminals and insurgents is simply to provoke and consolidate support for those groups."[1]

I am grateful to British researchers Scilla Elworthy and Gabrielle Rifkind for their insights into what motivates terrorists and what can be done to prevent their actions.[2] They note how the British rules of engagement in Iraq differed from those of the Americans. British troops were allowed to open fire only when attacked, using minimal force and directing it only at identified targets. The troops worked to build relationships in the local community. They walked the streets, drank coffee with local leaders, and wore berets instead of helmets. Unfortunately they lost the trust of the Iraqis when two men in Arab dress, said to be undercover British agents, were arrested by Iraqi police and later freed by the British in a military assault with tanks and helicopters. Two Iraqi civilians were killed in the attack that destroyed the jail. The situation in Basra deteriorated after that.

The stereotype of terrorists as poor, fanatical males is not helpful because many are well-educated young men from prosperous families. In some cases, women have been suicide bombers in Israel, Iraq, and Chechnya, but they are a minority. Several of the suspects in the World Trade Center and the London transit attacks were educated and living in the west. The common thread that appears in their life

- *Hearts and Minds* by Scilla Elworthy and Gabrielle Rifkind: www.demos.co.uk
- Oxford Research Group: www.oxfordresearchgroup.org.uk

experience is powerlessness, exclusion, trauma, and humiliation. The significance of humiliation as a source of anger and rage in Islamic men has received very little attention in the west or in Israel. The number of terrorists increases as anger and hatred increase. Among Palestinians and Iraqis, the drive to restore honor and dignity by using violence follows such humiliations as being forced to strip naked at checkpoints, being deprived of freedom of movement, or helplessly watching as their houses and olive groves are bulldozed. The videotapes of Abu Ghraib prison, and the degrading acts prisoners were forced to commit, fed the rage of those whose faith and culture were being dishonored.

People who are living in an uncertain, chaotic world, with no sense of control and no ability to influence their lives, may find comfort in the certainties afforded by fundamentalism. To prevent terrorism we must address the anger and rage that fuel it. One of Elworthy and Rifkind's key recommendations is to avoid more violence whenever possible. The killing of innocent civilians in Fallujah, the torture in Abu Ghraib, and the disrespect shown to women all allow terrorists to claim they are protecting the honor of the community.

Training armed forces personnel to show respect for the religious and cultural sensitivies of the population, to learn the basics of their language, and to understand why respect is so important would reduce some of the significant triggers of anger.

The solutions in this book include recommendations for governments, communities, schools, and faith groups that are working to reduce the risk of terrorism.

Ta'ayush Arab-Jewish Partnership volunteer work in Halisa.

12

A Culture of Violence

If a tribe's songs and dramas are centered on violence and warfare, if its young boys play war games and violently competitive sports from the earliest age, if its paintings, sculptures, and potteries depict fights and scenes of battle, it is a pretty sure bet that this is not a peaceful, gentle tribe.

— Myriam Miedzian, *Boys Will Be Boys*[1]

When violence and aggression are glorified as the ideal of masculinity, men and boys are trapped in a distorted expectation of what it means to be male. UNESCO recognizes that violence is not simply a response to conflict, but is expressed in all parts of culture, from child rearing to sports and entertainment. With this in mind, the UN declared the first ten years of the new century, 2001 to 2010, the International Decade for a Culture of Peace and Non-Violence for the Children of the World.

If we want to prevent violence, we must look at how we encourage and promote it. The world is dominated by American culture, and people in distant countries draw conclusions about what Americans are like from CNN. In fact, what they are seeing are the images of American culture that advertisers want shown. Ad agencies know that violent programs attract audiences whether the medium is TV, film, video games, or computer games. News editors use the guideline "If it bleeds it leads" to help decide which story to feature. The result is that we see a violent culture projected 24 hours a day, which causes us to integrate violence into the way we see the world. Unfortunately, movies and TV provide a steady diet of violence that is becoming more extreme and explicit as viewers become habituated to it.

Many facets of our culture are not visible to us because they are so familiar we think they are universal. Small children are often given toys that glorify violence and war. Many other cultures do not have such toys. Most of the cartoons on Saturday morning TV are extremely violent. They are not made less violent because the characters are cute little birds and cats. If we pay attention to dialogue in sitcoms, we see that what is meant as humor is often simply disrespect, sarcasm, foul language, and put-downs. Children imitate what they see, and so do we. Otherwise, advertisers would not spend millions for a 30-second time slot.

When I commented to a university class that films increasingly portrayed beautiful women as brutally violent murderers, a student made me a seven-minute collage of scenes from 15 current high-grossing films. They featured highly sexualized women carrying out horrendous murders and, in many cases, going free at the end. Her collage was almost intolerable to watch. Even

Violent computer games are one way we expose children to a culture of violence.

more appalling are the first-person video games available today, including one in which the player stalks a woman, rapes and kills her, and moves on to another.

Values in North American culture began to change about 80 years ago. Previously, success was associated with wisdom, courage, integrity, and patience. Now wealth has became the most valued characteristic. This change is not surprising when we consider that we are surrounded by messages that tell us that our longings to be loved, admired, and powerful can be satisfied by going shopping.

Underlying the culture of violence is the assumption that individual rights take precedence over any responsibility to the community. Corporations extend this assumption to mean that their rights trump the rights of communities that want environmental protection and social responsibility.

When prisoners from Iraq and Afghanistan were taken to sites that were not accessible to the Red Cross or the press, many human rights experts objected. They anticipated the torture and debasement of prisoners that occurred in Guantanamo Bay and Iraq's Abu Ghraib prison. What was shocking to the world was that political leaders tried to justify torture.

A measure of the violence or nonviolence of a culture is revealed in how it deals with those convicted of crime. Progressive societies make use of restorative justice programs that address the impact of the crime on the victim and, if possible, impose measures designed to rehabilitate the perpetrator and prevent recurrence of the crime. In some places, particularly in aboriginal communities, sentencing circles involve the whole community in determining how the convicted person will make restitution and eventually be accepted back into the community.

- Peaceful Childhoods Kit (From Physicians for Global Survival Canada):
  www.pgs.ca/index.php/Health/284
- UNESCO Culture of Peace: www.unesco.org
  "UNESCO or 60" is the opening page see box p. 15 for a UNESCO address that brings up "Peace is in our Hands.
- Voice of Women for Peace Workshop Kit:
  www.peace.ca/vowworkshopkit.htm

13

The Legacy of Gandhi

> Nonviolence is the greatest force at the disposal of mankind. It is mightier than the mightiest weapons of destruction devised by the ingenuity of man.
>
> — Mahatma Gandhi

We know the change we wish to see in the world — an end to the violent domination of others. We know that millions of courageous people have defeated violence by steadfastly refusing to recognize it as a moral force. By using nonviolence, or *ahimsa* as Gandhi called it, they have defeated overwhelming military might.

Gandhi was a towering figure of the 20th century. He made his life the personification of his teachings, and by doing so he showed that governments cannot rule without the permission of the governed. His intensive study of truth and his conviction that nonviolence can defeat military power led him to explore how nonviolence works, what furthers its goals, and what undermines its effectiveness. He was utterly

Mahatma Gandhi.

certain that the path he was taking would force the British Empire to give up control of India.

Mohandas Gandhi was born in India in 1869. As a young man, he went to Britain to study law. Although he practiced briefly in India on his return, he was soon sent to South Africa to represent an Indian firm. There he had an experience that transformed his life. He had purchased a first-class ticket on the train to Pretoria, but when a white person complained about his presence in the first-class coach, he was ejected and left to spend the night on the platform.

Gandhi, baffled and defiant, later described the incident as the watershed in his life. After that, he stood up against injustice at every opportunity and stayed in South Africa leading the resistance to laws that discriminated against Indians until 1914.

By the time he returned to India, he had become a well-known leader who had tested his ideas of the power of nonviolence in action. Millions of Indians referred to him as *Mahatma* or "great soul." He experimented with strikes, non-cooperation, and mass civil disobedience, and consequently spent large parts of his life in prison. Far from passively resistant, Gandhi sought strategies that forced the British to engage with the Indian people and either yield on an issue or use violence against unarmed demonstrators. Each time the British used violence, it decreased their moral authority and increased the Indian opposition.

Gandhi struggled to convince his followers not to respond violently to vicious beatings by the British, but to continue to refuse to yield to their authority. Again and again he confirmed that when his followers lapsed into violence, they were defeated by force and discredited.

We are fortunate that he recorded his thoughts about power and how it can be transformed, because his words are as relevant today as they were then.

Power is of two kinds. One is obtained by the fear of punishment and the other by acts of love. Power based on love is a thousand times more effective and permanent than the one derived from fear of punishment.

If patience is worth anything, it must endure to the end of time. And a living faith will last in the midst of the blackest storm.

A small body of determined spirits fired by an unquenchable faith in their mission can alter the course of human history.

We do not need to proselytize either by our speech or by our writing. We can only do so really with our lives. Let our lives be open books for all to study.

In his examination of truth, Gandhi studied philosophy and the religious texts of Christianity, Islam, and Indian faiths. He was profoundly influenced by the *Bhagavad Gita*, a Hindu religious book of moral discourses explaining the practice and philosophy of yoga.

The second half of the 20th century was filled with wars and the threat of nuclear annihilation, but it was also a time when Gandhi's legacy began to spread far beyond India. His ideas profoundly changed how many of those living under military dictatorships thought about the path to justice. Gandhi inspired many of those people to live their lives in service to the ideals he taught.

Gandhi was assassinated on January 30, 1948, less than a year after India gained its independence, but his legacy is still unfolding in nonviolent revolutions all over the world.

Today we have overwhelming evidence that nonviolence works and many examples of how it has worked in different cultures. We know it calls on that which is highest in each of us, and that, through nonviolence, small numbers of people can transform a whole society.

- Bombay Sarvodaya Mandal (Gandhian Book Center): www.mkgandhi.org
- *Gandhi*, 1982 film by Richard Attenborough
- Mahatma Gandhi Foundation: web.mahatma.org.in
- *The Story of My Experiments with Truth* by Mohandas Gandhi: www.nalanda.nitc.ac.in/resources/english/etext-project/Biography/gandhi/index.htm

14

The Power of Nonviolence

> The arc of the moral universe is
> long, but it bends toward justice.
> — Martin Luther King Jr.

Gene Sharp, a pacifist and political scientist, has documented thousands of nonviolent interventions and analyzed the factors that contribute to success. His writings have been widely distributed, including the underground democracy movements that transformed governments in the past half century. In 1991, when people took to the streets in Moscow to stop the coup against Mikhail Gorbachev, there were reports that they were passing copies of Gene Sharp's articles from hand to hand.

Nonviolence has a long and heroic history. Gene Sharp writes that in ancient Rome in 494 BC, the plebians protested their grievances by withdrawing to a hill outside the city. They refused to provide their usual services, and after several days the rulers agreed to provide better conditions for them. The hill became known as the Sacred Mount, and in 258 BC, when the Senate attempted to block reform, the army protested by marching to the Sacred Mount, where it threatened to build a new city.[1] The Senate yielded to its demands.

Gandhi's experiments with civil disobedience in South Africa in the early 1900s showed the power of non-cooperation to stop unjust government practices. When he returned to India, he continued to develop his ideas and used nonviolent resistance to challenge British rule. In 1930 he decided to defy the British monopoly on the production and sale of salt, a commodity that everyone needed and that the poor could easily make for themselves if they were allowed.

He first asked the viceroy, Lord Irwin, to amend the salt tax law. When he received no response, Gandhi proceeded to walk with his followers some 240 miles to the coastal village of Dandi.[2] At the seashore he picked up a lump of mud and salt that he boiled in seawater to make salt. He said, "With this, I am shaking the foundation of the British Empire."

All across India, thousands of people made salt or bought it illegally. A month later, Gandhi was jailed, as were 60,000 of his followers. The salt march was a turning point. The British had lost their moral authority, and by 1947 they had lost India.

Nonviolent actions are not passive, and they are not cautious. They require careful planning, great discipline, courage, and willingness to accept beatings and even death. The power of an unarmed individual facing a much stronger and well-armed adversary shows the strength of a moral principle that most people have integrated into the deepest level of their psyche — that it is morally reprehensible and, indeed, cowardly to attack or kill someone who is clearly weaker than you are.

Gandhi thought deeply about the principles that would have to apply if a people chose to

- Bombay Sarvodaya Mandal (Gandhian Book Center): www.mkgandhi.org/
- Mahatma Gandhi Foundation: web.mahatma.org.in
- *A Force More Powerful* and *Bringing Down a Dictator*: www.aforcemorepowerful.org

use nonviolence against oppression and injustice. His life, his many campaigns, and his writings provided the foundation for the civil rights movement in the American South, the end of apartheid in South Africa, and the velvet revolutions that have brought democratic change to a long series of despotic regimes.

Gandhi called this concept of action *satyagraha*, combining the Hindu words for "truth" and "holding firmly." Martin Luther King Jr. brought his Christian faith to nonviolent action, comparing the power of nonviolence to St. Paul's idea of love. King also saw it as more than just a strategy. It was a way of tapping into a greater power. His great skill as a preacher drew the different civil disobedience actions into a coherent movement with a solid base in Christianity and the churches in the southern United States.

Montgomery, Alabama, hit the world news when Rosa Parks was arrested for refusing to give up her seat to a white passenger on a bus in 1955.[3] As blacks mobilized, Martin Luther King Jr. became their charismatic leader. By 1960 there were sit-ins in 78 cities. Some 70,000 students were involved in demonstrations, and 3,000 went to jail. Boycotts of white firms, sit-ins at lunch counters, and demonstrations spread throughout the South. People took training in nonviolent civil disobedience, and systematic recruitment brought thousands more into the movement.

Finally, the Civil Rights Act was passed by President Lyndon Johnson in 1964, followed in 1965 by the Voting Rights Act. One of the legacies of the American Civil Rights movement is the song "We Shall Overcome," which has become the anthem for struggles for peace and justice in countries all over the world.

RUSSELL DAVIDSON

Rosa Parks.

15

Small Signs of Hope

In April we cannot see sunflowers in France, so we might say the sunflowers do not exist. But the local farmers have already planted thousands of seeds, and when they look at the bare hills, they may be able to see the sunflowers already. The sunflowers are there. They lack only the conditions of sun, heat, rain and July. Just because we cannot see them does not mean that they do not exist.

— Thich Nhat Hanh, *Living Buddha, Living Christ*[1]

Signs of hope are like the tiny, surprising seedlings of sunflowers. When I look for the signs of a culture of peace, I see the green shoots pushing up even in the desert of a war zone.

The rising influence of civil society in international relations is a major sign of hope, but most of my life is spent in the small sphere of everyday routine, not the heady atmosphere of the UN. The signs of hope are all around me in small expressions of the culture of peace. The public voice of civil society is based in thousands of actions, each seemingly small and inconsequential, like Thich Nhat Hanh's sunflowers. Each action builds the habits of respect, caring, and cooperation that shape the way we want our society to respond to the challenges of conflict.

A Few Sunflowers

In my home city of Victoria, the principal of a small school stands on the curb in the morning, greeting every child by name as they arrive. The whole staff took training in how to make the school a welcoming place. In several other schools, the children are raising funds for a girls' school in Afghanistan and are exchanging art with a school in Uganda.

Although church attendance continues to drop in Canada, the involvement of church people in social action and service continues to rise. Churches may not be full on Sundays, but they are full on weekday nights, when the homeless come in from the cold and are fed and sheltered. Churches are rallying around American military resisters who have come to Canada as the Vietnam draft dodgers did in the 1970s. The sanctuary movement is preparing itself in case the United States restores the draft.

Toronto has a program for grade 6 boys called "Boys for Babies." Each class is introduced to a toddler under two years old who comes to class once a month. The students follow the infant's growth and development for several months. They learn what to expect in terms of the child's vocabulary, diet, and milestones. The demand for the class is so great the teachers have trouble locating enough volunteer parents with toddlers.

The story of Hossam Abdala, a New York taxi driver, made the world news in August 2005.[2] The 30 year old returned bags full of diamond rings worth $200,000 to a Jewish businessman who left them in the trunk of his taxi. Abdala told reporters that the best part was that his father was so proud of him for doing the honest act expected of a good Muslim.

The Forgiveness Project is a website of stories of people who have chosen not to feed hatred in their hearts, but to try to find the capacity to forgive terrible wrongs. Jo Berry's father, Sir Anthony Berry, a British MP, was killed when the IRA bombed the hotel hosting the Conservative Party convention in Brighton, UK, in 1984. Jo chose to stop blaming an unseen enemy, and in 2000 she set out on a journey of healing that took her to meet Patrick McGee, the man who killed her father. They talked for three hours and struggled to hear and understand the other person's story. Both are now engaged in projects to help people work through their pain from the period the Irish call "The Troubles." Their story is on the Forgiveness Project website.

These acts of generosity, honesty, compassion, and wit counter the images of violence, anger, and fear that make us believe the world is a jungle. If all the acts of kindness were reported, we might see the world not as a jungle, but as a rain forest, nurturing and sheltering us. Showing children they are respected, putting your faith on the line to help the poor and disadvantaged, breaking down stereotypes, being honest, and knowing when to laugh are the seeds we plant in daily life that bring a harvest of hope.

In blaming and dehumanizing the enemy, our hearts shut down, we lose some of our own humanity, and we become part of the problem.

— Jo Berry

Jo Berry.

• Forgiveness Project: www.theforgivenessproject.com

16

Big Signs of Hope

Each time a person stands for an ideal, or acts to improve the lot of others, or strikes out against injustice, he or she sends forth a tiny ripple of hope. And crossing each other from a million different centers of energy and daring, those ripples build a current that can sweep down the mightiest walls of oppression and resistance.

— Robert F. Kennedy

Interconnections

Perhaps the most hopeful sign for the future is the widespread awareness that all the global issues that face humanity are interconnected. Peace, environment, sustainable development, human rights, participatory democracy, and the advancement of women are all dependent on each other. Global civil society is making these connections, and the networking of international movements is increasing rapidly. UNESCO's International Decade for a Culture of Peace and Non-Violence for the Children of the World is a major opportunity for communities to become involved in education and exchanges with the rest of the world.

International Law and the UN and the EU

The United Nations is more than a sign of hope; it is a milestone in human social development. For the first time the world has a forum for discussing disagreements and preventing armed conflict. UN agencies like WHO and UNICEF have demonstrated the benefits of international cooperation for the health and well-being of children.

The UN has succeeded in establishing treaties that ban the use of biological and chemical weapons. The path to the treaty banning antipersonnel landmines began with the actions of civil society and ended in a partnership between civil society and governments. The International Criminal Court (ICC) is another initiative of civil society and governments. The ICC puts war criminals on trial if their own country cannot or will not do so. As a result, brutal leaders can be held accountable for war crimes and crimes against humanity.

The European Union (EU) is another major achievement. In a region where wars had taken place, one after another, for centuries, the countries of Europe chose to form a cooperative union. The union has grown to 25 member countries. The complex issues that must be resolved in the EU are clearly trying the abilities of leaders to mediate differences; nonetheless, the EU is slowly stabilizing and finding its

Jody Williams and Lloyd Axworthy at Mines Action Canada's symposium on the 5th anniversary of the treaty signing.

- UNESCO: www.unesco.org
- UNICEF: unicef.org
- *War and Peace in the 21ˢᵗ Century*: www.humansecurityreport.info
- Women's International League for Peace and Freedom: wilpf.org
- World Social Forum: www.forumsocialmundial.org.br

way. The idea that one of the member countries would attack another is becoming unimaginable.

Civil Society

The rise of civil society is a major sign of hope. In almost every country the participation of groups and individuals is shaping the debates on global climate change, free market capitalism, the privatization of resources, human rights, rights of women, and armed conflict.

Opposition to the policies of the World Trade Organization, the International Monetary Fund, and the World Bank makes it clear that these institutions do not serve the public good and must be reformed. The World Social Forum was set up as a response to the World Economic Forum of wealthy and powerful corporate CEOs and government leaders held annually in Davos, Switzerland. The World Social Forum brings civil society together to discuss the serious global issues facing the world. The forum grew to 120,000 participants in 2005, and now conferences are divided into regions. Civil society supports global trade that is fair and equitable, rather than unregulated free market capitalism.

Women

The increasing participation of women in decision-making bodies is another positive sign of hope, even though the change is slow and insufficient. Developing countries are leading the world in mandating the participation of women in municipal governance. The UN Security Council Resolution 1325, which calls for full participation of women in all phases of peacebuilding and conflict resolution, is discussed in Solution 14.

World Public Opinion

I have a sense that we are at the beginning of a global social revolution — a sense that is supported by the surprising 2005 research report of the Human Security Centre at the University of British Columbia. *War and Peace in the 21ˢᵗ Century* shows a strong global trend away from war, particularly since 1991, and concludes that the world has become "war averse."

- 60 dictators have toppled, almost all without violence.
- The number of genocides dropped by 80 percent between 1988 and 2001.
- The number of international crises dropped more than 70 percent in the same time.
- The number of armed conflicts around the world has dropped 40 percent since 1991.
- Global military expenditure and troop numbers declined sharply in the 1990s.
- Some 100 armed conflicts have quietly ended since 1988.

The end of colonialism and the end of the Cold War changed the global political landscape. The report credits the dramatic increase in UN conflict prevention and peacebuilding efforts, the advancement of international law, and the increased influence of civil society with moving the world away from war.

17

The New Ground Rules

Formerly, a nation that broke the peace did not trouble to try and prove to the world that it was done solely from higher motives .... Now war has a bad conscience. Now every nation assures us that it is bleeding for a human cause, the fate of which hangs in the balance of its victory .... No nation dares to admit the guilt of blood before the world.
— Ellen Key, *War, Peace and the Future* (1916)

The past century brought unprecedented bloodshed, but it also brought a global shift in the norms of civilized behavior. People were exhausted by two world wars, and despite the earlier failure of the League of Nations, they were determined to found a strong international organization to prevent war.

The UN Charter begins "We the peoples of the United Nations determined to save succeeding generations from the scourge of war .... " It was indeed the peoples of the world who demanded a different world order. The UN Charter set new ideals for international relations, and leaders, both good and bad, signed on. Colonial rulers, military dictators, ruthless and corrupt politicians, and those who were serious about a better world order all signed the Charter.

Shortly after the UN was founded, the same mixture of leaders signed the Universal Declaration of Human Rights. Some of them probably had no intention of complying with the provisions of either document. In spite of the hypocrisy, however, the Charter and the Declaration have become the standards for civilized behavior. Nations are now embarrassed to be found out of step.

International agreements made through the UN address colonialism, racism, and discrimination against women, and integrate the ideals of inclusivity, tolerance, and justice. Civil society demands a moral commitment to fulfill the intent of global agreements to advance the common good. The Convention on the Rights of the Child, which came into force in 1990, is an example of an agreement that sets the bar very high. If states fulfilled their obligations under the convention, children would be protected in war zones, would be first to receive aid in difficult circumstances, and would be entitled to education and health care no matter where they lived. Because the convention has the force of international law, civil society is able to use it to pressure governments.

After World War II, the United States recognized the possibility of renewed hostilities if Germany were left in poverty and devastation, as it had been after World War I. Through the Marshall Plan, the US committed enormous financial support to reconstruct Germany. This forward thinking brought longstanding stability to Europe and led to the possibility of cooperation instead of enmity. The European Union is the result. Similar reconstruction of Japan, and constitutional change to prevent rearming, brought Japan peace and prosperity.

Gandhi's nonviolent overthrow of British colonial rule in India was another milestone in

- History of the UN: www.un.org/aboutun/history.htm
- International Crisis Group: www.crisisgroup.org
- UNIFEM (UN Development Fund for Women): www.unifem.org
- United Nations: www.un.org

the new norms of international behavior. The people of the Philippines applied Gandhian principles to their resistance movement and toppled Ferdinand Marcos. Their revolution was the first of what proved to be a long series of regime changes with little bloodshed. The fall of the Berlin wall in 1989 was followed by the collapse of the Soviet Union and the end of dictatorships in one Soviet satellite after another.

As civil society was finding its stride, women were taking up leadership roles. In 1985, the UN met in Nairobi to evaluate progress at the end of the Decade for Women. The Kenyan government expected about 4,500 women to attend the non-governmental organization (NGO) conference that accompanied the official meetings. Instead, 16,000 women converged on Nairobi, filling hotels and overflowing into the community, where Kenyans opened their homes to welcome them.

In Canada in 1985, women were protesting the Indian Act because it stipulated that aboriginal women who married non-aboriginal men lost their Indian status, while non-aboriginal women who married aboriginal men gained status. Anticipating scathing criticism in Nairobi, the Canadian government enacted Bill C-31 shortly before the UN conference. The bill restored full treaty rights to all aboriginal women. That is just one example of civil society's power to ensure that documents signed by governments are not dead files, but the guiding principles for governance.

The UN takes the education of women seriously because as female literacy improves, so does the health of a society, the economic status of women, and the ability of families to plan the number of children they want. Unfortunately, the lack of women's rights in Africa has led to the terrible toll of HIV/AIDS, with women making up nearly 75 percent of those infected between ages 15 and 25.

These new ground rules of justice, protection of the environment, human rights, and international law are as clear to civil society as they are to the nations that flout them. A small number of powerful people are trying to shed the global ethic that has taken 50 years and the sacrifices of millions of people to build, but civil society is not about to let that happen.

End of the Decade for Women Conference in Kenya brought 16,000 women to Nairobi.

ANNE S. WALKER, INTERNATIONAL WOMEN'S TRIBUNE CENTER

35

18

The Women Have Come to Stay

Women are not thinking of courage in relation to the power that means exercising might over people …. Rather it is the power of listening, of patience …. This is a new vision of power that we, as women, have together.

— Dame Nita Barrow

The advancement of women in the past 30 years parallels the rise of civil society. If we try to measure progress by women's incomes or their election to federal political leadership or their power in the corporate world, we are justified in feeling disappointed. On the other hand, if we look at civil society, we see the impact of women's activism in the movements for peace, the environment, and human rights.

Early feminists drew attention to some of the characteristics of male hierarchical societies that are not welcoming to women — competition, disregard for the emotional context, disconnection from the Earth and from caring relationships, and emphasis on the bottom line without regard for other values. Women's groups experimented with organizing in a nonhierarchical way, arranging chairs in circles instead of rows facing a platform, rotating responsibility for running a meeting, and emphasizing consensus. They elevated the importance of relationships and connections with the Earth and future generations. They insisted that emotional responses and better communication skills are as important as efficiency.

- Green Belt Movement: www.greenbeltmovement.org
- Nobel Peace Prize Laureates: www.nobelprize.org/peace/laureates
- UN Division for the Advancement of Women: www.un.org/womenwatch/daw
- UNIFEM: www.unifem.org

Gradually the processes and values women were demonstrating moved into the mainstream. We see them in schools and communities, in business meetings, and even in men's groups. Social movements adopted many of the women's processes. They set up nonhierarchical organizational structures and began to train people in communication skills and conflict resolution. Inclusive processes support the participation of minorities and expose assumptions about power that were previously invisible to most people.

Women began doing much more public speaking; they began taking on leadership roles in NGOs; and they encouraged girl children to work toward careers in sciences, law, and medicine. Women were early users of computer communications and have built international networks that connect women from remote areas to actions at the UN or national capitals.

Women are not newcomers to social activism. They began to take a role in western civil society when they demanded and got the vote, and when they demanded and (mostly) got rights before the law, property rights, divorce rights, and the right to protection from assault. The Convention on the Elimination of all Forms of Discrimination Against Women (CEDAW) has been signed by 180 countries, although a number of countries, including the United States, have not yet ratified it.

In developing countries, women are strong advocates for social justice. Since 1991, the Nobel Peace Prize has recognized five women, four of them from developing countries: Aung

San Suu Kyi (Burma), Rigoberta Menchú Tum (Guatemala), Shirin Ebadi (Iran), and Wangari Maathai (Kenya). The fifth, Jody Williams (United States), was recognized for her role in the International Campaign to Ban Landmines. In the first 90 years, only seven women were awarded the prize.

At a conference in Kenya, I first encountered the strong women of Africa. They were articulate and highly critical of the effects of the global economic system, continuing colonial oppression, and violence against women.

When a woman from the wealthy north suggested that it was important to raise money for the south, the African women became quiet and clearly uncomfortable. One finally said, "Sister, leave us to work out our lives here. You go home and change what your country is doing that is keeping us in poverty and misery."

It has taken me many years to learn all of the ways that my country and others in the north have set up structures that hold developing countries in the grip of debt. Gradually I have come to understand the words of Lila Watson, an Australian aboriginal poet, who wrote "If you have come to help me, you are wasting your time. But if you recognize that your liberation and mine are bound up together, we can walk together."

Meanwhile, women like Wangari Maathai took the future in their own hands. In 1977,

Maathai planted seven trees in her yard and encouraged other women to do the same. Thus began the Green Belt Movement to plant trees to stop the encroachment of the desert. Women planted so many trees they used up all the government seedlings. The government paid them to produce more seedlings and continue planting. They have now planted more than 30 million trees. Wangari Maathai was awarded the Nobel Peace Prize in 2004. For the first time the award recognized the interdependency between peace, the environment, and human rights.

Russell Davidson

Wangari Maathai, Nobel Peace Prize Laureate, 2004.

19

Getting the Word past the Roadblocks

We are not afraid to entrust the American people with unpleasant facts, foreign ideas, alien philosophies, and competitive values. For a nation that is afraid to let its people judge the truth and falsehood in an open market is afraid of its people.

— John F. Kennedy

The day I received a fax from Sylvia Schriever, a doctor on Greenpeace's *Rainbow Warrior* in the middle of the Pacific Ocean, I knew that the age of world citizens had become a reality. In the 1980s, faxes themselves were still a source of amazement, but if I could send an instant letter to a boat in the Pacific, I could correspond equally well with a doctor in a war zone.

Participatory democracy depends on the free flow of information. Fax machines, cell phones, text messaging, e-mail, and the Internet make it possible to alert people when decision makers propose unacceptable legislation. Responses can be coordinated very quickly, and background facts distributed so that individuals can write their own letters. Many government proposals have been scrapped in the face of a deluge of e-mails and faxes.

North Korea confiscates your cell phone when you arrive in the country and gives it back when you leave. The government knows that a

- Democracy for America: www.democracyforamerica.com
- Ethical Markets Television: www.ethicalmarkets.com
- Indymedia: www.indymedia.com
- MoveOn: www.moveon.org
- The Real News: www.therealnews.com
- True Majority: www.truemajority.com
- Truthout: www.truthout.org
- Win Without War: www.winwithoutwarus.org

closed society can only remain isolated if it prevents communication with the outside. However, it is becoming more and more difficult to control information as computer use increases. Trying to select some technology, but not all, is simply not workable. A country that wants the advantages of modern communications will have to become an open society.

When hundreds of Chinese students demonstrated for democracy and were killed in Tiananmen Square in 1989, faxes carried news and comments in and out of China despite all the government's efforts to prevent the spread of information. Some doctors who had seen victims dying in emergency were killed, but others were saved because fax machines made it possible to secretly arrange visas from governments that would accept them at their embassies and facilitate their travel out of the country.

The control of mass media by a small number of giant conglomerates limits the depth of mainstream news broadcasts and greatly biases reporting in favor of advertisers and the interests of corporations. The frustration of trying to understand a whole story when a program offers only a sound bite is driving more and more people to look for alternative sources of news.

The ability of individuals to upload video to a website without going through a television studio may be forcing the networks to provide more balanced coverage. As the technology advances, a growing number of websites are making videotaped speeches and films available online. This means that instead of viewing a

15-second clip of a speaker on the news, you can see the whole speech and understand the context. All without advertising.

One exciting development is The Real News, a channel that will broadcast on the web and on cable stations that choose to run it (see Solution 73). The programs will feature progressive journalists reporting on global content. It will be supported by members and will not be financed by government or commercial interests or be subject to government regulation of content.

Web networks connecting activist groups have made it possible to expand actions from one city to the world. In 2003, when US president Bush met with British prime minister Tony Blair in Washington, thousands of Washington-area residents attended a candlelight vigil at the Lincoln Memorial to protest the planned US-led invasion of Iraq. Win Without War, a mainstream antiwar coalition, and MoveOn.org, a million-member web-activist organization, issued a web-call for activists to hold vigils in their communities. Over 6,000 vigils were held in 136 countries.

When Cindy Sheehan was camped in a ditch near President Bush's ranch at Crawford, Texas, on August 17, 2005, activist organizations MoveOn, True Majority, and Democracy for America called for candlelight vigils. More than 1,627 vigils were held, with 50,000 people signed up in the United States. Thousands more vigils were held around the world in support of Sheehan, who was waiting for Bush to answer her question "What noble purpose did my son die for?" Although the president did not meet with Sheehan, the rapid response of global activist networks shows civil society's continued determination to end the occupation of Iraq.

Cindy Sheehan speaks out against the war in Iraq.

20

Democracies Up, Dictators Down

The oppressed without hope are mysteriously quiet. When the conception of change is beyond the limits of the possible, there are no words to articulate discontent so it is sometimes held not to exist. This mistaken belief arises because we can only grasp silence in the moment in which it is breaking.

— **Sheila Rowbotham**

In the late 1980s and 1990s, the overthrow of Eastern European governments, one after another, took many westerners by surprise. They had been unaware of the underground movements that prepared people for the pivotal moment when they could act.

In Poland, Lech Valesa, a young activist in the Gdansk shipyard, was leading a nonviolent movement against the communist government through his labor union, Solidarity. After a year and a half of confrontations between Solidarity and the government, Valesa was captured at gunpoint in 1981. "At this moment, you lost," he told them. He recognized, as had Gandhi, that when a government loses the permission of the public and must rule by force, its time is limited. Eight years later, Poland had free parliamentary elections and defeated the communists.

The Soviet Union was in the throes of change under the leadership of President Mikhail Gorbachev. In 1987, Gorbachev introduced *perestroika* (economic restructuring) and *glasnost* (transparency), which were meant to reduce the secrecy of decision makers and allow public debate and criticism of government policy. Gorbachev made radical changes in the foreign policies of the USSR. When I heard him speak in 1987 at the Moscow Forum for a Nuclear-Free World for the Survival of Mankind, he said that no country should be able to hold another by force and that the USSR would have to get out of Afghanistan. The audience found it hard to believe, but he had laid out the principles that would guide his leadership.

The changes in Poland led to Hungary opening the Iron Curtain and allowing its citizens to visit Austria. Mass demonstrations began in East Germany, and in October, Erich Honecker, the head of state, had to resign. The new government planned to end travel restrictions to the west, and one of the officials was asked by a reporter when the new law would take effect. He said he thought it was immediately. In response, thousands of people streamed to the gates, and the

Annual meeting of Nobel Peace Prize Laureates in Rome. Left to right: Dr. Sergie Kolesnikov, Mikhail Gorbachev, Mary-Wynne Ashford, Dr. Sergei Gratchev.

GORBACHEV FOUNDATION ITALY

guards allowed them to pass into West Berlin. People danced on the wall in an exuberant display of the joy of freedom.

True to his word that one state should not hold another by force, Gorbachev did not send troops to East Germany. People's movements in the other Soviet satellite countries were ready for the opportunity now presented. They rose up against dictators and ousted the communist governments in a dozen countries, with little blood shed except in Romania.

Tragically, in 1989, Chinese students also tried to use peaceful demonstrations to bring more democracy to China. Their attempt failed at the cost of hundreds of young lives. The role of the army is critical in a mass demonstration. If it remains loyal to the government, the resistance can be crushed. If it is already on the side of the people, the leaders will be toppled. Regrettably, in Tiananmen Square, the Chinese government brought in troops from the countryside who followed orders regardless of the loss of life, and the rebellion was quashed.

Democracy movements owe much to the courage of young people who are willing to confront tyranny. Often they challenge authority through their art, whether it is music, writing, theater, or other forms. Oppressive regimes cannot tolerate art that suggests there are

alternative ways to view the world. In August 2005, the government of Uzbekistan, in an attempt to prevent a democratic revolution, banned imported music and outside groups known to support nonviolent change. The Uzbek government had identified some of the powerful forces that threaten despotic rulers, but the seeds were planted long ago and are unlikely to be uprooted now.

Biblical scholar Walter Wink noted that the successful revolutions that started in 1989 involved 1.7 billion people; if we add up all the people involved in all the nonviolent movements of the 20th century, the figure comes to 3.4 billion people.[1] That is more than half the world's population on the way toward democracy. How can we doubt the power of nonviolent change? Since Professor Wink did his calculations, Georgia, Ukraine, and Kyrgyzstan have also replaced their rulers with democratically elected leaders.

- Common Dreams: www.commondreams.org
- Open Societies Institute: www.soros.org
- Walter Wink, *Jesus and Nonviolence*: www.thinkingpeace.com/Lib/lib080.html

21

The World We Want

Another world is not only possible, she is on her way. On a quiet day, I can hear her breathing.

— Arundhati Roy

One of the roots of war digs down into the psyches of ordinary people; it feeds off a place where poverty, inequality, oppression, and a lack of control over the fundamentals of life feed anger and humiliation. For centuries, it has been mostly young men who expressed their anger. Today, increasing numbers of young women are joining them. They know it is not right that rich people live in luxury, with fancy homes and big salaries, while poor families are deprived of the most basic control over food, warmth, land, water, and housing. Whether they live in the refugee camps of Palestine, the slums of Pakistan, or the back streets of Belfast, their response has often been primitive: to fight with whatever weapons they can find. The sense of injustice is a powerful moral force that can be expressed either through soul-force and non-violence or through hatred and war.

When a sense of injustice is taken up by a nation's leaders and distorted for personal power, it can lead to the most awful consequences. This is what happened in the 1930s, when Germany's and Italy's leaders persuaded their country's population that they had been shut out of empire-grabbing by the British, French, and Russians.

In Rwanda/Burundi, where population growth was putting intense pressure on the land, the violence of Hutu against Tutsi broke out first in those communities that had the least amount of land. In the genocide that followed, one of the motivations was to kill every member of a family line so that no one should be left to claim the land.

When we consider the amount of poverty and injustice in the world today, and the number of young people under the age of 30, it is remarkable that there is not more violence. Even in the worst of situations, there are heartwarming stories of constructive endeavor that show the human desire to build a caring, compassionate world is still strong and alive.

On Easter Island, a remote bit of land in the eastern Pacific, when the Polynesian settlers had cut down the last tree and lost most of their topsoil to unsustainable practices, they turned to warfare and cannibalism.

On Tikopia, a remote island in the western Pacific, the Polynesian settlers faced the same pressures of population growth. Instead of fighting, however, they united, and changed their way of living. They adopted strict population control, abandoned patch-cutting for forest permaculture, and stopped eating meat because they saw that the animals consumed too many resources. Today the Tikopians are very proud of their culture, and though they may not know

- Arundhati Roy: www.arundhatiroy.org.uk
- Easter Island: www.primitivism.com/easter-island.htm
- Grameen: www.grameen-info.org
- Mondragon: www.mondragon.mcc.es
- Sekem: www.sekem.com
- Sustainability: www.earthfuture.com
- Tikopia: en.wikipedia.org/wiki/Tikopia

the word "sustainability," they are practicing it. Their culture is male-hierarchical and traditional, but they live in peace.

What does it mean to build a sustainable world?

- It means building a fair, transparent, and unbiased democracy so that people can choose their representatives without fear of corruption or the theft of votes by the rich and powerful.

- It means that the population growth of a region must be voluntarily limited so that it does not exceed the carrying capacity of the land and its ability to produce food, energy, and water.

- It means establishing mechanisms that give communities democratic control over their land, water, and sources of energy so that they can grow healthy food for their own needs and build settlements they are proud of.

- It means establishing mechanisms that allow communities to build and control their own local economies, and to invest their savings locally, so that they are not at the mercy of distant corporations whose interests are anything but their own.

The people of Mondragon, in the Basque country of northern Spain, have done this; as have the people of Bologna, in Italy; the people in many aboriginal cultures around the world (provided they are left relatively alone and given absolute security of their land); the 2,000 people who work on organically managed farmland reclaimed from the desert in the business initiative called Sekem (vitality from the sun), outside Cairo, in Egypt; and the villagers who are part of the Grameen movement for financial self-sufficiency and village pride in Bangladesh.

Sustainability is a gift from the future that we can claim for the present if we set our minds to it. It is a fundamental precondition for a truly peaceful world.

Sekem, an Egyptian initiative, began with biodynamic agriculture and has grown to combine economic, social, and cultural endeavors for human development.

22

Learning to Stand

> Example is not the main thing in influencing others; it is the only thing.
>
> — Albert Schweitzer

People often tell me they want to do something, but they don't know what. Sometimes they start by helping organize events, writing letters, making phone calls, or working on newsletters. As they get to know people in a group, they know who they like to work with, who is a trusted source of information, and who could use a hand. They often find themselves doing what they never imagined — public speaking!

When I first decided to get involved in the antinuclear movement, I asked Dr. Elinor Powell, the president of the local chapter of Physicians for Social Responsibility, what I should do. She said "Nobody can tell you what you should do. You look around and think what might make a difference and do it. And if anyone asks you to help, you say 'yes'." With that advice, I went to a gathering of Women's Alternatives to Negotiating Peace and said "yes" to my first speaking engagement.

I wrote a speech comparing people to the instruments in a symphony and, fortunately, ran it past an organizer ahead of time. She said, "Get to the point. Don't waste time. Just tell the audience why we have to get rid of nuclear weapons." I realize now what good advice that was. Another piece of good advice is "Don't apologize." Many speakers begin by saying they can't cover the topic in the limited time they have ... or they didn't have time to prepare slides. It's better just to start your speech.

I remember spending hours preparing a speech to medical colleagues about a delegation of Canadian doctors who went to Moscow, Leningrad, and Tbilisi in 1986. I was intimidated to speak to my peers in case they asked a question I couldn't answer. I carried a binder with details about the Soviet medical system, the numbers and types of Soviet nuclear weapons, and the arguments for a Comprehensive Test Ban Treaty. I should have saved my time.

Their hands went up the moment I finished. "Were you followed everywhere?' they asked. "Were you scared? What did the doctors say — could you actually talk to them? Could you go out on your own?" They asked the same questions I had in my own mind when I left for Moscow. Basically, we all wanted to know if the Soviets were human. I ended up telling

RUSSELL DAVIDSON

The author preparing to give her first rally speech. Victoria Peace Walk, April 1985.

stories about hospitals, dinners, and the warm, generous-hearted people we met.

Slowly and painfully, I learned that if I was serious about getting people to become active against nuclear weapons, I needed to tell them what *they* wanted to know, not what I wanted them to know. As a teacher, I knew they would only retain three or four points, and that if I wove the points into stories, they were more likely to be affected. I gave them handouts to satisfy my need to tell them what I thought they should know.

When I spoke on the radio, I was in a terrible panic in case the interviewer stumped me with a question. Then I read that people don't actually remember what you say on the radio in an interview. They remember whether you sounded honest, concerned, and credible. If you did, they were likely to move toward your viewpoint without really remembering what you said. What a humbling bit of information! After that, I wrote down the two or three points I wanted to make and memorized a short, pithy saying for a sound bite. "We either learn to live together or we will die together" or "Human beings and nuclear weapons cannot co-exist." I

started saving good quotations and posting them on my refrigerator.

Finally I realized that I didn't have to know everything. All that mattered was that I didn't want nuclear war and neither did the audience. People filled in details I didn't know, and if I couldn't answer a question, someone in the audience could. The important thing was just to start.

My life became enriched by the people I met, many of whom had been working since the 1960s to ban nuclear weapons. My closest friendships developed over e-mail with people I had met only a few times in person. My meetings with Physicians for Global Survival every six months became my times of spiritual sustenance and renewal.

Groups Providing Background Information

- Democracy in Action: www.democracyinaction.org
- Oxford Research Group: www.oxfordresearchgroup.org.uk
- Peace Pledge Union: www.ppu.org.uk
- Physicians for Global Survival (Canada): www.pgs.ca

23

Transforming Our Thinking

Tempting as it may be to conform to prevailing orthodoxies, resist them .... Question every assumption and every argument ... keep alive your precious power of independent, open-minded, critical enquiry.

— Richard Levin, president of Yale University, 1994

Building a movement to create a culture of peace means more than joining a protest group or writing letters to try to influence a decision maker. It also means showing who you are to people who are in your sphere of influence everyday — your family, your next-door neighbor, your hairdresser, your grocer. We can transform our society one by one, starting with those closest to us.

At a retreat of our Canadian doctors' group, members told what transformed their thinking and compelled them to work for nuclear disarmament. All of us could describe either a moment or a gradual process that brought us to a commitment to action. For one it was seeing the Tatsenshini River wilderness and knowing that it could disappear forever in a nuclear war; for another it was looking at his new-born granddaughter and thinking of her future. Another read a scientific article and suddenly connected it with his life. For many, the experience came from attending a lecture or seeing a film.

Research shows that people are more likely to go through transformation if they are comfortable, feel safe, and are emotionally involved. If they trust and admire the person they are listening to or the author they are reading, they are more likely to shift their views. They need to feel respected for their current beliefs in order to be able to give them up. When their beliefs are challenged, they are more likely to freeze. They need to have enough information to make informed judgments, and they need answers to questions. They feel more comfortable shifting position if they are part of a group, if they feel supported, and if they can see the next step for them in the new paradigm.

One summer I taught a university course in global education. One of the students was a friendly young man whose passion was hockey, not studying. I had taught him previously, and he now told me honestly that he had no particular interest in global issues; he just wanted to graduate.

The major assignment for the course was to examine a global issue and find the hopeful solutions that experts were advancing to deal with it. Each student gave a 15-minute presentation of an issue and the best solutions available. They handed out two-page summaries to their classmates. At the end of the course, each student took home the summaries of the positive steps being taken to deal with 15 of the most serious problems facing the world. The topics ranged from global climate change to the rights of aboriginal people. As the last student finished her presentation and class members gave their impressions of what we had learned, the young man came to me. He said, "I have never thought about any of these issues before. I have only cared about hockey. Now that I know, I'll never be the same again, will I?"

He won't be the same again. You can't go backwards once you have wakened to the state of the Earth. Even if you don't choose to become an activist in a group, your awareness changes your conversations and what you notice going on around you. It isn't so much a loss of innocence as an expansion of consciousness to include what is eternally important and where you fit into the whole scheme of things. I think he was affected so deeply because the issues were presented by his friends and peers, rather than by me. He saw them struggling with their despair and finding hope in the steps that are already underway.

All of the students were struck by the multiple crises we face, but all saw that the solutions have common threads:

- Care about other people.
- Care about living things.
- Stop wasting and destroying.
- Think before you act, but do act.

All of the solutions told us to make a smaller footprint on the Earth and to be aware of how we affect the seventh generation after us. We felt close, as if we had been given special knowledge for a reason. That feeling faded as the days went by, but not the sense of hope we gained from each other.

The Nuclear Weapons Inheritance Project is based on dialogue among students from different countries. Here Chinese and European medical students meet in Beijing to discuss the nuclearized world they have inherited.

- Educators for Social Responsibility: www.esrnational.org
- Global Issues: www.globalissues.org
- Project Ploughshares: www.ploughshares.ca
- The Initiative For Inclusive Security (formerly Women Waging Peace): www.womenwagingpeace.net

24

Building a Global Movement

> Look closely at the present you are
> constructing. It should look like
> the future you dream of.
>
> — Alice Walker

The global movement to end war has been growing for over a hundred years and continues in the myriad ways that people, both alone and in groups, act with peace and justice. Every so often there is evidence of how widespread this movement has become — like the marches in February 2003 to oppose the war in Iraq.

We are not going to end war this year, but to get to the world we want — a world without nuclear weapons, without massive expenditures on conventional weapons, without the illegal arms trade, without money laundering to buy weapons, and without the poverty that both causes war and results from it — we have to visualize the steps that are needed to get there.

We need a 50-year plan to end war, a plan that gives us goals we can act on and that can be achieved in ten-year steps. We need a strong, reformed UN and respect for international law. So how do we get there from here?

German medical students and doctors protest the Iraq war.

NGOs are outraged at the failure of nuclear weapons states to keep their promise to eliminate nuclear weapons. As a result, they are uniting to form massive campaigns for nuclear disarmament that involve other social movements as well. The movements to restore a healthy environment, to ensure human rights, to end poverty, and to prevent war are dependent upon each other, and many of us are working in all of them. If women, environmentalists, human rights organizers, antipoverty activists, health care activists, educators, musicians, faith groups, and children all call for nuclear disarmament, our voices will be heard.

War and the preparations for war destroy the environment on a scale never seen before. The damage caused by the Asian tsunami and Hurricane Katrina don't begin to compare with the devastation that would be caused by a nuclear war. Ending the war culture needs to be a priority for all of us, and it doesn't have to take away from what we are doing. We just need to link our work to turn up the volume. Save the environment — stop war. End poverty — stop war. Protect human rights — stop war. Fund health care — stop war. End violence against women — stop war. Care for children — stop war.

Governments gain the political will to make change when the public no longer tolerates their inaction. As the pressure builds, we must be ready with a clear vision of the steps that need to be taken to reduce the incidence of war and terrorism: a phased reduction of nuclear weapons, with inspections and verification, and a gradual shift to reliance on the UN to provide

- Abolition Now: www.abolitionnow.org
- Amnesty International: www.amnesty.org
- Code Pink: www.codepink4peace.org
- Global Action to Prevent War: www.globalactionpw.org
- United for Peace and Justice: www.unitedforpeace.org

security, with a resulting reduction in the need for all armaments. Governments will not suddenly trust the UN to ensure the security of their country and people. Instead, the UN must show its capability and build confidence.

Global Action to Prevent War (GAPW), a group of distinguished scholars, lawyers, and experienced activists, has developed a 50-year plan to build our common security without war. It begins with steps that can be taken in the next five to ten years and shows how implementing them would change the global context so that further steps would become possible. Each decade of the vision will move the whole world to greater security.

Global Action suggests that to succeed in mobilizing broad support, a program of action to prevent deadly conflict should take into account the following steps:

- Avoid inadvertently increasing some risks of war while reducing others.
- Strengthen the commitment to nonviolent conflict resolution.
- Offer substantial economic benefits.
- Include the means to overcome resistance to change.

The program underscores a commitment to the rule of law and to peaceful dispute resolution in three ways:

- It enhances the influence of global institutions for war prevention.
- It limits the accepted uses of force to deter and defend against aggression,

genocide, and other forms of organized violence.

- Step by step, it replaces national armed forces with UN and regional forces to be used in a nonpartisan way.

The plan builds on existing treaties and agreements which show that ending war is not a utopian dream, but a goal that can be fully realized within a few short decades.

The Global Action plan shows that it can be done if we all work together. Now it is up to us to do it.

GLOBAL ACTION TO PREVENT WAR

Global Action to Prevent War launches Nationwide Campus for Peace Project in Nigeria. Canadian High Commissioner to Nigeria David Angell and Dr. Vincent Mkanju, Director of Peace Education Centre in Nigeria attend the Award Ceremony attended by more than 4,000 students.GAPW Achiever and Peace Advocate Awards were given to notable Nigerians.

Part II

101 Solutions

1

Be the Change

> We must be the change we wish to
> see in the world.
>
> — Mahatma Gandhi

People in every land long for an end to violence and fear, and many feel hopeless,
fearing that change is impossible. In fact, the
tide is already turning, as the stories in this book
show. The change is happening in the choices
ordinary people are making in their daily lives as
they try to live with greater understanding of
those in conflict with them. Many people in
conflict zones are seeking solutions that bring
justice to both sides, and many people are showing that even after horrific losses, it is possible to
reconcile and move on.

When I think of people who live the change
they want to see in the world, I think of Jeannie
Ferber, a writer from New Hampshire. Jeannie
started a small project to take books to children
in remote villages in the Ural Mountains of
Russia. With Nikolai Arjannikov from Moscow,
she travels each year, in the dead of winter over
almost impassable roads, to tiny, isolated communities, where they give Russian books to the
schoolchildren. In her exquisite diaries, Jeannie
tells how children in her American community
share their joys and fears with children in Russia
over a phone-bridge, and how the project has
transformed both communities.

A decade ago, the Canadian Centre for Days
of Peace brought together officials of many UN
agencies and civil society organizations studying
humanitarian ceasefires. The mornings began

We support violence, terror and war when we —

- choose to dominate others by force and confrontation.
- think that rules apply to others but not to us.
- raise our children to see life as a competition between winners and losers.
- teach history as a list of battles instead of a record of social progress.
- finance and invest in enormous military industries.
- accept the promotion of hate and war without question.
- allow our media and our entertainment industries to glorify war and violence.

We support peace and justice when we —

- choose cooperation, justice, and the rule of international law.
- choose to build community with others.
- raise children who respect others regardless of their differences.
- support education for critical thinking, cooperation, and service to others.
- ask who benefits from war, arms industries, and the promotion of hatred and fear.
- stand up for justice and human rights.
- demand that our elected officials govern for the good of all, not just the rich and powerful.
- think of ourselves as sharing the earth and protecting it from harm.

with short ceremonies to help us remember why we were there. One morning, Douglas Cardinal, who is the architect of Canada's Museum of Civilization and a Native elder, led us in a sweet grass smudging. He spoke slowly, each word full of thought. Each sentence was a lesson in how to live. He held out the peace pipe, showing its straight handle, and placed it pointing from his heart to us. "We must speak straight from the heart," he said. Then, referring to the work that brought us together, he asked us to remember that "every act is a sacred act."

In my own life, deciding to try to live the change has been a real challenge. I'm not good at it yet, but I am lucky to be surrounded by people who inspire me to seek the peaceful way in difficult times. The values that support war are difficult to ignore — the drive to have more than everyone else, to have status and power, to dominate and control others. Choosing to value people and relationships over objects is extraordinarily difficult because we are immersed in a culture of acquisition and envy. Watching television makes it worse, especially for children, who are drawn into believing that owning something will make them happy. We cannot fill the emptiness inside with more stuff. Only connectedness to others, to the Earth, and to our own spirit can make us full.

It helps to make a start — today, right now — together.

School boys help unload books at Proharovka, Russia.

- *Coming Back to Life: Practices to Reconnect Our Lives, Our World* by Joanna Macy, New Society, 1998
- *The Impossible Will Take a Little While: A Citizen's Guide to Hope in a Time of Fear* by Paul Loeb, Basic Books, 2004
- *Make a Hole in the Fence* by Jeannie Ferber and Nikolai Arjannikov, Andover Green, 2002 (www.accesstoideas.org)
- *The Peace Book: 108 Simple Ways to Create a More Peaceful World* by Louise Diamond, Conari, 2001

2

Stand Up. Speak Out. Join with Others

> All that is needed for evil to triumph is that good people do nothing.
>
> — Attributed to Edmund Burke

This is a time when we must take a stand for the gains made by civil society over centuries of struggle with powerful elites in many countries.

The United Nations has advanced the power of international law and established standards of behavior between nations. The UN Declaration of Human Rights began as a piece of paper but has become the benchmark for the acceptable treatment of citizens by governments. Although we may take these rights for granted, they are the pillars on which we base the prevention of war.

Our best hope for the future is to build security together, using the UN and international law to ensure that the weakest are protected against those who would use raw power to dominate them. Proposals for UN reform include bringing civil society into decision making so that the interests of the nation-state do not neglect the interests of all the peoples represented. As individuals, we can show that we stand for new ways to resolve conflict without violence.

- Stand up for international law, the UN, and the nonviolent resolution of conflict by wearing a T-shirt, a button, peace sign earrings, by putting a bumper sticker or a license-plate holder on your car, hanging a wall poster, or putting a candle in your window. Why?

The Preamble to the Charter of the United Nations

We the Peoples of the United Nations Determined

to save succeeding generations from the scourge of war, which twice in our lifetime has brought untold sorrow to mankind, and to reaffirm faith in fundamental human rights, in the dignity and worth of the human person, in the equal rights of men and women and of nations large and small, and to establish conditions under which justice and respect for the obligations arising from treaties and other sources of international law can be maintained, and to promote social progress and better standards of life in larger freedom,

And for these Ends

to practice tolerance and live together in peace with one another as good neighbours, and to unite our strength to maintain international peace and security, and to ensure by the acceptance of principles and the institution of methods, that armed force shall not be used, save in the common interest, and to employ international machinery for the promotion of the economic and social advancement of all peoples,

Have Resolved to Combine our Efforts to Accomplish these Aims.

- American UN Association: www.unausa.org
- Canadian UN Association: www.unac.org
- Progressive Portal: www.progressiveportal.org
- Syracuse Cultural Workers catalogue: www.syrculturalworkers.com
- United for Peace and Justice: www.unitedforpeace.org

Because the hardest step is the first one — declaring yourself out loud. And the best thing is you'll find you're not alone.

- Talk talk talk. Don't miss a chance. Talk to your hairdresser, your babysitter, your uncle, your kids' teacher, your next-door neighbor. They may be sitting on the fence, feeling alone, uncomfortable, and not confident enough to ask a question. You may be the one to give them the space to make their choice. Remember your personal story is the most powerful.

- Write a check. Nonprofit groups spend enormous amounts of time and energy raising money to cover the expenses of sending out newsletters, hiring a person to answer the phone, researching and writing sample letters to government leaders, teaching people about the issues, organizing lectures and film screenings. A donation is more than a financial gift; it is a statement of support for, and solidarity with, those who are putting themselves on the line.

- Join a group and multiply your effectiveness and theirs. Find your niche in the group, because everyone is needed. Remember, for every famous speaker who moves a crowd to action, there are dozens of people preparing the ground: booking the theater, making the posters, sending the ads out, calling the press, hiring a janitor, making the coffee, keeping the books, printing the programs, finding the sponsors, and writing the thank-yous.

I remember an informal meeting with Mother Teresa after she addressed the UN General Assembly. A young man from Latin America stood up with tears in his eyes. "Mother, did you tell them in the General Assembly that they must fund human needs instead of funding war?" She looked at him and smiled, shaking her head. "Don't you see?" she said. "They already know what to do."

They already know what to do. Her words have stayed with me for years. Perhaps we all know what to do. What if we all just do it?

"They already know what to do." Mother Theresa at the United Nations, speaking to nongovernmental organizations, 1988.

M.W. ASHFORD

3

Turn Up the Volume

> The most common way people give up their power is by thinking they don't have any.
>
> — Alice Walker

In the middle of the Cold War I was getting dressed to speak at the annual Peace Walk when my 82-year-old mother said, "I don't know why you are doing this. It doesn't make any difference, you know, because the audience already agrees with you."

"I know, but it seems better to do something than nothing. What do you think would work?"

"Oh, I'll tell you," she replied. "Bumper stickers."

"Bumper stickers?"

"Yes, when I drive downtown I see bumper stickers on every second car, and they are all against nuclear weapons. I think if that many people are against the bomb, then I should pay attention."

So few cars have bumper stickers today that my car stands out like a flashing billboard. "Doctors say No Nukes!" Our local peace group printed up bumpers stickers and then bought a scrap roll of the vinyl from the same print shop. We invited kids to make their own bumper stickers using permanent acrylic felt markers. To our surprise, people offered to pay more for the homemade ones than the commercial designs.

There are many ways to turn up the volume on civil society, even when the mainstream media seem to have turned off the microphones on dissent. You might choose to earn media attention by doing something that makes a buzz. Some cities have ceremonies on Hiroshima Day, August 6, to remember that the first atomic bomb was dropped that day and to promise that it will never happen again. In Japan, lanterns represent the souls of those who died in the atomic bombing. In many North American and European cities, people float paper lanterns, painted with their hopes for the future, at dusk. The ceremonies attract attention and media coverage (see Solution 22).

One year, in the pre-dawn hours of August 6, a group of my friends stenciled white outlines on the city pavement to resemble the silhouettes on Hiroshima sidewalks where people were vaporized in the heat of the bomb, leaving

Lantern floating ceremonies remember Hiroshima and Nagasaki bombings with the commitment "Never again."

M.W. ASHFORD

56

- Institute for Media Policy and Civil Society: www.impacs.org
- International Campaign to Ban Landmines: www.icbl.org
- Physicians for Global Survival (Canada) resource kit: www.pgs.ca
- Syracuse Cultural Workers catalogue (Offers bumper stickers): www.syrculturalworkers.com

only shadows etched on the stones. We painted with a watery mixture of chalk and milk powder that would wash off easily in the rain. When we suddenly encountered police officers at 5:00 a.m., we realized we should have told them of our project in advance. To our great relief, they were fascinated and supportive.

Physicians for Global Survival (PGS) has a resource kit on its website that provides instructions for making the lanterns to float on Hiroshima Day and the paint mixture to do the shadow project.

When PGS launched its bombsaway.ca website against US ballistic missile defense (BMD), we got help from the nonprofit society Institute for Media Policy and Civil Society (IMPACS). We wanted to know how to attract people to the website. IMPACS told us that bus transport companies usually give nonprofits a low rate for bus advertising, so in Vancouver and Toronto we used posters in the university buses and a billboard at a busy intersection in each city. Then TV stations interviewed medical students speaking against BMD. Our site got 250,000 hits in the six weeks of the campaign.

During the worldwide campaign to ban landmines, one group made an enormous pile of single shoes to represent landmine victims who had lost a leg in an explosion. The message was graphic and personal. Another landmine action that got wonderful coverage was a mock minefield. Students tried to cross it without tripping a wire that triggered a sound which meant they had touched a hidden mine. The students held mine detectors as they inched over the field, but few made it across without a sound.

IMPACS provides online courses so nonprofits can learn professional skills for writing letters to the editor that will be published, writing press releases, and giving interviews. Here is my summary of IMPACS' formula for writing an op-ed piece, the short opinion pieces printed opposite editorials in newspapers.

1. Open with a compelling statement, position, or argument — a personal connection to the issue.

2. Connect your personal story to the bigger picture.

3. Answer the question "Why should I care?"

4. Bring the story home with local or national information.

5. Cite information from a new study or international statistics.

6. Offer solutions.

7. Say what we can do where we live.

8. Tell readers exactly what you want them to do and how.

9. Conclude by returning to your personal story in an empowering way.

4

Break Down Stereotypes — Meet the Other

> If you want to make peace, you don't talk to your friends. You talk to your enemies.
>
> — Moshe Dayan

USSR

The first time I went to the Soviet Union in 1986, I expected Moscow to be black and white, not technicolor, because we had seen so many black-and-white TV images of tanks in front of the Kremlin. I was unprepared for the storybook colors of the onion domes of St. Basil's Cathedral or the soft fall shades of the poplar trees in the Moscow parks, so similar to where I grew up in Edmonton, Canada. What was most amazing was the warm, enthusiastic welcome we received from the doctors in Moscow, Leningrad, and Tbilisi. Suddenly my stereotypes dissolved. They simply didn't fit these people who were friendly, witty, irreverent, and frank — and as worried as we were about nuclear war.

M.W. ASHFORD

North Korean doctors at the Pediatric Hospital in Kaesong City receive donated ciprofloxacin from American Dr. John Pastore after floods devastated the country. (IPPNW, 1999)

In the dark days of the Cold War, doctors from the US and the USSR met to talk about the threat of nuclear war. Refusing to be bound by ideological differences, they pledged to raise public awareness in both countries that medicine has almost nothing meaningful to offer in the event of a nuclear war. For this work, International Physicians for the Prevention of Nuclear War (IPPNW) won the Nobel Peace Prize in 1985.

Other groups also went to the USSR to see the Evil Empire for themselves and didn't find it. Engineers and schoolteachers, journalists and filmmakers came back with stories of dinner parties, bear hugs, and toasts to friendship. People exchanged photos of children and grandchildren, and everyone smiled to bridge the language gap. On both sides, people wanted to end the terrifying threat of nuclear war.

These exchange visits took tens of thousands of people from the west to meet with Soviets, and a smaller number of Soviets to visit the west. They shared their experiences with hundreds of thousands of people, making it difficult for the leaders on either side to insist that the enemy was aggressive, brutal, inhuman, and not at all like us. By the time Gorbachev and Reagan met in Iceland, the public was demanding nuclear disarmament and an end to the Cold War.

North Korea

Today, doctors from IPPNW go to North Korea to meet with colleagues there in an attempt to build bridges to peace through health. North

- American Friends Service Committee (Quakers): www.afsc.org
- Indian Doctors for Peace and Development: www.idpd.org
- International Physicians for the Prevention of Nuclear War: www.ippnw.org
- Mennonite Central Committee: www.mcc.org

Korean doctors are trying to practice in very difficult circumstances because of the severe shortage of electricity. Almost everything we do in western medicine depends on electricity, from X-rays and lab studies to heating water and sterilizing equipment.

I led two delegations of doctors from outside. We took medical supplies and medications as well as textbooks on CD-ROM, and we presented continuing education lectures to help update the physicians, who have received little medical literature since the fall of the USSR. They spoke of the need for peaceful reunification of the Korean peninsula and the need for more medical exchanges.

India/Pakistan

In India and Pakistan, medical students and doctors meet together to address the urgent danger of war between their countries and the real possibility that it would lead to a nuclear exchange. Recently, travel restrictions between India and Pakistan have been eased, and many doctors and students from India have been able to meet with colleagues in Pakistan for the first time.

One Indian medical student, Ankita Choudhary, wrote to thank her Pakistani hosts:

I had no past connections with Pakistan .... No ancestral homes .... No long lost relatives .... But there were many in our delegation and millions back in my country with such ties. One doctor, while speaking of these relatives and Indo-Pak relations, broke down into tears and sobbed, and he sobbed with such painful sighs, he made the whole audience cry.

I know I should've written about more relevant things like what was discussed in the conference, the statistics, technical presentations on Confidence Building Measures, talks with the political leaders, doctors' contribution ... etc. .... In the end what really matters are these little things that made such a difference. The way our Pakistani friends dissolved our fears, demolished those man-made walls of hatred and enmity built by fanatics, and stretched our horizons of friendship and bonding, with being "just themselves."

5

Committed to reducing violence by getting in the way.

— Christian Peacemakers

Speak for the Voiceless

Witness for Peace

Thirty years ago, Central America was the site of brutal massacres and repression of peasant farmers, mostly Mayan, who were calling for human rights and land reform. In the US-backed, low-intensity war, huge numbers of people were kidnapped, tortured, mutilated, and slain in El Salvador, Nicaragua, and Guatemala.

In Nicaragua, the United States backed the Contras against the Sandinista government. The Contras operated from Honduras, attacking villages and disrupting the harvest. Many church groups in North America gave support to the farmers, and hundreds of people traveled to Central America to stand physically in solidarity with the oppressed. Men and women from Witness for Peace (WFP) went to work in the fields, picking coffee and helping rebuild the infrastructure. By their unarmed presence, they protected many whose lives were threatened. No Nicaraguan village was ever attacked while a WFP delegation was present.

As the violence became more and more horrific, tens of thousands of peasants fled their countries to live in refugee camps, where they stayed for years, clinging to their dreams of returning home. Eventually, peace agreements were signed and refugees began to return. Despite government agreements to repatriate them, returnees in each country lived under constant threat of being killed by armies or paramilitaries.

Returnees requested international accompaniment on their journey home and demanded that governments agree in writing to the presence of these witnesses before they would agree to be repatriated. The accompaniers were threatened and harassed, some were jailed, and a few were killed, but they saved many lives by their courageous acts.

Peace Brigades International

Today, a number of organizations, such as Peace Brigades International (PBI), provide volunteers to witness and accompany those whose lives are threatened because of their human rights work. Other organizations doing this work include Amnesty International, Witness for Peace, International Service for Peace (SIPAZ) in Chiapas, and Christian Peacemaker Teams (largely Brethren, Quaker, and Mennonite). These groups provide popular education, unarmed bodyguards, grassroots activism, and

MICHAEL JOSEPH

Witness for Peace (*Accion Permanente por la Paz* in Spanish) and PBI volunteer accompanying a peace commission in Colombia.

nonviolent peacemaking in various parts of the world.

Nonviolent Peaceforce

A new initiative on a larger scale is the formation of a global organization that will mobilize and train a multicultural, nonviolent, standing peace force. The Nonviolent Peaceforce will "deploy to conflict areas to help create the space for local groups to struggle, dialogue and seek peaceful resolution while protecting human rights and preventing death and destruction."[1] The goal is to have 2,000 members by 2010.

The force uses four carefully developed and tested strategies: accompany threatened individuals, bear witness in threatened communities, monitor elections, and stand between combatants. Its first project is in Sri Lanka, where a ceasefire agreement has broken down.

Mel Duncan, one of the founders of the peace force, wrote of the power of witnesses to stop the killing of refugees:

> On the island of Negros in the Philippines in 1989, over 500 refugees gathered in a church hall were threatened to be killed by death squads. The Catholic bishop, Antonio Fortich, after hearing of the successes of Peace Brigades International and Witness For Peace, called on religious leaders from around the world for help. Within 24 hours 25

- Christian Peacemaker Teams: www.cpt.org
- Nonviolent Peaceforce: www.nonviolentpeaceforce.org
- International Fellowship of Reconciliation: www.ifor.org
- International Service for Peace (SIPAZ): www.sipaz.org
- Peace Brigades International: www.peacebrigades.org
- Peaceworkers: www.peaceworkers.org.uk
- Voices in the Wilderness (VitW) (US-based group working in Iraq): www.vitw.org
- *Taking a Stand: A Guide to Peace Teams and Accompaniment Projects* by Elizabeth Boardman, New Society Publishers, 2004.
- Witness for Peace: www.witnessforpeace.org

> religious representatives had joined the bishop and the 500 refugees in the church hall asserting that anything done to the refugees would also have to be done to them. They also promised to tell the world what happened. The death squads failed to carry out their threat.[2]

We can't all go to stand in solidarity in conflict zones, but we can give the two things these groups really need: financial and moral support. We can donate to help them cover the costs of training, maintaining field services, and organizing and sending people abroad. We can also set up speaking engagements for the witnesses when they return so that their work is known to the world.

6

Resist War Propaganda

The marvelous richness of human experience would lose something of rewarding joy if there were no limitations to overcome. The hilltop hour would not be half so wonderful if there were no dark alleys to traverse.

— Helen Keller

Immunize yourself against the incitement of hatred. Remember that truth is the first casualty of war. Here are two examples:

- When Iraqi troops invaded Kuwait before the first Gulf War, reports circulated about Iraqi soldiers stealing incubators from Kuwaiti hospitals and leaving the babies who had been in the incubators to die. That story was exposed as a lie after the war when the woman who made the statement was identified as the daughter of a Kuwaiti official.

- The press reported in 1999 that a genocide was occurring in Kosovo, with 100,000 to 200,000 bodies buried in mass graves. This news convinced many people that military intervention was again necessary. In September 2004, according to Lawrence Martin of the *Globe and Mail*, the Canadian forensic team searching for mass graves reported that there was no evidence of genocide and, in fact, there were fewer than 1,000 bodies in the alleged mass graves.[1]

Support the Troops and Oppose the War

In the first Gulf War, people who supported the war wore yellow ribbons and said those who protested were unpatriotic. Music from World War II romanticized the young men (and women) who went to war on our behalf. In a dreamy reminiscence of a different war, we pictured handsome Johnny marching home. And we forgot that in today's wars, 95 percent of the casualties are civilians — about half of them children. In other words, when we support war, we support killing those who are not combatants and who do not have a voice in their government. Ask yourself what if we did this to everyone? What if someone did it to us? We need to choose the other alternatives that do not include bombing from 35,000 feet.

A common strategy to confuse the issue is to label those who oppose war as traitors, cowards, draft dodgers, peaceniks, hippies, fuzzy-headed idealists, professional protestors, or communists rather than responding to their arguments. Another strategy is to deride the UN as weak and indecisive if it refuses to support the war plan. The UN was formed to prevent war. Period.

Watch for stories of brave dissenters taking a stand against armed conflict. There are many, but they appear for one day and then vanish into the void. In Israel, for example, a group of pilots refused to fly missions to the Gaza strip because they disagreed with killing people indiscriminately to enforce an Israeli occupation. There are over

Yesh Gvul (There is a limit) sponsored alternative torch lighting ceremony in Jerusalem on Israel's Independence Day, April 26, 2004.

1,200 soldiers, reservists, and young draftees who have refused to serve in the Occupied Palestinian Territories, and according to Yesh Gvul, an Israeli peace group, about 300 have been jailed.

Take the following steps when you want to check out the facts and not get caught up in the lies of the warmongers:

- Ask who will benefit from the war, or as the journalists say, "Follow the money."

- Ask "Is oil the reason for the war? Diamonds? Coltan, the mineral needed in cell phones?"

- Be suspicious that you are being sold a bill of goods when the radio plays "When Johnny Comes Marching Home."

- Be suspicious when you hear "You are either with us or against us"; "War is inevitable"; "Force is all they understand"; "No other means will work"; "This is the exceptional case"; "This war is for democracy, freedom, truth, justice, God." And remember, countries don't go to war to get little girls back into school.

- Question authority. Don't believe someone just because they are on TV or in print.

- Talk to the other side — organize a conference to bring together moderates to talk about the current issue.

- Look at the alternative media for alternative solutions such as unarmed observers, weapons inspectors, third-party negotiations, or economic incentives.

Some alternative media you might want to check out:

Websites
- Media Lens: www.medialens.org
- Search for Common Dreams: www.commondreams.org
- Truthout: www.truthout.org

Radio and television sources
- CBC: www.cbc.ca
- NPR: www.npr.org
- PRI: www.pri.org
- Democracy Now (with award-winning journalist Amy Goodman): www.democracynow.org
- PBS: www.pbs.org

Print sources
- *The Guardian*
- *Le Monde Diplomatic,* (English edition) comes out monthly in *The Guardian*
- *The Nation* magazine
- *The New Internationalist*
- *Yes! Magazine*
- *Zed Magazine*

Writers to watch for
- Naomi Klein, Bill Moyers, George Monbiot, Jonathan Schell, Greg Palast

- Ask what the Secretary-General of the UN is saying because he is more likely than political leaders to call for alternatives to bombing.

- Beware of false comparisons — we aren't facing Hitler and the Americans aren't back in Vietnam.

- Remind yourself of all the dictators who have been deposed by nonviolent means.

7

Don't Pay for War — Invest in Peace

> If I can't build my retirement based on the performance of these companies, there won't be a world to retire to.
> — Client speaking to Deb Abbey of Real Assets about ethical investment

Invest in Ethical Funds

When we invest through our pension funds or mutual funds, we are often unwittingly supporting military industries. We don't have to put our money into making the world a worse place; we can invest in companies that support the values we want to live by, and we can take shareholder actions to move companies a little more toward the light. Luckily, we don't have to do this alone. There are ethical investment groups that are doing the research we need and offering good returns on money invested in socially progressive companies.

The Domini Social Investment Index in the United States provides information about ethical investment in socially responsible companies. Companies on their index must have less than

Greenpeace calls on BP Amoco's shareholders to abandon Northstar Project. London, UK.

(c) GREENPEACE/DAVISON

(c) GREENPEACE/DAVISON

2 percent of their investments in military industries. In Canada, Real Assets is an investment firm that screens companies to ensure they put less than 1 percent of their investments in military manufacturing. Real Assets also checks the way companies treat their employees, the number of women on their boards, and whether they have an environmental conscience. Deb Abbey, then CEO of Real Assets, reported taking action because the Canada Pension Plan invests in Haliburton and in tobacco. Haliburton is one of the major corporations supporting the US war and occupation of Iraq. She suggested that Canadians write to their government and ask it to shift to more socially sound investments.

Speak Out at a Shareholders' Meeting

Investors sometimes buy shares in a company so they can speak at the shareholders' meetings. Often churches do this as a way to influence corporate leaders to pay attention to the products they sell, as well as the working conditions of their employees, especially those working in factories in developing countries. During the apartheid era in South Africa, shareholder resolutions in many transnational corporations called on the corporations to sell off their investments in South Africa. This pressure helped to end apartheid. Many shareholders are now demanding that they be allowed to review the compensation packages of highly paid corporate executives. The shareholders are cognizant of the fact that at the beginning of the 21st century some 358 billionaires have a greater net worth than the 2.4 billion poorest people in the world.

Right Livelihood Awards

"The idea of 'right livelihood' is an ancient one. It embodies the principle that each person should follow an honest occupation which fully respects other people and the natural world. It means being responsibile for the consequences of our actions and taking only a fair share of the earth's resources.

"In every generation there are groups of people and individuals around the globe who valiantly uphold the principles of right livelihood. They should be the stars in our human cosmos, but their work often entails personal sacrifice, being opposed by powerful forces around them."

www.rightlivelihood.org

Choose the Right Livelihood

The Right Livelihood Awards are given annually to people who work for peace and social justice. The organization's website offers an inspiring list of people who are rarely recognized for the light they bring to the world. Canadian nun and biophysicist Sister Rosalie Bertell has received this award for her lifetime of writing and speaking about the dangers of low-level radiation and the use of depleted uranium in weapons. She has also been awarded the Order of Canada.

It is not always possible to choose to work at peacebuilding for a living, but many people decide to work part time in order to have time to volunteer with an NGO. Someone once told me that money is what we exchange for our time on Earth. Suddenly I realized my time on Earth doesn't have a price tag, and the old saying "time is money" trivializes the fact that we can only live this moment once. It made me see that I need fewer things and more moments to treasure.

Fund Democratic Change

The Simons Foundation in Canada funds research and education on nuclear disarmament and is a significant supporter of government/civil society consultations on disarmament and peace.

Multibillionaire George Soros backed the nonviolent revolutions in Serbia, Georgia, and the Ukraine through his Open Society Institute.

At the same time, our donations to small nonprofit organizations make a big difference to the effectiveness of their campaigns and send the message that we are behind them, cheering. Election observers traveled from North America and Europe to help in the re-run elections in the Ukraine. Many of them joined the protests that led to new elections and then stayed to observe the election process. Local communities supported their expenses. Investing ourselves in peace means putting our money and our time behind our conviction that there are better responses to conflict than military force.

- Domini Social Index: www.domini.com
- Open Society Institute: www.soros.org
- Real Assets: www.realassets.ca
- Right Livelihood Awards: www.rightlivelihood.org
- Simons Centre for Peace and Disarmament Studies at the Liu Institute for Global Issues: www.ligi.ubc.ca/Centres
- Social Investment (Canada): www.socialinvestment.ca
- Social Investment Forum (US): www.socialinvest.org

8

Resist the Oppressor

> It's like Newton's third law of action and reaction. When you raise the level of repression, resistance goes up as well.
>
> — Ivan Marovic, Otpor (Serbian resistance movement)

War is not over when an occupying force declares victory. In fact, if the weaker party does not concede defeat, the war continues, sometimes as armed insurrection, but often as underground resistance that makes the people more and more difficult to govern. Massive weaponry does not ensure control of a population. Stable government requires the consent of the people.

Use Nonviolent Resistance

Gandhi mobilized the Indian people in a long campaign of non-cooperation and resistance to British rule that eventually led to Indian independence (see "The Legacy of Gandhi" and "The Power of Nonviolence" in the Introduction). He was convinced that *satyagraha* (soul-force), was stronger than military might and that people must act from their spiritual strength.

Martin Luther King Jr. and his followers studied Gandhi's writings as they built the American civil rights movement.

Prepare for the Right Moment

Decades after Indian independence, the Philippines was governed by Ferdinand Marcos, known as the Hitler of the East.[1] The resistance to the dictator had been building for years, with people studying Gandhian principles of nonviolence in an underground movement that was supported by the churches. Many people were jailed or killed. The turning point came when two key military leaders defected. Archbishop Jaime Cardinal Sin used the independent Catholic Radio to call people to block the streets

to prevent Marcos from capturing the defectors. People camped on the downtown streets day and night, singing and praying. There was a festive atmosphere, with food and entertainment. When the army approached, nuns and priests knelt in front of the tanks, and the army refused to fire on the people. Eventually the armed forces defected. After four days of unified public defiance, Marcos fled to Hawaii.

American author Gene Sharp has written several books about successful strategies of nonviolent resistance. Robert Helvey, a colleague of Sharp and a former military officer, prefers to call the nonviolent actions "political defiance" to show that the work is strong and confrontational, not weak or passive. It requires courage and creativity to capture the imagination and commitment of the public, and to inspire people to risk their lives by standing up against oppression. The movie series *A Force More Powerful*, by Peter Ackerman and Jack Duvall, documents the overthrow of oppressive regimes through nonviolent actions in India, Chile, Poland, and Serbia.[2]

Although the difficult and dangerous underground work must be done by local people, the support of outside experts in nonviolent resistance increases the likelihood that their actions will succeed.

Slow Down

After the brutal dictator Augusto Pinochet took over Chile in a military coup in 1973, people struggled against the military rule with increasing determination. Thousands were "disappeared," tortured, and killed. By the beginning of the

Arpillera showing women showing they are hungry by banging their empty pots and pans. Fires of burning tires create an acrid, thick smoke. This was done to keep the police and military out while the women demonstrated against the dictatorship in Chile.

1980s there were weekly protests that included slowdowns and strikes, and at 8:00 p.m. everyone would bang pots and pans or honk their car horns. When a slowdown was called, everyone drove very slowly, spoke slowly, counted money slowly ... but to the frustration of authorities, there was no apparent leader to arrest.[3]

Women smuggled out hand-embroidered wall hangings called *arpilleras* that told the rest of the world the story of the disappeared, the brutality of the regime, and the protests against the Pinochet government. Networks outside Chile raised money for the women by selling the *arpilleras* through churches and women's groups. Eventually Pinochet was toppled.

Keep on Singing

Resistance sometimes takes the form of singing banned songs, as happened in Lithuania under Nazi occupation during World War II. At every opportunity, choirs sang to hold onto their identity.

In Czechoslovakia, the rock band Plastic People of the Universe formed in 1968 as the Russian tanks rolled into Prague (see Solution 54). The band came to symbolize the radical underground opposition to Russian power. Although the band was not overtly political, its members were harassed and repeatedly arrested because they were nonconformist. Oppressive governments cannot tolerate free-thinking

groups. When the band members were arrested again in 1976, their trial stimulated the formation of Charter 77, an organization of artists, students, writers, and dissidents led by poet Vaclav Havel, who later became president of the Czech Republic.

Resistance may become an important strategy to prevent war in the next few years as US policies to fight terrorism expand. The war in Iraq must be brought to an end, and the legitimacy of the UN and international law restored. Roll up your sleeves and do what you can.

- *A Force More Powerful*:
  www.aforcemorepowerful.org
- Gene Sharp: www.peace.ca/genesharp.htm

9

Raise Caring, Compassionate, Thoughtful Children

If we are to reach real peace in this world,
If we are to declare war on war,
We must start with the children.

— Mahatma Gandhi

Over the past 30 years or so, we have learned a great deal about child raising and have developed strategies that make it easier and less stressful to deal with the great challenges of parenting.

Show How It's Done

We know that children learn how to behave by watching adults and other children and that they learn their values the same way. What we do speaks louder than what we say. Some of the people children watch and copy, besides their parents, are on television; some are their care-givers or babysitters or neighbors.

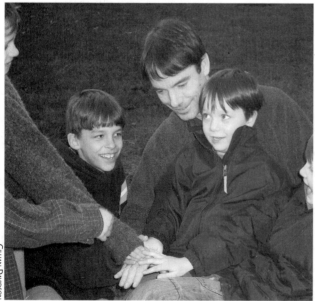

Practicing a cheer before a game.

If we hit children when they do something wrong, they may stop what they are doing (at least while we are there), but they have learned that it's okay to hit. Sometimes we seem to go on autopilot when a child misbehaves, because more than 90 percent of us were raised by parents who spanked us. It is not easy to think of an alternative when we are angry. Some people think that if we don't spank our children, they will grow up with no discipline or will perhaps run all over us. We worry they will be spoiled. In fact, treating chil-dren fairly and respectfully is most likely to lead to children treating others with similar respect.

Listen and Then Use Your Words ... Respectfully

We are the generation that can stop the vio-lence. Stopping spanking doesn't mean allowing bad behavior; it means using other strategies to teach children how to behave. We help most effectively when we listen carefully to each other and talk through what has happened. Learning to listen, to respect others, to forgive, and to share our feelings honestly are important lessons for children; they are important lessons for all of us.

Queensland, Australia, has mandated that all schools in the state use *The Family Virtues Guide.* Teachers are being trained to teach this different approach to moral education, and parents are enthusiastically welcoming it.

Be an Involved Dad

In the past, parenting was thought to be the responsibility of the mother. Now we know that

GILLIAN DAVIDSON

- *Above All, Be Kind: Raising a Humane Child in Challenging Times* by Zoe Weil, New Society Publishers, 2003.
- *EcoKids: Raising Children Who Care for the Earth* by Dan Chiras, New Society Publishers, 2005
- *The Family Virtues Guide: Simple Ways to Bring Out the Best in Our Children and Ourselves* by Linda K. Popov, Dan Popov, and John Kavelin. Plume Books, 1997
- *How to Talk So Kids Will Listen and Listen So Kids Will Talk* by Adele Faber and Elaine Mazlish, Avon, 1999
- Peaceful Childhoods Kit: www.pgs.ca
- Teaching Children Virtues: tadpoleclub.com/daystar
- Virtues Project: www.virtuesproject.com

the father has a powerful impact on raising boys who can choose not to resort to violence.[1] Men are beginning to recognize that their role in teaching boys how to work out conflicts without force may be the most important gift they give their families.

When parents are not together, the male role model may be a friend or relative who makes time to be a mentor to a young boy. Children who learn to value politeness and respect have an easier time getting along with others at school and in the community.

Show the Importance of Serving Others

Some experts say that the most important source of meaning in life is service to others. Parents who teach children the value of service give them a sense of worth that helps sustain them through difficult times. Schools and church groups that set up programs where young people take on service projects for the elderly or handicapped help the community and, perhaps even more, help the youth to know they are valued. Similarly, children who have responsibility for the care of animals also develop a sense of meaning and service that is an important part of their emotional development.

Turn off the TV

If you reduce the amount of television your children watch, you might find parenting much easier. I did. When I turned off the television, except for an occasional special movie that we watched together, two of the things that drove me crazy stopped — the pounding and wrestling that started with every commercial break, and the begging for snacks and toys that were advertised on Saturday morning. Yes, we endured a lot of complaining, but it was worth it. The children quickly filled their time with games, sports, reading, music, and playing with friends.

You might try a week without TV to see what happens with your family. Pediatricians now recommend no TV under the age of two. They link television with increased childhood obesity, possible problems with attention, and loss of time building relationships with others.

10

Pray, Meditate, Reconcile, and Forgive

> **Teach this triple truth to all:**
> A generous heart, kind speech, and
> a life of service and compassion are
> the things which renew humanity.
> — **Buddha**

Many of us have felt a call to action that has stirred us to join the great movements for peace, social justice, and the environment. Action, for some of us, is an expression of our religious faith. For others it is an expression of love and compassion for those who are suffering, or it expresses a deep connection to nature. Some describe themselves as spiritual but not religious — they have a sense of a transcendent purpose, but do not subscribe to an organized religion. Others do not relate to something outside themselves but recognize an internal series of principles that guide their actions.

In my case, it was the nuclear issue that made me consider the ultimate existential questions of "Who am I?" and "Why am I here?" In 1984, after hearing Dr. Helen Caldicott lecture, I lay awake for three nights wrestling with my deep reluctance to take a stand against nuclear weapons. First I argued with her in my mind.

"I am not sure that your facts are right."

"So check them out. They are from the Pentagon and the US government."

"I am not that kind of person."

"What kind of person?"

"That placard-carrying, strident, marching kind of person. I don't believe they can save the world."

"No, I agree, it's going to take mothers, doctors, teachers, writers, public speakers .... "

"Yeah." As a woman doctor and a former teacher/columnist/public speaker, I was running out of excuses.

"I don't have time to take on anything more."

"Who does?"

"I need to work and save money for my kids."

"And if there is no planet?"

The questions shifted over the next nights to the core questions of my existence. Why is there life instead of nothing? Why am I alive now, at this time in history? Am I personally meant to do something? Is there a God acting through us, assuming that we will take action to save the Earth?

Finally, without answers, I acquiesced. I began to work against nuclear weapons, knowing that now I would not back off, that I would put myself on the line.

Once, in Kazakhstan, I attended a huge antinuclear-testing protest organized by the Nevada-Semipalatinsk movement. Americans who lived downwind from tests in the US state of Nevada joined with tribespeople from the Soviet test range in their rejection of further tests in either country. One morning a group of doctors from outside Kazakhstan spontaneously gathered in the hotel bar at 7:30 a.m. to meditate and reflect together. The astonished bar staff carefully stopped vacuuming and closed the door behind us. One of the doctors said "I think there is a reason for us to be here — we who have the advantages of money and education, who choose to be here now instead of on a ski weekend." As a result of the protest, Mikhail Gorbachev stopped Soviet nuclear testing.

The power that is beyond our understanding is called by many names in different faiths. I have gradually come to rely on that unknowable

- Christians for Justice and Peace: www.sojourners.com
- Downwinders (Movement against nuclear testing) www.downwinders.org
- Fellowship of Reconciliation: www.ifor.org
- *Peace is Every Step: The Path of Mindfulness in Everyday Life* by Thich Nhat Hanh, Bantam, 1991
- Ten Ways to Stop War with Your Spirit: www.earthfuture.com/stopthewar/spirit.asp
- Tikkun Community (An interfaith group based on Judaism): www.tikkun.org/community
- Women Praying for Peace: www.women-praying-for-peace.org

presence both in my medical practice and in my work against violence and war. I think of it as spiritual, but sometimes I call it love. In meditation or prayer one can sometimes almost touch a central meaning that connects all people and all beings. I find the practice of seeking that which is of God in each person to be a powerful way to stop judging and condemning those I disagree with.

In the past 20 years I have met thousands of people who have committed themselves to making a better world. They run the whole gamut from the deeply religious to atheists. They have chosen to live their lives with the goal of bringing peace to their communities and the world. I have been deeply affected hearing their reasons and listening to what sustains them.

Those who have been able to forgive and reconcile with their former enemies have drawn on a deep wellspring to find the strength to let go of the need for revenge and choose a different future. It is in community with others who are willing to try to take that same path that we are most likely to build a new way to live together.

M.W. ASHFORD

Protest at the Soviet nuclear test range in Kazakhstan, 1990 stopped Soviet nuclear bomb tests.

11

Support Women's Values

Security is mostly a superstition. It does not exist in nature, nor do the children of humans as a whole experience it. Avoiding danger is not safer in the long run than outright exposure. Life is either a daring adventure, or nothing.

— Helen Keller

According to John Zogby, president and CEO of Zogby International pollsters, differences between men and women have been evident since the Vietnam War, when a Gallup poll found 73 percent of men but only 59 percent of women supported the war.[1] "There is always a gender gap on matters of war and defense. You'll find women less willing to go to war, less willing to spend on defense, and more attuned to health-care needs, educational needs, and child-care needs," Zogby stated.

A week before the beginning of the 1991 Gulf War, 67 percent of men and only 45 percent of women in the United States supported the bombing. In March 2003, a Zogby poll asked whether people would strongly support a war against Iraq. While 45 percent of men did, only 21 percent of women were in favor. Far more women are against nuclear weapons and ballistic missile defense. Women consistently call for negotiations instead of armed conflict.

Women discussing the word "security" generally focus on their personal safety rather than the security of their nation-state. They speak of being unable to walk alone in certain areas, or of having to decide whether to board an elevator or accept a first-floor hotel room. Of course, security also means not being in danger of being killed in war.

Many theories that try to explain the reason for these differences between men and women suggest that they are the result of variations in child rearing, but an interesting discovery about women's hormonal responses to severe stress may have something to contribute to our understanding of this gender difference. When stressed, women secrete oxytocin, which is the hormone that makes us bond. Called the "tend and befriend" hormone, oxytocin is produced during labor and delivery and is one of the reasons for the powerful attachment formed between mother and baby. Men, on the other hand, produce testosterone when they are stressed and thus become more aggressive. It seems counterproductive to me, but we send men to negotiate peace treaties.

When people suggest that if we had more women in power we would be more peaceful, others counter that Margaret Thatcher, Golda Meir, and Indira Gandhi were not examples of more peaceful leaders. That may be true, but as the number of women in a group rises above the critical level of one third, there seems to be a change in the group dynamics. There is more emphasis on social justice issues and efforts to support community, and the process becomes more cooperative and inclusive of all participants.

- Canadian Voice of Women for Peace: home.ca.inter.net/~vow
- Code Pink (Women for Peace): www.codepink4peace.org
- Jewish Women's Archive (For Bella Abzug's biography and more): www.jwa.org
- Peace by Peace (Connecting Women for Peace) www.peacexpeace.org

In Canada, when a minority Liberal government expressed its intention to join the US ballistic missile defense program, it found that not only did the Canadian public oppose the plan, but so did the Women's Caucus of the Liberal Party. The women's opposition made it impossible for the government to go ahead because it could not be certain of winning the vote in Parliament.

Two of the world's great leaders in peace and disarmament, Cora Weiss and the late Bella Abzug, have inspired thousands of women with their vision, their chutzpah, and their unfailing humor. Cora Weiss, president of the Hague Appeal for Peace, is renowned as a peace activist. A leader in the anti-Vietnam-war movement, she traveled to North Vietnam and organized an exchange of mail between families and POWs in Vietnam. She then accompanied some returning POW pilots to the United States. She leads a huge coalition of organizations dedicated to ridding the world of war and to making peace a human right. According to Cora Weiss, www stands for world without war. The Global Campaign for Peace Education is the focus of the Hague Appeal for Peace.

Bella Abzug (1920–1998), a New York lawyer and three-time member of the House of Representatives, was a tireless advocate for labor rights, the rights of women, and nuclear disarmament.[2] Famous for always wearing large hats, she told the story that when she was a young lawyer, she was always asked to get the coffee, so she began to wear a hat and gloves to indicate

RUSSELL DAVIDSON.

Bella Abzug in her famous hat.

that she was not the secretary. "After a while," she added, "the gloves came off."

"In a perfectly just republic," wrote John Kenneth Galbraith in 1984, "Bella Abzug would be president."

Bella Abzug's memorial was the first ever held in the UN General Assembly. Geraldine Ferraro said of her, "She didn't knock politely on the door. She didn't even push it open or batter it down. She took it off the hinges forever."

12

Join Activist Women

We don't want to fight the old
system. We want to build a new one.

— Susan Collin Marks

Men and women see the issues of war and peace differently, run their meetings differently, and campaign differently. The feminist analysis of the causes of war calls for social change, a move away from patriarchal structures toward partnership between men and women. The male-dominated governments of the United States and the USSR argued that a missile gap would leave one of the countries vulnerable, despite the fact that together they had enough missiles to kill everyone on Earth 20 times over.

Once, at a peace meeting mostly attended by men, a woman whispered to me, "Have you noticed that the men are counting missiles and the women are calling for revolution?"

I am convinced that we all have both masculine and feminine aspects that we express at different times, and that a better balance of the two in our governments would help lead the world toward peace. That is, we need to elect more women, but we also need to elect men who are willing to use collaboration instead of competition.

It was a woman, Dr. Helen Caldicott, an impassioned physician and speaker, who led millions, including me, to take action against nuclear weapons. She is known for her famous book *Missile Envy* and is the subject of Bonnie Klein's National Film Board of Canada movie *If You Love this Planet*. The film, which won an Oscar, was banned in the United States at the time. Today Caldicott leads the Nuclear Policy Research Institute, which is vigorously opposing US nuclear policies.

Here is a list of women's organizations that include international experts and at the same time welcome women who have never before been activists.

UNIFEM is the UN Women's Fund. It is committed to women's empowerment and equality. In the field of peace and disarmament, UNIFEM is a central organization in the action to implement Security Council Resolution 1325, which ensures that women are on all peace negotiation teams and post-conflict meetings (see Solution 14 for ways to join this work).

Women's International League for Peace and Freedom (WILPF), founded in 1915, is the oldest international women's peace organization in the world. Its project "Reaching Critical Will" focuses on increasing the effective participation of NGOs in international discussions of the Nuclear Non-Proliferation Treaty (NPT), particularly at the UN. WILPF monitors discussions and committees relating to the NPT and posts authoritative commentary on the website, with suggestions for action before crucial votes at the UN. WILPF also organizes actions to implement Security Council Resolution 1325. WILPF has chapters all over the world.

The Acronym Institute for Disarmament Diplomacy was founded by Rebecca Johnson in 1995. It engages governments and civil society at the UN by providing reports, analysis, and strategic thinking on peace and security. Johnson is a highly regarded expert who doesn't mince words and whose reports on treaty discussions and multilateral approaches are eagerly sought by national delegations at the

- Acronym Institute: www.acronym.org.uk
- Canadian Voice of Women for Peace: home.ca.inter.net/~vow
- Code Pink for Peace: www.codepink4peace.org
- *The New Nuclear Danger: George W. Bush's Military-Industrial Complex* by Helen Caldicott, New Press, 2001 (revised 2004)
- Nuclear Policy Research Institute: www.nuclearpolicy.org
- UNIFEM: www.womenwarpeace.org
- WILPF in the US: www.wilpf.org/us-wilpf/default.htm
- Women's International League for Peace and Freedom: www.wilpf.org

UN. Acronym provides accurate and timely analysis of the discussions that are in progress in various official meetings without reflecting the interests of any national government.

Canadian Voice of Women for Peace (VOW) was founded in 1960 to bring a women's and feminist perspective to issues of peace, human rights, social justice, and development. Its current projects include working to delegitimize war. It has been cited by UNESCO for its contribution to women and a culture of peace. VOW sends delegations of observers to UN conferences and trains many who want to learn how to navigate and strengthen the UN system. It is working to have the new Canadian War Museum feature exhibitions on the role of Canadians in building peace. Women have played a major role in the Canadian peace movement, and VOW would like to have the museum renamed the Canadian War and Peace Museum. VOW has chapters across Canada.

Code Pink is a US organization founded in November 2002 in response to the repeated Code Orange alerts in the United States. It quickly spread in opposition to the re-election of George W. Bush, using hot pink buttons and sneakers, marches, and demonstrations to increase its visibility. In recognition of the number of jobs lost under the Bush administration, Code Pink's "Give George Bush a pink slip" banners were giant pink slips. *The Nation* commented that Code Pink is not an organization but a phenomenon: a sensibility reflecting feminist analysis and a campy playfulness.

Code Pink women call for giving the pink slip to George W. Bush. Los Angeles, 2005.

13

Vote for Women/ Run for Office

In a strange twist of social progress, some of the poorest and most male-dominated countries have stepped ahead of the west in legislating that at least 30 percent of the positions on local councils must be held by women. Bangladesh, Nepal, Sri Lanka, Afghanistan, India, and Pakistan are leading a movement that brings women into decision making.[1]

The problems facing women who are elected to the local councils are staggering. Not least is the resistance from some of the men who held power before. In one place in Pakistan, the men turned the women's chairs to face the wall. In another they hung a curtain to separate the

I sense that the time has come for the growing and hardy band of women legislators to demand that governments everywhere get their priorities right and recognize that if we want peace and human security in the world, we must replace the culture of war with the culture of peace. I am not saying that a world run by women would necessarily be a completely peaceful world, but my political and diplomatic experience indicates to me that the prospects of achieving a more humane world would improve with more women in the decision-making processes of governments.

— Senator Douglas Roche's last speech to the Canadian Senate, March 31, 2004

women from the men. Fortunately, there is a movement to empower the newly elected women to take on their responsibilities.

In the state of Bihar, India, 45,000 women were elected. Most of them had no experience in public office, and many were illiterate. Acharya Ramamurti, a man in his 90s, is leading week-long training workshops to teach women about nonviolence, human rights, and the role of local government. One result of the increased participation of women is an increase in their literacy. He calls the trained women *Mahila Shanti Sena* or Women's Peace Corps.[2]

Women are concerned about the health of families and education, especially of girl children. One of the most significant policies that can be implemented at the local level is to ensure that schools have bathrooms with private cubicles for girls. This simple change allows girls to stay in school after they reach puberty, when previously they had to drop out.

RAMA SINGH

Acharya Ramamurti.

- Ben's Guide to US Government for Kids: bensguide.gpo.gov
- University of Maryland Women's Studies Database (Women in government and politics): www.mith2.umd.edu/WomensStudies/ GovernmentPolitics
- Emily's List (US political network supporting women candidates): www.emilyslist.org

In North America, almost 80 years after women got the vote, only about 30 percent of the councilors elected in our cities are female. The percentage drops to just 14 percent to 20 percent elected federally and in states and provinces. There have been strong women leaders in the United Kingdom, India, and Israel, but organizations do not seem to shift toward women's values until the group is about one-third female. In both east and west, more women must be elected to federal office if we are to move foreign policy away from war and in the direction of greater cooperation and support for international law.

According to some experts, when countries require that there be equal numbers of male and female candidates standing for office, the number of women elected increases dramatically. In France, the new parity law passed in June 2000 applies to municipalities with populations of more than 3,500.[3] In 1995, when there was no parity law, women obtained 25.7 percent of seats on local city councils. After parity, the percentage of women elected to council increased to 47.5 percent. At the same time, the percentage of women elected at the county level, where the parity law did not apply, increased only marginally, from 7 percent to 9 percent.

South Africa's new constitution has built in support for women's equity and representation that corresponds to the gender composition of the country. Tragically, the impact of the HIV/AIDS epidemic in that country is much more severe for women than men. The loss of women, combined with the need for those women who are healthy to be caregivers to children and sick adults, means that it will be difficult to bring more women into government.

Polls in Cambodia tracking people's views about women in government showed an interesting similarity to those in the United States.[4] The majority of Cambodians polled believed that women would be less corrupt in office than men. In the United States, the *New York Times* reported that 80 percent of people believe that electing women would result in improved education, social services, and health programs.

14

Demand Action on Security Council Resolution 1325

Here's a brilliant, powerful solution that needs some civil society muscle behind it. If I believed in performance-enhancing steroids (which I don't), I'd want to give them to SC Resolution 1325. Here's the story.

Women's organizations have been observing and monitoring UN action and inaction on peace and disarmament for decades. In 2000 they wrote a resolution to be discussed by the Security Council. Of course they could not present it in the chambers at the UN, but the Security Council agreed to meet with them across the street from UN headquarters in New York.

There the women described war's disproportionate effects on women and girls. They argued that women are always forced to live with the tragic consequences of men fighting wars: loss of husbands, sons, and fathers; injuries, illness,

The doors were open just wide enough for women to squeeze into a Security Council debate. But concerned women and men must act upon the words of Resolution 1325 and use those words and those stacks of papers to jam the doors permanently open, to enter the rooms where peace agreements are negotiated and into the rooms where peacekeeping operations are planned.
— Sara Poehlman-Doumbouya and Felicity Hill[1]

poverty, and rape; being forced to flee as refugees; some women being forced into prostitution to survive. They also argued that women bring particular skills and experience that make a significant difference to resolving conflicts without resorting to arms.

To address these issues, Resolution 1325 calls for the UN to ensure the following:

- Participation of women in peace processes.
- Gender training in peacekeeping operations.
- Protection of women and girls and respect for their rights.
- Inclusion of gender issues in the UN's reporting and implementation systems relating to conflict, peace, and security.
- Consideration of the consequences UN decisions might have for women.

The resolution outlines 18 steps to be taken by the UN Secretary-General, the Security Council, member states, and all parties to armed conflicts.

The Security Council members returned to the UN building and immediately passed the resolution unanimously. Now, how could that be? Did they not understand the meaning of the resolution and the profound changes that it would bring? Or did they have their fingers crossed and pass it without the intention to implement it? Whatever they may have been thinking, the resolution is binding, but it has

Women's working conference in 2004 to advance the implementation of Resolution 1325.

- Initiative for Inclusive Security (A program of Hunt Alternatives Fund): www.womenwagingpeace.net
- Canadian Women 4 Women in Afghanistan: www.w4wafghan.ca/
- Mano River Women's Peace Network (Poems, art, stories by women in war zones in Africa): www.marwopnet.org
- PeaceWomen (WILPF website on Resolution 1325): www.peacewomen.org/un/sc/1325.html
- UNIFEM toolkit of actions on 1325: www.womenwarpeace.org
- Voice of Women Canada: home.ca.inter.net/~vow/circles.htm

not been implemented, and women are demanding action.

Why is this resolution so important? Because when women's perspective is not taken into account in the peace process, conflict situations are exacerbated. Women hold communities together in times of conflict as caregivers, providers, counselors, and negotiators. Women are able to cross between groups and mediate when men have been unable to do so.

Dear

In October 2000, the UN Security Council unanimously passed Resolution 1325.

This extremely important resolution states, among other things, that women will be involved in all the implementation mechanisms of peace agreements.

Unfortunately, the implementation of R1325 is not happening. As a result, in situations where women could have a major impact on peacebuilding and conflict resolution, they are still outside the process. This agreement is important because women bear the hardship of war disproportionately, and because women bring unique skills and experience to the peace process.

The United States and Canada identify themselves as part of the "Friends of 1325" government group. Please take this resolution beyond friendship and into action so that women can take their place in peacebuilding, where they are so badly needed.

Sincerely,

When women are involved in the peace process, as they were in East Timor and Guatemala, the transition is calmer and people feel committed to the peace process. Experiences in Northern Ireland, South Africa, Guatemala, and elsewhere show that bringing women to the peace table improves the quality of the agreements reached and increases the chances they will be implemented effectively. In Rwanda, where new structures to include women have been institutionalized, there is growing evidence of a qualitative difference in governance for peace.

You can join in this action by writing to your Canadian member of parliament or your US representative to ask for action in implementing Resolution 1325. There are few actions that could have a greater effect than adding women to the teams working on peacebuilding, because women are more likely to bring a human face and a willingness to work out win-win solutions than men. To read the whole resolution, see the resources above.

15

Resist Militarism and Foreign Bases

> Nothing could be worse than the fear that one had given up too soon and left one unexpended effort that might have saved the world.
>
> — Jane Addams

Greenham Common

When the United States stationed cruise missiles at Greenham Common air base in the United Kingdom, 36 women formed a group they called Women for Life on Earth and walked 120 miles from Wales to Greenham Common to protest. They chained themselves to the perimeter fence, and on September 5, 1981, they established the first Greenham Common Peace Camp.[1] When the base commander was asked what he was going to do about the women camping outside the fence, he dismissed them, saying that they could stay there as far as he was concerned. They took him at his word, and the last women left the last camp nearly 20 years later.

Greenham Common became the most famous peace camp in the world.[2] It was symbolic of feminist protest because of its rejection of patriarchal structures. Members steadfastly refused to designate a leader or to formalize a structure of governance for the camp. Women came from all over the world to join the peace camp for short or long periods and to provide food and support for the campers. They blockaded roads to disrupt the cruise missile convoys as they left the base on exercises. Often they would follow a convoy in the middle of the night, and when the trucks stopped, the women would quietly paint peace symbols and flowers on the missiles.

When Newbury district council tried to evict the campers, the councilors were swamped with letters, cards, and petitions from all over the world objecting to the eviction. An action called "Embrace the Base" brought some 30,000 women from Britain and Europe to surround the base, holding hands to form a continuous circle of protest. They hung toys and flowers on the fence, and some made huge quilts with eyes on the side facing the base. The banners said, "Mother is watching you." Hundreds of people were arrested for taking down sections of the fence. Many women served time in jail. The Greenham women used the arrests and court cases to bring attention to their cause.

Eventually, the Ministry of Defence announced in 1993 that it no longer needed the base, and Greenham Common was reclaimed for public use. The last peace camp came down on January 1, 2000.

Trident Ploughshares

The UK protest shifted to the Trident submarine base at Faslane, Scotland, where the Trident Ploughshares group, made up mostly of women, carries out frequent actions to blockade the base and to damage the equipment and aircraft used in war. They call for a nuclear-weapon-free Scotland and hold themselves accountable, notifying the authorities of their actions, knowing that they can face five to ten years in prison. In their defense, they cite the World Court advisory that, in general, the threat or use of nuclear weapons is not legal under international law. They state that their actions are taken to prevent a greater crime and are therefore reasonable in the eyes of the law. They have been acquitted repeatedly (see Solution 79).

In June 1999, three women boarded a research vessel at Faslane and threw all the

- Ground Zero: www.gzcenter.org
- Trident Ploughshares: www.tridentploughshares.org

computers and files overboard. The women then tidied up, placed their pamphlets neatly on the counters, and called the media to let them know they were aboard awaiting arrest. The military police saw the tidy vessel and asked if the women had gone to all this trouble just to put

out their pamphlets. It wasn't until the next morning, when the workers arrived, that they realized what had been done. The women were acquitted because international law (the World Court) supersedes national law in Britain. The British government considered appealing the decision but was reluctant to give the women another platform to make their arguments. The case was front-page news for weeks in Scotland, but almost nothing was reported in North America.

Philippine Women's Movement
Women in other countries have also taken high-profile actions against foreign military bases. In the Philippines, women campaigned for decades against the US Clark air base and Subic Bay naval base because of the violence and abuse associated with them and the prostitution of women and children in the area around the bases. The bases were established in 1947. The Philippine government finally voted not to renew the US lease on them in 1992.

Ground Zero
The US group Ground Zero protests against the Trident submarine base in Washington state. Members have been arrested countless times, but the courts have been unable to convict them (for more on their actions, see Solutions 36 and 38).

LEENUS LARSSEN

Trident Ploughshares swimmers Anna Goransson and Emma Larssen.

16

Speak for the Children

Do your work as though you had a thousand years to live, and as if you were to die tomorrow.

— Mother Anna Lee

Women speak on behalf of our children and our children's children to call for a world without war. We must not leave a legacy of environmental destruction from the production and use of modern weapons, and we must not leave our descendents huge stockpiles of toxic weapons. Our children trust us to care for them and protect them. Women who have never taken political action before will do almost anything to protect their children. When they speak for the young, and when they join with women from all over the world, they are speaking for the future of all humanity.

How can we speak for the children?

- We can take them with us when we rally and march to remind ourselves and the political leaders what is at stake in the war system.

- We can bring rhetoric down to reality by addressing the impact of government policies on the children in our arms.

- Television cameras are drawn to babies, so put the baby in a T-shirt with a message.

- We can write to our newspapers to say that we take part in events that bring together people working for peaceful solutions to global problems because of our love for our children, our families, and our Earth.

Women Strike for Peace

In the 1960s, doctors suspected that the fallout from atmospheric nuclear tests would cause strontium 90 to build up in children's teeth and bones. They collected baby teeth to confirm their suspicions. Women were outraged when the tests showed strontium 90 deposited in the teeth and, by implication, in their children's bones. Mothers began marching against the continued testing of nuclear weapons.

Women Strike for Peace (WSP) was founded in 1961

Women Strike for Peace July, 1962.

as a protest against atmospheric nuclear tests by the United States and the Soviet Union that were poisoning the air and their children's food. Historian Amy Swerdlow reported that 100,000 women from 60 cities came out of kitchens and jobs to demand an end to the arms race, not the human race.[1] The women chose to use a simple language, "the mother tongue," because they believed that the special status of mothers could persuade the nation that the health of the next generation was in jeopardy.

WSP gained wide publicity when women pushing strollers picketed the White House, the Pentagon, and UN headquarters in New York. In 1963, US president Kennedy and Soviet leader Khrushchev, faced with ongoing protests bolstered by the moral strength of women arguing for their children's health, moved to sign the Partial Test Ban Treaty, which ended atmospheric testing of nuclear weapons.

WSP was investigated by the House Un-American Activities Committee. "The mothers refused to grant the investigation legitimacy. Employing a politics of humor, irony, evasion and ridicule, they turned the hearings into a circus. They brought cribs, suckled infants and created an instant child-care center. They hoped to persuade the public that their defense of children was morally superior to the arms race."[2]

WSP was in some ways a forerunner of the Greenham Common Peace Camp (see Solution 15) in rejecting formal systems of organization identified with men. Without membership lists or any central organization, and with no hierarchy, its members frustrated the investigators. Historians credit them with helping to bring an end to the McCarthy era in the United States.

The tradition of women resisting militarism and war continues in the United States, particularly with the Code Pink demonstrations against the occupation of Iraq (see Solution 12). Cindy Sheehan has become a symbol of that resistance.

Committee of Soldiers' Mothers of Russia
On the other side of the world, the Committee of Soldiers' Mothers of Russia works against the war in Chechnya.[3] Members stage hunger strikes and picket government offices to protest officers' abuses of soldiers. Food and clothing shortages made the situation for young recruits so appalling that the mothers appealed to President Yeltsin to have the autumn 1998 draft cancelled.

- *Traditional Motherhood and Radical Politics in the 1960s* by Amy Swerdlow, University of Chicago Press, 1993
  (Includes the story of Women Strike for Peace).

- Committee of Soldiers' Mothers:
  soldiersmothers.ru soldiersmothers@pisem.net

- History of Women Strike for Peace:
  www.ratical.org/radiation/WSP1961.html

17

Learn Nonviolent Conflict Resolution

If peace is subversive, in God's name what is war?
— Margaret Laurence, Canadian novelist

For decades, women have practiced varied forms of conflict resolution every day as they scheduled their family's activities and stretched money to make everyone happy. Someone had to facilitate the give and take of daily life. A generation ago they used the same strategies that their parents used, such as threats, spanking, and withdrawal of privileges — with many of the same frustrating outcomes.

Young parents today have several advantages in raising their children. The fathers are much more likely to be involved in parenting from the time their children are babies, and both parents are more likely to have taken a parenting course or read about different child-rearing methods. They also often have experience with nonviolent conflict resolution.

Over the past 20 years, psychologists, teachers, lawyers, and others have been thoughtfully developing better ways to communicate so that we don't make each other angry or try to solve problems by striking out at each other. During the 1980s, many people were exploring ways to decrease the threat of a nuclear confrontation between the superpowers. At the same time, courts in the United States and Canada were jammed with cases, and there was a need for alternative dispute resolution. The last few decades also brought insights into child behavior and development that led psychologists, teachers, and social workers to try new approaches to child-rearing that had much in common with the strategies of dispute resolution.

Good parenting and good conflict resolution both require clear communication and empathy skills. Fortunately most communities and schools now offer programs to teach these skills to children as well as their families. I watch my own grown-up children with amazement because they have learned a whole new approach to raising their children. I wish I had known some of the key ideas that would have helped me through their sibling rivalries and the days when whining made me want to take up the cudgel.

Take a Course

You can learn basic conflict resolution in most communities, often through your children's school. Many colleges and universities offer courses in anger management and alternative dispute resolution, as well as parenting courses.

Many parents learn conflict resolution skills when their children begin using a new way to communicate at home. One skill they learn is to give "I messages." This means that instead of accusing someone, you tell them how their words affect you by saying "When you do X, I feel Y." One of my friends was stopped in her tracks when her four year old said to her, "Mom, when you say that to me, I feel like you don't love me anymore." One child I know learned she could get through a conversation with her drunk father by applying what she had practiced at school.

Read a Book; Buy a Tape or a Video

Self-help materials for solving conflict in families and communities abound. My children swear by *How to Talk so Kids Will Listen and Listen so Kids Will Talk*. I am fond of the ideas of Marshall Rosenberg, founder of the Center for Nonviolent

- Educators for Social Responsibility: www.esrnational.org/home.htm
- *How to Talk So Kids Will Listen and Listen So Kids Will Talk* by Adele Faber and Elaine Mazlish, Avon, 1999
- *The Joy of Conflict Resolution: Transforming Victims, Villains and Heroes in the Workplace and at Home* by Gary Harper, New Society Publishers, 2004
- Marshall Rosenberg: www.cnvc.org
- Peaceful Childhoods kit: www.pgs.ca

Communication. He uses puppets to teach how to speak a language of respect and caring.

Order a Kit; Organize a Workshop

It's hardest to be respectful to those we live with. Kids are very sensitive to put-downs and patronizing. Physicians for Global Survival (Canada) offers a kit for peaceful childhoods that includes materials on peaceful child rearing; children and war toys; guns and children; and children and media. In the United States, the Educators for Social Responsibility's Resolving Conflict Creatively Program offers workshops called "Keeping Peace in the Family."

Teach the Men

The ideas of nonviolent conflict resolution are being taken up worldwide, especially by women. An Australian SBS TV documentary showed the influence of women in the Kurdistan Workers' Party PKK in Iraq.[1] The PKK is the organization that has used suicide bombings and guerrilla attacks to try to achieve an independent Kurdish state in Turkey and Iraq. The group that was featured in the documentary has given up armed conflict and terrorism in order to work for democratic reform. This story gets even more astonishing when you learn that there is a quiet social revolution in progress in their camps in northern Iraq.

About half the members of the featured group are men and half are women, with separate quarters. The women and men treat each other as equals; in fact, the local leader is a woman. The women are giving the men a year-long course about feminism (with an exam). The camp is described as a serene place where most of the people are busy reading political literature, as well as works on existentialism and feminism. Their major concern is that they may be bombed and killed before they are able to convince the world that they have given up armed violence and are working for democratic solutions.

violence-free zone

Peaceful Childhoods Kit, Physicians for Global Survival, Canada.

CATHERINE O'NEIL, EMERGING DESIGN, OTTAWA

18

Bear Witness to Atrocities

> The age of generals has ended; the
> era of women has begun.
> — Coalition of Women for a Just Peace

Women in Black

To know that your child is missing and may be suffering torture must be the worst form of torture, and the loss of a child is surely the most agonizing experience for a parent. In Argentina, 30,000 people were "disappeared" under the military regime. Many were known to be tortured and killed; the fate of many others is unknown.

A group of women clothed in black, led by Estela Carlotto, refused to be intimidated by the death squads. They decided to break the silence and bear witness by standing silently at the Plaza de Mayo. Wearing white scarves bearing their child's name, they kept their regular vigil, their presence alone a blatant accusation of murder and brutality. "My whole life is committed to this; I'm going to fight so that this can never happen again," said Carlotto. By challenging the authority of the oppressive regime, their vigils broke its power and laid the groundwork for its collapse.

Estella Carlotto was awarded the United Nations Prize for the Defense of Human Rights and France's Order of the Legion of Honor. Women in Black was awarded the Millennium Peace Prize by UNIFEM and International Alert. Women in Black in Israel/Palestine and former Yugoslavia were also nominated for the Nobel Peace Prize and the Right Livelihood Award.

Today, Women in Black is a worldwide network of women opposed to injustice, war, militarism and other forms of violence. They work for a world where difference does not mean inequality, oppression, or exclusion.

Women for a Just Peace

Women in Black is a member of many coalitions of women's groups, including Women for a Just Peace in Israel. In 1988, Israeli and Palestinian women began standing together at a busy intersection in Jerusalem, holding up a placard

EASYBUENOSAIRESCITY.COM/GDIAZ©

The scarves that identified the Mothers of the Plaza de Mayo are commemorated in the pavement in Buenos Aires.

- Israeli section of Jerusalem Link: www.batshalom.org
- Jerusalem Centre for Women: www.j-c-w.org
- Jewish Coalition of Women for a Just Peace: www.fire.or.cr/junio01/coalition.htm
- Research on Women in Black: www.cynthiacockburn.org
- Women in Black: www.womeninblack.org

showing a large hand and the words "Stop the Occupation." Women on the Israeli side call themselves *Bat Shalom*; those on the Palestinian side, Jerusalem Center for Women. Within months of their first appearance, vigils had sprung up around the country.

In 2001, Women for a Just Peace called for women around the world to hold vigils in support of their protest against the occupation. In response, some 10,000 women held 150 vigils in different countries. Currently Women for a Just Peace is working for the implementation of Resolution 1325 (see Solution 14) and particularly for the participation of women in the peace process in the Middle East. The two organizations bring together organizations of Jewish and Palestinian women, citizens of Israel, to work together for a just peace based on the following principles:

- An end to the occupation.
- The full involvement of women in negotiations for peace.
- Establishment of the state of Palestine side by side with the state of Israel, based on the 1967 borders.
- The recognition of Jerusalem as the shared capital of the two states.
- Israel's recognition of its share of responsibility for the results of the 1948 war.
- Cooperation in finding a just solution for the Palestinian refugees.
- Equality, inclusion, and justice for Palestinian citizens of Israel.

- Opposition to the militarism that permeates Israeli society.
- Equal rights for women and all residents of Israel.
- Social and economic justice for Israel's citizens, and integration in the region.

Women in Black in Vojvodina, Serbia, and Montenegro has more than a hundred women's groups addressing violence and discrimination against women. Concerned people outside the region can make the difference between persecution and safety for the women coming forward in public. If we let government leaders know the world is watching, the women are much less likely to be hurt. We can write to their government, sending a copy of the letter to our own leaders, to express our concern for the women and the issues they are raising.

The Women in Black website keeps an updated list of local organizations all over the world, with the days and times of their regular vigils. Women are welcome to simply dress in black and join the group in silence. In some places they identify themselves with a placard, but ask that individuals not bring signs or petitions, so it is best to use your discretion the first time you join them. New groups are welcomed, so if you can't find one, you can start your own.

19

Reject the Glorification of War and Violence

> We used to wonder where war lived, what it was that made it so vile. And now we realize that we know where it lives, that it is inside ourselves.
>
> — Albert Camus

Glorifying war and violence as the triumph of heroic masculinity makes it easy to sell war as the best possible solution to international conflicts. But public attitudes are shifting rapidly. In our communities, violence against women and children is no longer accepted as private business but is addressed by the police and by social programs. The world is slowly and steadily moving away from war, with fewer wars each year. The result is that selling war is becoming more difficult because the public knows that there are alternatives to bombing and killing.

We still must face the fact that we live in a culture of violence and are only slowly awakening to the effects of the violence that is in our living rooms every day on television. You can click on your remote control any hour of the day or night and find a gun battle, an exploding car, a murder — or an equally violent cartoon. What can you do?

- Turn off the TV. It shouldn't be necessary to censor movies that are violent, but it seems that the industry is not willing to voluntarily limit the extreme material that is now available. As a society we have the right to demand entertainment that will help us raise children who respect others, who are compassionate, and who care about the world we live in. As parents, we must set a higher standard.

- Join a media group to take action against the violent entertainment. Don't accept violence as a thrilling expression of manhood instead of the outdated and dysfunctional way in which some men try to dominate others. Speak out against war by challenging the images that show war as a glorious, patriotic endeavor and ignore the infliction of pain and the injury, suffering, and death for political gain.

- Walk out of movies that are violent, especially when the violence is gratuitous and senseless. Ask for your money back as you leave. Phone or write to the advertisers who sponsor violent TV programs. We can demand better. Let the advertisers know that we want something to inspire us — something authentic and meaningful, something that shows the heights to which human beings can rise instead of the depths to which they fall. If the advertisers raise the

GILLIAN DAVIDSON

Turn off the TV and encourage cooperative play.

bar, the writers and producers will rise to their expectations.

- Watch comedies — they're good for your health! Norman Cousins wrote of the power of humor to heal illness. He was the editor of *Saturday Review* and wrote many books including *Anatomy of an Illness as Perceived by the Patient*. Cousins credited the hours he watched funny movies with curing his autoimmune disease. Since he wrote of his experience, research has shown that when people watch violent television, their adrenalin levels rise and stay elevated for a period of hours. When they watch a neutral show, like gardening, this does not happen. And when they watch something humorous or inspiring, like the Marx Brothers or a documentary about Mother Teresa, their endorphins go up and stay high for hours. Endorphins not only make you feel good, they boost your immune system.

It makes you wonder why airlines show violent movies on flights and then are surprised they have to deal with anger and rudeness as tired people push their way through airports after they land. Why not show movies that will leave people feeling great for hours? Let's add the airline public relations departments to our lists for letters.

When children are asked to evaluate whether a TV show is suitable for children, they will often say that it is no problem for them, but it could be a bad influence for other children. I recall one six-year-old child who, after watching a movie, asked, "Shouldn't they stop us from seeing this?"

The American Medical Association, the National PTA, the American Academy of Pediatrics, and the Canadian Pediatric Society have all concluded that violence on television and in other forms of entertainment increases violence and aggression in normal children and adults.

- Adbusters: www.adbusters.org
- *Armed Conflicts Report* (Project Ploughshares): www.ploughshares.ca
- Consumer Reports for Kids Online: www.zillions.org.
- Media Awareness: www.media-awareness.ca
- Media Watch: www.mediawatch.com
- New American Dream: www.newdream.org
- US National Institute for Media and the Family: www.mediafamily.org

20

Speak Truth to Power

> There is no democracy without peace and no peace without women.
> — Coalition of Women for a Just Peace

Speak Truth to Power

Theodore Taylor was one of the designers of the hydrogen bomb, but later he became a powerful spokesman against nuclear weapons. I sat beside him on a flight to the Soviet test range in Kazakhstan in 1990 and asked why he left his job at Livermore Labs. He told me that his wife and his mother refused to buy his argument that his work would make war so horrifying that it would never happen again. "Finally," he said, "I didn't buy it myself."

The turning point for him was seeing a map in a war planning room and finding small circles around cities to show the area of total destruction if they were hit by a nuclear bomb. He saw circles around Moscow, Leningrad, Odessa, Glasgow, Rio de Janeiro ... and suddenly realized the system had gone mad. Shortly after that he left and began speaking about the urgency of nuclear disarmament.

- *Breaking Ranks* by Melissa Everett, New Society, 1989.
- Conflict Research Consortium of Colorado University: conflict.colorado.edu
- Crisis Group: www.crisisweb.org
- The Network University: www.euconflict.org.
- Oxford Research Group: www.oxfordresearchgroup.org.uk
- United States Institute of Peace: www.usip.org
- The World March for Women: www.marchemondiale.org

Write Truth to Power

Years ago, the Oxford Research Group (ORG) determined who actually made decisions about nuclear weapons in the countries with nuclear capability. ORG found that the 650 key people might be in government, industry, or the military. The group began to correspond respectfully with those individuals in order to learn more about the thinking behind their decisions.

The power of this strategy was shown when Scilla Elworthy, founder of ORG, supported a group of musicians in London who began writing to the head of the British armed services. Their intention was to establish a dialogue about British policy on nuclear weapons, and they wrote to him every three months. They would build on a press report of something he said and, without being confrontational, would present the view that perhaps security would be better served by the reduction and elimination of nuclear weapons.

Each time they wrote, they received a one-line reply saying that their letter had been received. Nothing else. After three years, just as they began to wonder if it was possible to establish a dialogue at all, the head of the British armed services retired and was welcomed into the House of Lords. In his maiden speech he made the points set out in their letters over the years. They phoned him and he invited them to join him for a glass of sherry. Scilla Elworthy has been nominated for a Nobel Peace Prize for the work of the Oxford Research Group.

Show Truth to Power

In her book *Breaking Ranks*, Melissa Everett writes about people who gave up their careers in US military industries when they suddenly confronted the meaning of their work. One senior official told of the impact of passing a solitary man who stood every day outside the entrance to the Lawrence Livermore Laboratory, holding a placard opposing nuclear weapons. The anonymous protester played a significant role in the official's eventual decision to resign his job.

The power of truth was shown in the US civil rights movement when blacks began sitting in places where they were not allowed, like the front of the bus or the segregated lunch counter. When the invisible was made visible, truth made it impossible to sustain the injustice of segregation. The strength of truth speaks to us when children from war zones write and draw pictures about war. They paint the bombs, the dead, the ambulances, and the children mourning, which is how they experience daily life.

There is a new and exciting project for women around the world that started in Quebec. The Women's Global Charter for Humanity is a proposal to build a world where exploitation, oppression, intolerance, and exclusion no longer exist and where integrity, diversity, and the rights and freedoms of all are respected. The charter is the result of a long process of consultation and discussion involving women's groups from 60 countries.

Women met in Kigali, Rwanda, to adopt the charter in December 2004. The charter, which you can download from the World March for Women website, was carried around the world in a relay — the World March. Women are making a quilt to record the journey of the charter. If you want to be involved, you can check out their activities on the website. My favorite part is listening to the exuberant theme song with joyous African rhythm. I'm going to join them.

Women met in Kigali, Rwanda in December 2004 to adopt the Charter for Humanity.

> Every child is potentially the light of the world as well as the cause of its darkness.
>
> — City Montessori School, Lucknow, India.

Nonviolent Conflict Resolution

Perhaps you have wondered, as I have, whether peace education really makes a difference in reducing violence. The story of the City Montessori School (CMS) in Lucknow, India, certainly dispelled any of my doubts.[1] The Montessori School is the largest private school in one city in the world. It has 29,000 students at 20 different campuses. The school is based on the teachings of Gandhi and Maria Montessori, and its goal is to inspire children and youth to think in terms of the welfare of all the people of the world. Over 250,000 students have passed through the City Montessori School since it was founded in 1959.

Lucknow is a city about 87 miles (140 kilometers) from Ayodhya, which is recognized by Hindus as Lord Rama's birthplace, but which is also the site of a sacred Muslim mosque. In 1992 the mosque was destroyed by Hindu extremists, who tore it apart brick by brick. The resulting Muslim outrage burst into riots across India, killed some 3,000 people, and devastated communities.

Lucknow's population is about 40 percent Muslim, and residents anticipated riots within hours of the destruction of the mosque. The city magistrate, however, asked the City Montessori School to convene a meeting of religious leaders so they could plan together how to prevent the eruption of violence in Lucknow. He asked the school because of its long history of teaching the values of universal brotherhood and the cultivation of virtues. It appears that by 1992, not only had tens of thousands of students been inspired, but the large number of adults who had been educated there also made the school a highly respected intervenor.

Each day the religious leaders met to pray for peace and to work together to reduce the tensions in the community. Each evening they returned to their own congregations to urge them to maintain communal harmony.

City Montessori School

Communal Harmony March by CMS students. Students are carrying symbols of different religions: Hindu, Muslim, Christian to stop hatred and give peace a chance.

- City Montessori School in Lucknow, India: www.cmseducation.org
- Educators for Social Responsibility, Metro New York (Ideas on conflict resolution and stopping put-downs): www.teachablemoment.org
- Physicians for Global Survival: www.pgs.ca
- *Towards a Non-Violent Society* by Joanna Santa Barbara, 2004

Tens of thousands of children marched with their teachers and parents behind rented jeeps with loudspeakers, spreading the message that the God of the Hindus and the God of the Muslims is the same God, and imploring people not to resort to violence. Astonishingly, they were successful, and Lucknow was spared the destruction that occurred in other cities.

Most schools in North America teach children some classes on communications skills, empathy, and nonviolent conflict resolution. Many teach about how painful it is to be put down by a classmate, even if the words were intended as a joke. Television often reinforces the hurtful behavior instead of the supportive language we all need to use.

A teacher told me a story about a task she gave her grade 6 class and the lengthy debriefing that resulted. The children worked in pairs and had just one chair. The child not sitting in the chair had to work out how to get the other child off the chair without touching him or her. Most of the pairs quickly worked out an agreement to share or take turns. One pair even agreed to pay each other ten cents when they wanted to sit on the chair.

Two pairs of boys, however, became very frustrated and couldn't reach a solution. They said the boys on the chairs wouldn't get off without force and there was no way to make them. The teacher surmised that perhaps girls are more often taught negotiating strategies than boys are. She led the whole class in a discussion about how often we assume that only force will work because we have not been taught how to use our words to search for solutions. Once

the boys learned new negotiating skills, they were able to apply them in different situations.

The arm wrestle game is a common exercise used to help children and adults recognize how often we jump to the conclusion that if someone wins, someone must lose. In the game, two people sit opposite one another with their elbows on a desk and their right hands gripping. The teacher tells them that they must not talk, and that each time one person's hand touches the desk, the other person will get a cookie. In the beginning, most people struggle furiously to keep the other person from getting a cookie. Then suddenly they stop and alternate, allowing their hands to be pressed down, so that each of them will get a cookie.

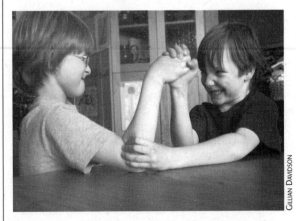

Two boys just before they realize that they win more if they cooperate than if they continue to compete.

22

Refuse To Be an Enemy

I destroy my enemies when I make them my friends.

— Abraham Lincoln

Break Down Stereotypes of the Enemy

During the Cold War, children in the west knew little about the Soviet Union and its people. In fact, all of us, children and adults alike, had stereotypes of the Soviets that we had absorbed from television. We thought of drab, unsmiling people, parades of weapons and troops, and journalists posed standing in front of parked tanks. At the same time, children's fears of nuclear war were of great concern to psychologists because children expressed anxiety and despair for the future. I was often invited to talk about my visits to Soviet schools and hospitals. I wanted to reassure children that millions of adults all over the world were working to prevent nuclear war and that children did not have to carry that burden. What children could do was learn to see other people not as enemies, but as friends they hadn't met yet.

Make Friends around the World

We connected the children in our communities with children in the Soviet Union. I thought of the words "you've got to be taught to hate and fear" when I was in a grade 1 class in Canada and about to show slides of children in Soviet Georgia dancing in a ballet class and painting sidewalks for a fall fair. The teacher asked the class what they knew about children in the Soviet Union. We were stunned when one little boy snorted, "They don't have children in the Soviet Union. They kill them all!" His comment led to a rich discussion about how we learn about people in other countries and how sometimes we might not get the whole story from television.

Many schools boards and ministries of education provide addresses for students who want to write to pen pals in countries where there is conflict but sufficient stability that children can communicate. The arrival of immigrant and refugee families in a school can also provide a teachable moment so children begin to understand the reality behind the television news.

Make a Lantern To Show Your Hopes for the Future

In Hiroshima and Nagasaki, people float lanterns on a river with prayers for those who died in the atomic bombing of their cities on August 6 and 9, 1945 (see Solution 3). In other countries, Hiroshima Day is remembered by the floating of lanterns for peace.

A doctor from the United States began teaching schoolchildren to make simple paper lanterns with messages of peace and friendship inscribed on them. The children exchanged the lanterns with schoolchildren in the Soviet Union. Many of the lanterns from the Soviet Union had photos of the children, and some even had a lock of hair attached. The lantern exchange often led to pen pals beginning to write to one another.

If you want to organize a Hiroshima Day event, get your friends to make lanterns at school and then store them until August 6. You might want to provide materials at the event so other children and adults can make lanterns. Suggest that people draw or paint images of what is most important to them, symbolically releasing their wishes and prayers for the future onto the water.

- Instructions for creating paper lanterns from Physicians for Global Survival: www.pgs.ca/updir/Resource_Kit.pdf
- Instructions for folding paper cranes and other resources: www.sadako.com
- McMaster Peace Festival: www.humanities.mcmaster.ca/gandhi/
- *Sadako and the Thousand Paper Cranes* by Elinor Coerr, Dell, 1977

You can make lanterns using a foam base, with bamboo skewers holding the lantern shades up (instructions are on the Physicians for Global Survival website), or you can become more creative and make a lantern with a recycled milk carton floating on a foam meat tray. To decorate it you can use tissue collages or inserts or simply draw pictures of whales, trees, and flowers or write family sayings or poems. Put a small votive candle in the center of the float, holding it in place with toothpicks.

At sunset, have people sing as the lanterns are released onto the water. In many cities the ceremony includes music, dance, and short readings. Arrange to have people in canoes or boats collect the lanterns afterward so the materials can be reused and recycled.

Fold a Crane for Peace

Another key date for a peace gathering is October 2, Gandhi's birthday. Hamilton, Ontario, holds a Gandhi peace festival that includes children's activities at the library. Usually someone reads *Sadako and the Thousand Paper Cranes*, the true story of a little girl who was a toddler in Hiroshima when the bomb fell. When she was 12 she got leukemia, and while she was ill, her friend told her that if she folded a thousand cranes, the gods would grant her wish. When Sadako died, she had folded more than 600 cranes, and children continue to fold cranes in her memory today. There is a statue of Sadako in Hiroshima. Thousands of paper cranes hang on threads over it, and written at the foot of the statue are the words "This is our cry. This is our prayer. Peace in the world."

Children learn to fold paper cranes at the public library on Peace Day in Hamilton, Canada.

23

Stand Up and Speak Out

> Don't worry that children never listen to you. Worry that they are always watching you.
>
> —Robert Fulgham

Speak Out

In 1983, when the threat of nuclear war filled the world with dread and hopelessness, the American student Samantha Smith wrote to Soviet leader Yuri Andropov.[1]

> Dear Mr. Andropov,
> My name is Samantha Smith. I am ten years old. Congratulations on your new job. I have been worrying about Russia and the United States getting into a nuclear war. Are you going to vote to have a war or not? If you aren't, please tell me how you are going to help to not have a war. This question you do not have to answer, but I would like to know why you want to conquer the world or at least our country. God made the world for us to live together in peace and not to fight.
> Sincerely,
> Samantha Smith

Here is an excerpt of Mr. Andropov's reply:

- Al Jazeera: english.aljazeera.net
- CNN: edition.cnn.com
- Colombian Children's Peace Movement: edition.cnn.com/SPECIALS/1999/children/stories/child.soldiers/
- Samantha Smith: www.samanthasmith.info/History.htm

> Dear Samantha,
> Yes, Samantha, we in the Soviet Union are trying to do everything so that there will not be war on earth .... No one in our country — neither workers, peasants, writers nor doctors, neither grown-ups nor children, nor members of the government — want either a big or "little" war ....
> We want peace for ourselves and for all peoples of the planet. For our children and for you, Samantha.
> I invite you, if your parents will let you, to come to our country ... and see for yourself: in the Soviet Union, everyone is for peace and friendship among peoples.
> Thank you for your letter. I wish you all the best in your young life.
> Y. Andropov

Samantha did go to the Soviet Union, where she traveled and met people on the streets and in their homes. She spoke on Soviet television, watched by 200,000 people, and became a beloved heroine to the Soviets. Tragically, Samantha and her father died in a plane crash when she was 13. The Soviet people were as grief stricken as the Americans at the loss of her life.

Mikhail Gorbachev, when he was president of the Soviet Union, wrote about how he came to sign a treaty reducing nuclear weapons. He said that the hundreds of thousands of letters he received from children affected him deeply.

An 11-year-old girl in the United States wrote a letter in a comic book asking children who were afraid of nuclear war to write to her so she could take the letters to President Reagan. She received 70,000 letters, which she took to the White House.

Call a Peace Vote

The Children's Peace Movement in Colombia has been nominated three times for the Nobel Peace Prize for its actions, including its leadership in calling for a peace vote.[2] Colombia is one of the world's most violent countries, with a long history of armed conflict. In 1996, children from different organizations throughout the country gathered and founded the Children's Peace Movement. The organization has grown to more than 100,000 members. The children organized a peace vote in which 2.7 million children voted on which human right was the most important. They voted overwhelmingly for the right to life and peace.

The children's vote was followed a year later by an election in which, for the first time, the guerrillas agreed to a ceasefire on election day. Ten million adults approved a peace mandate.

Farlis, a Colombian girl, said, "Contemporary societies think their children are cute, sweet, beautiful, but they don't see beyond their noses. So we also want to show the rest of the world that the role of the child must be elevated. There are moments in acute crises in countries when children have to make up part of the solution, because all the countries say children are the future of the country. But we are not the future, we are the present, a present which we all have to build together."[3]

If children today want to write respectfully to ask what is being done to prevent war, they must somehow make a bridge between the west and the Arabic countries. Perhaps if North American children wrote to Al Jazeera, the Arabic language news network, and children from Arabic countries wrote to CNN, the exchange of letters would show the world how frightened children are for their future. Perhaps leaders on both sides would take the time to respond, letting the children know what they are doing to make the world safer.

RUSSELL DAVIDSON

Samantha Smith.

24

Organize Student Action

> There are no passengers on spaceship earth. We're all crew. To your stations, crew!
>
> — from Mile Zero

In 1986, four Canadian students (two boys and two girls) in grade 11 and 12 took a year out of school to travel across Canada, speaking to high school students about the threat of nuclear war. One of them said education was too important to be left to schools. One boy had a driver's license, so they went from coast to coast in an old station wagon, followed by a film crew from the National Film Board.

The film about them, *Mile Zero*, is touching, funny, and very powerful, even today. By the end of their trip they had spoken to over 100,000 students and were featured at the Peace Walk in Vancouver with 250,000 people before they traveled to speak in Moscow.

Did they have any effect? In one city they suggested an action for local students. The

legislature was debating whether to make Ontario a nuclear-weapon-free zone (NWFZ). The local member of parliament planned to vote "No." The students were asked to phone the member's office to say, "I'm not old enough to vote in this election, but I will be in the next one, and I want you to vote "yes" tomorrow on the NWFZ." The next day they followed up by calling the member's office again to ask if there had been any phone calls about the vote. The secretary said they had never had so many calls on an issue, and the member voted "Yes."

What about students in conflict areas? Re'ut-Sadaka is a Jewish-Arab youth movement for peace. *Re'ut-Sadaka* means "friendship." The movement was established in 1982 by a small group of young people in Tel Aviv. Israeli and Palestinian youth have few opportunities to meet one another because they speak different languages, live in different areas, and have different religions. Knowing that without frequent contact people tend to reinforce their prejudices and the bias they see on TV, they decided to come together to create a dialogue between Arab and Jewish youth.

Their goal is to promote mutual respect and tolerance, support equal rights and respect for democracy and pluralism, and develop young leadership in Israel. Every year *Re'ut-Sadaka* works with over 500 Jewish and Arab young people and reaches thousands more by speaking in Jewish and Arab high schools. Many thousands have attended lectures about the values of tolerance and understanding and the ways in which they can help shape a new social and political reality of coexistence.

NATIONAL FILM BOARD OF CANADA

The SAGE Tour

Students who crossed Canada on the Students Against Global Extermination (SAGE) Tour to speak in high schools about the threat of nuclear war. From left to right, Maxime Faille, Desiree McGraw, Alison Carpenter and Seth Klein.

In the program One Year of Life for Coexistence, five to eight Jewish and Arab high school graduates live and work together for a year. Their goals are to educate others, plan community projects, and live the ideal of coexistence. *Re'ut-Sadaka* won a Fifty Communities Award from the Friends of the UN for its work.[1]

Student actions bring energy, creativity, and fun to the work of building peace in your own community and in the world. Here are some ideas:

- Organize a teach-in to give information about a current issue. Invite speakers, make handouts, and have an action to be done — a petition to sign, posters to make, something to sell to fund your project.

- Lead a workshop for students who want to learn public-speaking and facilitation skills. Ask your school for resource people, or go together with students from another school to bring in a media person or a Toastmasters member to help you. Practice with microphones and develop a sound bite that could be used if you were interviewed. Imagine yourself on the late news. (Sound bites are now just over 19 seconds! Make it easy for the editor. Pause before and after you say your bite.)

- Notify local TV reporters and college or community radio stations or newspapers about your activities. They will often cover student

- Amnesty International: www.amnesty.org
- Bullfrog Films: www.bullfrogfilms.com
- *Mile Zero* (Film from National Film Board of Cana[www.onf.ca
- Re'ut-Sadaka (Jewish-Arab Youth Movement for Peace) www.bkluth.de/reut
- Toastmasters International: www.toastmasters.org
- World Federation of UN Associations: www.funa.org

actions. Remember that young people are magnets for cameras. You are attractive, articulate, committed, and idealistic — just the kind of people who look great on TV!

- Set up a film night. For movie suggestions, check with Amnesty International or the National Film Board in Canada, or Bullfrog Films in the United States. Watch for documentaries coming to local theaters. Ask an expert to speak after the film.

- Run a role-playing exercise on conflict resolution, or contact your local United Nations Association to help you set up a model UN. You and your friends will play the roles of the ambassadors faced with a tough resolution like whether or not to abolish nuclear weapons. What would you say if you were the Chinese ambassador, or the Russian or American ambassador?

> **If you don't know how to fix it, don't break it.**
> — Severn Suzuki, age 12, speaking to UN delegates in Rio de Janeiro, 1992

...he young people do a talk show called *Say What?* The children wrote, revised, and prac-...ed in school and then rehearsed with a ...entor who worked in radio. They learned very quickly that professionals have no time for goofing around. Their thoughtful comments and self-discipline meant they were allowed to present five half-hour shows on current global issues.

The Internet offers students many opportunities to join campaigns that are working on peacebuilding projects. Many schools teach young people to make their own websites and allow students to show their concern for issues or write a blog. Schools can set up a petition or letter online for their students to sign.

...ı.dren ...ıcaı of what oth- ...ıı of what they watched ...ıves). The students viewed, and in their next class commented on, the shows. They decided they would give an award to the channel that showed programs that did not promote violence. Then they wrote a polite letter to another channel explaining why they were opposed to its Saturday morning programs and what they would rather see. The award-winning TV station interviewed the children and then covered their visit to the second station.

Produce a TV or Radio Program

A class of grade 5 students in Victoria, Canada, became interested in writing for radio. The local university radio station agreed to let

Media Pointers for Children

- Practice using a microphone so that you don't speak too far from it or so close that you make people's ears pop.

- Write some notes on a small file card so that you know the point you want to make, but don't read it from the card.

- For radio, write two key words on the card to remind yourself of the two points you want to make.

- Practice a few times so that you can hear what happens when you breathe or when you giggle. Listen to hear if you say "uh" or "like." With a bit of practice, you won't.

- For TV, read your notes over and then leave them behind. When you are interviewed,

Author with a seven year old speaker at Victoria Lantern Ceremony, 1987. The child recovered from his moment of panic and spoke beautifully about "what peace means to me".

GILLIAN DAVIDSON

- *Tell the World* by Severn Suzuki, Doubleday, 1993
- David Suzuki Foundation: www.davidsuzuki.org

look at the person asking you questions, not at the monitor. The interviewer may tell you exactly where to look so that you appear natural to the viewer. Speak fairly slowly and clearly so that the audience can understand you. Remember, they may not speak English well, and they need you to make yourself clear.

- See if you can come up with a very short statement of your view, and learn to say it easily. For example, some of the slogans from the antinuclear movement are: "War is not healthy for children and other living things" or "You can't hug a child with nuclear arms."

- You make the biggest impact when you tell your personal story. You may have read a news item that made you want to take action, or you may have seen a movie about the subject. Say how it affected you and what you are doing about it.

Get the Word Out

Letters to the editor written by children are often published because they present a fresh perspective. Don't forget that the page of letters to the editor has the biggest audience in the newspaper.

If you and your friends plan an action that includes a photo opportunity, you may well get coverage, especially in a community newspaper.

In 1989, David Suzuki's daughter Severn and four of her 11-year-old friends formed the Ecological Children's Organization (ECO). After a few years of local projects, they heard about the 1992 UN Conference on Environment and

Development in Rio de Janeiro and decided to raise money to go and tell the UN leaders to take strong action to fight for their future. Initially David Suzuki didn't take them too seriously, but the girls were determined. As they began to draw support from the community, they held a fundraising event at the Vancouver planetarium and saw their goal within reach. They surprised everyone, especially themselves. Raffi Cavoukian, a popular children's entertainer and friend, became a strong supporter and matched the fund so the girls from ECO could go to the conference. Raffi even accompanied them.

Severn, along with three children from other countries, was invited to give a speech to the UN plenary. Her short talk left the listeners in tears. You can read what she said in her book *Tell the World*, or order the video showing the young people who spoke at the UN Summit (from the Suzuki Foundation).

Young performers from the Colombian Children's Peace Movement at the Hague Appeal for Peace, 1999.

26

Welcome Diversity

Fifty years from now it will not matter what kind of car we drove, what kind of house we lived in, how much money we had in our bank accounts, nor what our clothes looked like. But the world will be a better place because we worked with children to educate them about world peace and understanding.

*— Lucy Way, chair of
Children's International Summer Villages*

We learn to value those who are different from us when we meet with mutual respect and warmth instead of fear and suspicion.

Conservative critics often deplore the fact that in some of Vancouver, British Columbia's inner-city schools, 70 percent of the students have English as their second language. The critics claim that teachers spend all their time dealing with these children rather than teaching core subjects. Some parents believe that teachers have little time for students who are fluent in English, and they worry that their children's education will suffer as a result. They wonder if they should remove their children from these schools because they won't be getting a good education.

Do we sometimes mistake a blessing for a curse? Other parents pay a fortune to send their children to international schools where large numbers of students have English as their second language. They want a broader education enriched by diversity for their children.

We Are All Related

Fortunately, there are teachers in the public system who see the diversity of the school population as a gift to be celebrated. Cunningham Elementary, an inner-city school in Vancouver, enriched the lives of its students, their families, and the whole community through a two-year project based on the theme "We Are All Related." Under the direction of art teacher Sharole Brown, students studied cultural values and made collages of family photographs and historical and cultural symbols. The high quality of the project led to wide community

support, art gallery exhibitions, a gallery tour, and a book illustrated with the children's collages, their understanding of the meaning of "We Are All Related," and quotations from their elders.[1]

The World We Want

In 2003 the Faculty of Education at the University of Victoria in Canada invited children to submit artwork depicting the theme "The World We Want." The idea was to connect students in Victoria with those in Kabul, Afghanistan, and in Sulaymaniyah in the Kurdish part of Iraq. The Canadian army provided paper to the children in Kabul and transported the drawings back to Canada. The artwork from Sulaymaniyah was smuggled out in the middle of the night and given to a contact at the University of Tehran, who carried it to London and then couriered it to Victoria.

When children's drawings began to arrive from war zones, Canadian students saw life as it had been under the Taliban in Afghanistan and as it was in the chaos of occupation through the eyes of children their own age. Images of men shooting, women weeping, buildings on fire all told the stories of pain and fear of Afghan and Iraqi children. Some of the translated notes from injured children were almost unbearable to read. One Afghan drawing showed a bird cage with a cover partly off to show the restrictions on women; another showed a woman standing a little above the earth, with shackles chaining her to the ground.[2]

- Education Without Borders:
  www.educationwithoutborders.ca
- Grassroots Holistic Healing: www.grassrootshealing.com
- Hands Across Borders:
  www.handsacrossborderssociety.org
- Kurdistan Save the Children Fund: www.ksc-kcf.com
- PRIA (International Center for Learning and Promotion
  of Participation and Democratic Governance):
  www.pria.org
- Project Hope: www.projecthope.ps
- Raffi News: www.raffinews.com
- Teachers for a Better Belize: www.twc.org/belize
- World We Want: www.childrensglobalarts.ca
- *We Are All Related: A Celebration of Our Cultural Heritage*
  by the students of G.T. Cunningham Elementary
  School, 1996

By 2005, when another collection of artwork arrived from Kabul, the children were clearly responding to positive changes in their lives. They drew women at ballot boxes, children playing, women free and smiling, and beautiful birds. One drawing showed children holding hands with a Canadian soldier. Members of the fire department in Langford, British Columbia, brought the artwork back to Canada after they had delivered donated fire equipment to the Kabul firefighters (see Solution 63). The future is still uncertain in Afghanistan, and the country outside Kabul is extremely dangerous, but for the moment, children are beginning to have hope.

Canadian children's entertainer Raffi Cavoukian and his Troubadour Foundation support this project. Raffi calls on us to honor children as participants in our society, endowed with innate and intuitive intelligence. He says we must make a global commitment to all children that they will be kept from harm and neglect and will inherit a world that is sustainable and free of environmental devastation.

Since 2003, the World We Want project has expanded to other countries including Zanzibar, South Africa, Nigeria, Algeria, India, Belize, Iran, Chile, Israel/Palestine, and Korea. Schools in all countries are welcome to join the project.

Children's art in Afghanistan changed from painful images in 2003 to hopeful ones in 2005.

ROBERT DALTON

Taliban men stab a baby and shoot a woman.

ROBERT DALTON

Women cast their ballots in the election.

27.

Establish Peaceful Schools

Establishing lasting peace is the work of education; all politics can do is keep us out of war.

— Maria Montessori

Over the past 20 years we have learned a great deal about how to create peaceful schools, and the results are showing in reduced school violence in both the United States and Canada. Some of the major successful programs are: peer mediation, communication and empathy skills, anger management, conflict resolution, bullyproofing, bias reduction, parenting education, media literacy education, outdoor education, cultural pride, meditation, peace studies, and changing school atmosphere. Programs that build peaceful schools mirror what is needed for peaceful societies.

When I did my doctoral research on programs to prevent adolescent violence, I found that there was an easy way to determine which school programs were likely to reduce violence. They were the ones that built the young person's sense of connectedness and meaning in life. Connectedness means we understand that body, mind, and spirit are all one, that we matter to someone, and that we belong to the Earth. Locker searches and metal detectors don't reduce violence; that's because they build alienation, not connectedness. When police organize midnight basketball games, they make

- Bullying prevention: www.bullying.org
- Family Channel: www.family.ca
- I Power I: www.bully.org
- Rock Solid: www.rocksolid.bc.ca
- Search Institute: www.search-institute.org

a difference because they build relationships that matter.

Peer Mediation

Peer mediation is an effective way for schools to reduce playground violence.[1] In this program, selected students in grade 5 or older receive professional training to mediate playground fights. The mediators wear special beanies or T-shirts. When a mediator spots a scuffle, he or she asks the students if they would like help to resolve things. If the students agree, they go with the mediator to work out a solution. When the students have a solution, the mediator writes it out and turns in a report. Mediators must report to the teacher on duty if fighters refuse mediation, but students rarely refuse.

When the whole school adopts peer mediation, the aggression on the playground drops so much there is often nothing for the mediators to do. One school tried cutting the number of mediators on the playground below four, but at that point aggression escalated again.

Resilient Children

There is a field of psychology concerned with resilient children — those who turned out well despite coming from high-risk families. Some had parents who were criminals, alcoholic, or addicted. Some had brothers and sisters who followed the same path. Yet these children grew up and became teachers, social workers, or police officers. When they were asked what made them different, most of them spoke of a person who came into their lives at a difficult time and believed in them. Some referred to a feeling they were specially called to show an example of rising above their circumstance. Many described themselves as deeply spiritual but not religious.

These adults are called "resilient" because they have responded to hardship by becoming stronger. The Search Institute in the United States has identified characteristics that support young people growing up to be positive, healthy, caring adults. They call these "assets." Having more than three non-parent adults who care about you is an example of an asset. Spending at least an hour a week doing service for others is another. Knowing your school and community care about you is a major asset.

Building Connectedness

How would you design a school and curriculum to strengthen a sense of meaning in life and connectedness, not only for students, but also for the teachers?

- Build schools small enough that bonds can form among students, teachers, staff, and parents.

- Connect with the natural world outside by designing gardens that attract birds and butterflies.

- Welcome children and let them know they matter.

- Actively involve parents in the school.

- Model respect and inclusivity.

- Include all staff members in training to build community.

- Support cultural identity.

- Respond to the beauty of nature.

- Teach ways to take a stance in the face of personal hardship.

- Include service to others as a source of meaning in life.

- Respond to the needs of kids in poverty: provide breakfast, access to showers, washers and dryers, secondhand clothing exchanges.

There are many schools like this already, both public and private. They make you want to sing.

Rogers Elementary School in Victoria, Canada is a "Green School." Here children are planting the school garden in spring 2006.

105

28

Teach History for Transformation

Does a student have the capacity to be affected by events that happen to others if the dangers of indifference have never been taught?
— Student quoted on the Facing History and Ourselves website

"Just tell us how the simulation goes. We're all experienced high school history teachers. We don't need to go through the whole exercise."

I hesitated for a moment. I was doing a teachers' workshop on aboriginal issues, using a role-play exercise from British Columbia's grade 4 curriculum, so perhaps they were right. On the other hand, every time I had done the activity with university students, I was stunned by the power of such a deceptively simple process.

"Would you be willing to put up with this and do it anyway?" I asked. They were too polite and good-natured to roll their eyes, and despite their obvious reluctance, they broke into small groups.

With a marking pen and a piece of flip-chart paper, I drew a line map of the Nass River Valley, where the Nisga'a people were negotiating their land claim with the provincial government. "Okay, each of your small groups will get a chunk of this territory, so please come up and draw a colored line around your land."

The teachers divided up the area and then copied the map of their territory to take back to their group.

"Now I would like you to put a small settlement on your map. Please draw one little person

to represent ten people. For every ten people you will need to draw one building. Each building requires two trees, so please draw them. Every ten people require one food source, so you may draw either one deer or one fish. Each food source needs four trees to support it."

The teachers sighed but were soon laughing and drawing smoke coming out of the chimneys of their little houses, smiles on the faces of their deer and fishes, clothes on the little people. They transferred their drawings onto the master map.

The door of the classroom opened and a stranger in a trench coat, carrying a black briefcase, strode in. He pulled a huge pair of tailor's shears from his briefcase. With a fat black marker he drew a circle around each house — sometimes including fish, trees, and deer, sometimes only a tree or two. Then he took the shears and cut holes out of the map, removing the sections he had marked. Without a word, he handed each group their small piece of paper. Then he took the large map off the wall, folded it, and stuffed it into his briefcase. He sat at the back of the room.

Confusion and anxiety filled the room.

"What do you think has just happened?" I asked.

"He has taken our land and left us with not enough fish or deer or trees to survive," they replied.

"Yes."

"Well, what are we supposed to do next?"

"What would you like to do?"

"Well, he can't do that. I mean, it's our land and we'll die. We have to tell him that."

- Facing History and Ourselves: www.facinghistory.org
- Rethinking Schools: www.rethinkingschools.org
- The Treaty Process in BC: *Shaping the Future.* A Resource Guide for Grade 4 Teachers. British Columbia Ministry of Education, Program Standards and Education Resources 1998

They approached the man, only to discover they had to find a translator to speak for them. "You haven't left us enough to survive!"

"The Queen," he said with a bored sigh, "would never let her subjects starve." Then he went back to examining his fingernails.

At that point I drew attention to the time-line on the board. Three hundred years ago the population of aboriginal people in British Columbia was estimated at more than 400 thousand. In 1911 the census reported 20,000 people.

The room erupted into shouts. One man suggested they arm themselves and attack.

"There is an armed ship in the harbor," the stranger said quietly.

"What if we…" someone started, and then the room grew silent as the teachers reconnected with the history they knew and taught.

"I have taught this for 25 years," said one man. "I have never before felt this enormous anger, frustration, and helplessness. Now what?"

We debriefed together about how they felt, what they wanted to do, and how their feelings affected their reasoning about the treaty negotiations in progress.

Simulations and role plays are strong tools to build understanding. Theater, dance, poetry, and music can also touch and transform us. A US group, Facing History and Ourselves, specializes in training history teachers to bring this kind of transformational learning to reducing racism and anti-Semitism in particular. Its website shows the impact of this work with teachers.

Draw a small settlement with the resources needed to support your population.

RUSSELL DAVIDSON

Legend:
one little person represents ten people
ten people need one house and one food item
each house needs two trees
each food item needs four trees to survive

Student worksheet.

107

29

Teach to Understand Each Other

The real voyage of discovery consists not in seeing new landscapes but in having new eyes.

— Marcel Proust

My class of student teachers was working on a display of their personal heritage so that they could teach children the same project. Heritage fairs, like the more familiar science fairs, challenge students to construct projects in different media. They use posters, video, music, dance, theater, or even cooking to show the past in a dynamic way.

When students began to ask questions of their relatives, they were often shocked to learn of the hardships endured by their grandparents or parents. Of course, everyone in North America can trace their ancestry to either immigrants or aboriginals. Many groups — including aboriginal, Asian, German, Irish, African or Latino — have been subject to exclusion at different times. Many came to North America as a result of war.

As students found old passports and health certificates, letters, diaries, and photographs, a dawning awareness of the struggles of those who move to a new country began to inform their understanding of current refugees and immigrants.

Bud Patel, one of the teachers, wrote, "Who am I? I am a Canadian, but I was born in Kenya of Indian parents. My parents have returned to India. So am I an Indian or an African? I have lived most of my life in Canada, but I can't play hockey. My wife has blonde hair, and my children — are they Indian or Canadian?"

As the class pored over the displays, they noticed recurring cycles of intolerance and acceptance, exclusion and integration. They could connect a classmate with his immigrant mother who had been held in a TB sanatorium, separated from her children, or one whose parents had been relocated during World War II because they were Japanese. They were moved by the stories of residential schooling suffered by the aboriginal students' parents.

Souvenirs of the boat passage, wedding photos, or a christening dress pulled us into the histories we were hearing. Many of the students commented that their parents and relatives were thrilled that their stories were being heard and remembered by this generation. I suspect that many of my students still remember the stories we heard in that class. I certainly do. By

George and Hana Brady, c. 1935.

THE BRADY FAMILY ARCHIVES

the end of the project we had a sense of ancestral kinship and an obligation to give a hand to someone from a marginal culture struggling in our own communities.

Artifacts from the past or from another country have an amazing power to capture our imagination and take us inside the lives of others. A small suitcase in a Holocaust museum in Japan caught the attention of the curator, Fumiko Ishiota. She found herself obsessed with discovering the history of its owner. A note written on the suitcase said "Hana Brady, May 16, 1931," and the German word for "orphan." Ishiota spent years following clues about Hana's life, from her early childhood in Czechoslovakia to her death in a Nazi prison camp at the age of 13.

Eventually she tracked down Hana's uncle, who now lives in Toronto, and went to meet him. The two pieced together Hana's story, which was made into a feature documentary for CBC Radio and then into an award-winning children's book, *Hana's Suitcase*. Children in Japan learn about Hana when they visit the museum and see her suitcase and photos. They respond with poems and drawings that show how much her story touches them.

At a peace meeting in Seattle, I heard another story about artifacts leading us to understand others. In the middle of the Cold War, when North American children could not imagine that Soviet people were human beings, a group in Seattle made a trunk of items different people had brought home from visits to Moscow. They took the trunk to schools where children could try on a policeman's greatcoat and fur hat or a flowered shawl, take apart a set of matrushka dolls, or sip tea, made in a samovar, from cups in little silver holders. As the children looked at books in Russian, the adults spoke of the importance of not seeing others as the enemy.

When a Soviet ship arrived in the harbor, the group invited the sailors to visit and share a meal with the American community. I am convinced that people like the members of that Seattle group, who were determined to see Russians as people, not faceless enemies, laid the groundwork that allowed Reagan and Gorbachev to come to an agreement to start reducing nuclear weapons.

- Earth Renewal: www.earthrenewal.org
- Educators for Social Responsibility: www.esrnational.org
- *Hana's Suitcase: A True Story* by Karen Levine, Allen and Unwin, 2003.
- Peace Education: www.worldpeace.org/youth
- Tolerance.org: www.tolerance.org/teens
- UNICEF Voices of Youth: www.unicef.org/voy/takeaction

30

Join the International Campaign to Ban Landmines

When children disabled by landmines speak with heartbreaking honesty of turning the tears they have shed to a determination to make a better world, we are both humbled and inspired to join them. Young people the world over are among the strongest activists in the global landmines campaign.

JOHN RODSTED, INTERNATIONAL CAMPAIGN TO BAN LANDMINES

Cambodian activist, Tun Channareth of the International Campaign to Ban Landmines meets with UN Secretary General, Kofi Annan.

We shed all the tears we had to. Now what we have to do is to live and show the world that although we have fewer limbs, we are all the same. We have one heart, one mind so we are all human beings. Therefore, we have to keep on living because we can contribute to the development of the world.

— Statement of the Ban Landmines! International Children Conference, 2004

The Ban Landmines! International Children Conference (BLICC) brought together 1,300 children from 11 countries to meet in Japan in 2004. Many were survivors of landmine explosions — survivors who are committed to ridding the world of landmines and to helping other children who need rehabilitation after landmine accidents. Long after war is over, landmines lie hidden in the ground until they are triggered by a farmer, a child, or a valued farm animal.

About 39 million mines have been removed since the treaty to ban landmines was signed in 1997. That enormous progress was made possible by public support for de-mining. Mine removal is carried out not just by professionals like the Mines Action Group, but also by local people, many of them women, who are trained in this extremely dangerous work. More than 80 million landmines remain in the ground, and, tragically, some countries are still laying new mines in conflict zones.

Here's what young people can do.

- Learn about landmines and how millions of adults and children pushed governments to outlaw them in 1997 (see Solution 33).

- Write to governments that have not yet signed the landmines treaty. Tell the leaders that landmines kill and maim the innocent long after the soldiers have gone home. Landmines are a weapon of mass destruction that operates in slow motion.

- Fundraise to support de-mining and to help those injured by landmines. Children who lose an arm or a leg need a series of artificial limbs as they grow up and must be refitted as often as every six months. They also have special needs for education and training that will allow them to make a living in adulthood. Their families are often living in desperate poverty. This is a case where money raised outside the country makes an enormous difference to the children and to their society.

- International Campaign to Ban Landmines: www.icbl.org
- International Committee of the Red Cross: www.icrc.org
- Mines Action Canada: www.minesactioncanada.org
- Night of a Thousand Dinners: www.1000dinners.com
- War Child: www.warchild.ca
- International Network of Youth Against Landmines: www.aplaceof.info/inyal/members.html

- "Clear a Path to a Safer World: Adopt a Minefield" is the slogan of Night of a Thousand Dinners. You can take up the challenge by hosting a dinner on the first Thursday in November. Invite family and friends to join you for a potluck meal or wine tasting, view a video, and donate to adopt a minefield. The project's goal is "to put an end to landmines one meal at a time." The Thousand Dinners website is full of ideas for entertaining, sample press releases, and even recipes.

- Do a presentation at your school to get more students involved. Show a video or a slide show you have downloaded from one of the websites listed below. War Child works closely with the music industry to help war-affected children. It raises funds through concerts and the sale of CDs, and works in many countries to assist injured children and to promote the rights of the child.

- Produce a play or puppet show about children's lives in countries where landmines still remain after war. Children are often badly injured by stepping on a mine when they go to help in the fields or play by a roadside.

Hearts

Wanna be a miracle for this earth

Never forget what we're given

Pure, sweet hearts we have had since birth

And a very precious place to live in

All of us have our minds

All of us have our hearts

All of us can dream together

For a better world

Can we have one world with peace and love

If I pass on this flame of hope

Say aloud, we are friends and will be for life

As we spread light around the globe.

— Official theme song of the Ban Landmines! International Children Conference (BLICC)

31

Catch Inspiration on the Net

If you don't take action, it doesn't matter what you think.

— Betty Williams, Nobel Peace Prize Laureate, 1976

> Now of course, we don't want to eliminate fear completely. That's why we have clanging bells and flashing lights at railroad crossings. And badness knows, there is plenty of badness in the world. But when we use evil to fight evil — well I'm not a math whiz, but it seems to me we're increasing, not decreasing, the evil in the world. And it's not just the math, it's the aftermath: A world stuck in greedlock, ruled not by the highest common denominator but the lowest common dominator.
>
> — **Swami Beyondananda**

Luckily, I am not stranded on a desert island without Internet access, because I am sustained by the images of groups in every place you can imagine, taking action for peace and justice — and posting the stories and the photos on websites. I can see children in India doing a service project, or women taking books and supplies to Kabul so that girl children can be educated. The evidence of global change is massive and thrilling. Here are my favorites.

Progressive Journalism

Truthout has free daily news commentaries and video clips of speeches and interviews.

Democracy Now, with Amy Goodman, provides analysis of US policy and events.

Activist Women

Code Pink 4 Peace encourages American women to work for positive social change through proactive creative protest and nonviolent direct action.

PeaceXPeace helps women form action circles in their community and connect with circles networked around the world. Excellent resources and ideas for action.

Canadian Women 4 Afghan Women supports human rights, women's rights, setting up schools, and filling libraries in Afghanistan.

The *Women's Global Charter for Humanity* is on the *World March of Women* site (see Solution 20). The music from Africa is wonderful and downloadable as sound or sheet music for your local choir.

Peace Choirs offers royalty-free music for choirs and a network around the world.

Connecting Peace, Justice, and the Environment

The *Earth Charter* provides the basis for a sustainable, caring world.

Serious Fun

When I need a little humor, I go to the various *Raging Grannies* sites all over the world. The Grannies in Tucson post the lyrics to "There's No Business like War Business." (They sang "God 'Help' America" at a recruitment center where they tried to sign up to serve in Iraq.)

Ben Cohen, one of the founders of Ben and Jerry's Ice Cream, is a leader in bringing the business community into social activism. His site, *True Majority*, features "serious fun," with the famous oreo cookie stacks that demonstrate what could result if 15 percent of the Pentagon budget were used for social good. Chip the dog explains about nuclear arsenals.

WWW.WAKEUPLAUGHING.COM

Swami Beyondananda.

Swami Beyondananda is a stand-up comic who uses humor to make serious points about how we live and what we could do to make a better world.

Direct Action

Take part in the International Campaign to Ban Landmines' *Night of a Thousand Dinners* (see Solution 30).

MoveOn is the most famous of all sites for mobilizing people to take political action in the United States.

> *Muslim Peacemaker Teams* work in Iraq with *Christian Peacemaker Teams*.
> *Nonviolence International*
> *United for Peace and Justice*
> *Voices in the Wilderness*
> *War Child*

Media Strategies

Search for Common Ground provides information on new media strategies, campaigns, and global information.

Institute for Media Policy and Civil Society (IMPACS) teaches how to use media to turn up the volume on civil society. It offers inexpensive, live, online courses on writing opinion editorials, writing for the web, or giving speeches.

Teachers

Check out *Educators for Social Responsibility* for lesson plans, strategies, and suggestions on how to teach controversial subjects. Lists courses and seminars around the country.

Conflict Analysis

> *International Crisis Group*
> *Project Ploughshares*
> *Center for Defense Information*

- Canadian Women 4 Afghan Women: www.w4wafghan.ca
- Center for Defense Information: www.cdi.org
- Code Pink 4 Peace: www.codepink4peace.org
- Democracy Now: www.democracynow.org
- Earth Charter: www.earthcharterusa.org
- Educators for Social Responsibility: www.esrnational.org
- IMPACS: www.impacs.org
- International Crisis Group: www.crisisgroup.org
- International Fellowship of Reconciliation: www.ifor.org
- MoveOn: www.moveon.org
- Muslim Peacemaker Teams in Iraq: www.cpt.org/iraq/iraq.php
- Night of a Thousand Dinners: www.1000dinners.com
- Nonviolence International: www.nonviolenceinternational.net
- Peace Choirs: www.peacechoirs.net
- PeaceXPeace: www.peacexpeace.org
- Project Ploughshares: www.ploughshares.ca
- Raging Grannies: www.geocities.com/raginggrannies
- Search for Common Ground: www.sfcg.org
- Swami Beyondananda: www.wakeuplaughing.com
- Tikkun Community: www. www.tikkun.org/community
- True Majority: www.truemajority.com
- Truthout video: www.truthout.org/multimedia.htm
- Truthout: www.truthout.org
- Tucson Raging Grannies: www.wilpftucson.org/Grannies.html
- United for Peace and Justice: www.unitedforpeace.org
- Voices in the Wilderness: www.vitw.org
- War Child: www.warchild.ca
- World March of Women: www.marchemondiale.org

Religious Perspective

International Fellowship of Reconciliation is a well-known Christian organization.

Tikkun Community is an interfaith group based on Judaism (*Tikkun* means "to heal, repair, and transform the world").

32

Support Heroes and Visionaries

> Courage is resistance to fear, mastery of fear, not absence of fear.
>
> — Mark Twain

A teacher, deploring the corruption of political leaders, once said to me that there aren't real heroes any more for young people to admire. I am not clear about the heroes she thought once existed, or why young people admired them, but in writing this book I have become aware that there is no shortage of heroes who are willing to risk their lives to bring peace to countries at war.

Voices in the Wilderness

Kathy Kelly is one of those heroes. She has been awarded honorary doctorates, nominated repeatedly for the Nobel Peace Prize, and thrown into prison in the United States again and again.[1] She went to Iraq in 1992 as part of the Iraq Peace Camp, which maintained a presence throughout the bombardment and invasion. She has returned to Iraq 22 times since 1996, each time taking food and medicine, in contravention of the UN/US sanctions imposed on Iraq. She helped found Voices in the Wilderness (VitW), a group that has organized over 70 trips to Iraq to take needed supplies to the people. VitW has been fined $22,000 for breaking the sanctions and has no intention of paying the fines.

VitW calls for an end to the occupation of Iraq and the cleanup of all depleted uranium, cluster bombs, and landmines left behind by the occupying forces. Out of respect for the human rights of the Iraqi people, VitW members ask that Iraqis, not outsiders, be hired to rebuild the country. They call for health care for all Iraqis and US veterans who have suffered physical or mental injuries in the war. They also call for the United States to pay restitution for the destruction of the country over 14 years of war and sanctions.

Iraq is required to pay war reparations for its invasion of Kuwait. So far, the UN has approved payment of $52.1 billion of Iraq's oil revenues to individuals, companies, and governments. In June 2005, Kathy Kelly and a VitW group gathered outside the UN building in Geneva to demand that further war reparations be postponed.[2] Instead they called for oil money to be used to meet

Civil infrastructure has not been rebuilt in Iraq. These children are swimming in a sewage outfall.

GERRI HAYNES

the most basic needs of Iraqis for food, safe water, medicines, and shelter.

Kathy Kelly spoke to an accountant who was part of the UN's compensation assessment process. He told her that he was terribly troubled by policies that lined the pockets of wealthy companies and contributed toward the suffering of innocent people. Looking bemused, he said, "Accountants can find a kind of relief in just working with numbers. Numbers don't talk back."[3]

Nonviolent Peaceforce

Another visionary group, Nonviolent Peaceforce (NP), takes a different approach.[4] NP brings together leaders with many years of experience in nonviolent intervention and research. Founded in 1992, NP builds on the notion that a group of trained and highly skilled people could help reduce armed violence in a conflict zone. With the backing and moral support of some 5,000 interested people, they have set up a pilot project with 50 trained people working in Sri Lanka.

These 50 people use techniques that have been effective at reducing the likelihood of armed violence in other regions. Members of the NP force frequently accompany local civil society activists, provide a protective presence in villages and at public events, and monitor demonstrations and other volatile situations. They provide links to resources, local leaders, other NGOs; consult with local activists and advisors; and provide a safe place to meet (see Solution 94).

The goal of NP is to have a force of 2,000 trained and experienced people in the field, with 5,000 more as backup. The membership is multiethnic, multi-faith, and intergenerational. Their training is complex and demanding, and they are using the Sri Lanka project as the subject of research into the effects of third-party intervention in conflict zones.

> Three of the first words I wanted to learn in Arabic were "Don't do that!" I wanted to shout the phrase at playful boys who, in the blasting heat, would cup their hands, dip into the sewage ditch running alongside the road, and pour water over their heads to cool off. By the end of the summer, my companions and I would sometimes clap our hands over our eyes and shout: "OK, my turn," then pucker our lips as the boys poured water over our heads. The alternative was to pass out under the harsh sun as the temperature rose to 140 degrees.
>
> — Kathy Kelly

- Nonviolent Peaceforce: nvpf.org
- *Taking a Stand: A Guide to Peace Teams and Accompaniment Projects* by Elizabeth Boardman, New Society Publishers, 2005
- Voices in the Wilderness: www.vitw.org

33

Move the World — Build Successful International Campaigns

> It isn't enough to talk about peace. One must believe in it. And it isn't enough to believe in it. One must work at it.
>
> — Eleanor Roosevelt

The treaty to ban landmines was a triumph of the second superpower — world civil society. A small group of six organizations pulled together a meeting of some 50 people in 1992 to develop a strategy to get a ban on landmines. Five years and a Nobel Peace Prize later, the treaty was opened for signatures in Ottawa.

I have been to many meetings, but never before did I attend a meeting like that one in 1992 in a convent in London. Jody Williams of the Vietnam Veterans of America Foundation was the lead organizer. The people at the meeting were experts in the fields of landmines, medicine, international law, and journalism. They knew exactly how to build a campaign with a loose, flexible structure and credible leaders from strong organizations. They also knew that in two days they had to convince everyone in the room that landmines must be banned and that a ban was possible.

The first day we were taught by those who knew

Student walking on mock minefield during a demonstration of demining activities.

firsthand the devastation wrought by landmines: a surgeon who showed us blast injuries and how he had to amputate above all the exploded flesh and shattered bone; a de-miner who showed us the dangerous and painstaking process of probing every two centimeters of ground; a rehabilitation specialist who showed us the future for a Cambodian child with a missing leg.

In 1992 there were about 120 million mines in more than 60 countries, with more being laid every day. Every mine would remain active long after a war was over. One speaker told us that "Cambodia is being de-mined an arm and a leg at a time." When the International Committee of the Red Cross told us exactly how a ban would fit into international law, it was apparent that the goal was possible.

We broke into groups to develop strategies to move forward rapidly. Journalists from alternative media asked for photos and stories of victims, de-miners, and surgeons. They told us that we needed striking images to attract the press and television cameras. Expert campaigners set out the steps to engage people of influence, including sympathetic military leaders. The campaign had to be clear and concise, with a simple, consistent message. Jody Williams set up a communications network to funnel ideas and information from each campaign out to the world. Some groups were on e-mail, but most were updated by frequent faxes and letters.

Within six months of the meeting I noticed the first photo articles in magazines and heard the first radio shows discussing a ban on landmines. Excellent short videos were distributed

- Ban Landmines USA: www.banminesusa.org
- Canadian Landmine Foundation: www.canadianlandmine.org
- Coalition to Stop the Use of Child Soldiers: www.child-soldiers.org
- International Campaign to Ban Landmines: www.icbl.org
- War Child: www.warchild.org

throughout the network so members could make school presentations that would bring students into the campaign. Medical journal articles described the injuries, surgery, and rehabilitation of victims. The campaign snowballed as new groups joined the work.

Jody Williams and Stephen Goose, of Human Rights Watch, have reported on the lessons learned from the landmines campaign that can be applied to other campaigns.[1]

- Civil society can be the driving force for change, even change involving international security.
- Coordinated action by NGOs, like-minded governments, and UN agencies can bring rapid success.
- Small and medium-sized countries, acting in concert with civil society, can achieve major diplomatic successes even against the opposition of major powers.
- Working outside the traditional forums for disarmament can make an agreement possible.

When Princess Diana became an advocate for a ban on landmines, she brought enormous prestige to the campaign. Lloyd Axworthy, Canada's foreign minister at the time, took up the issue and called like-minded states together to discuss a treaty. As the talks progressed rapidly, he surprised the delegates by inviting them to return to Ottawa the following year to sign a ban. This campaign was a unique collaboration between civil society and governments around the world.

The campaign has shifted to the monumental task of de-mining in countries that are still littered with landmines. Women often take up the task of de-mining in order to protect their families and provide for them. They accept the risks because the work pays well and because they have few alternatives if they have been widowed.

Many schools and community groups take up the campaign and adopt a minefield as a service project. They raise money to support the training of local people who will take on the task of de-mining. The projects are popular because they are nonpolitical humanitarian actions that clearly make a difference.

Cambodian deminer at work.

JOHN RODSTED INTERNATIONAL CAMPAIGN TO BAN LANDMINES

34

Reclaim Democracy

The penalty good people pay for indifference to public affairs is to be ruled by evil people.

— Plato

As corporate money tries to throw its weight around, civil society is practicing jujitsu. It is a struggle in every country to keep elections clean, but Canada took a huge step forward in 2003 when Parliament passed Bill C-24, which set new limits on political donations.[1]

- Corporations, unions, and other organizations can now donate only to candidates, not parties.

- They can donate no more than $1,000 annually, and they are prohibited from funneling donations through subsidiaries, employees, or anyone else.

- Individuals can donate no more than $5,000 to each party, including donations to any individual candidates.

- The limits apply to donations for candidates vying for a nomination as well as for election, and spending limits are in place for both nomination races and election spending.

Each party will receive an annual subsidy from public funds based on the number of votes it received in the previous election. The amount is $1.75 for each vote above a set minimum. This public subsidy is meant to compensate parties for the expected shortfall in their revenues from the loss of donations, and the amount may be adjusted in the future. The government wants to ensure a balance, with subsidies that are high enough to cover baseline expenses, but low enough that parties must still appeal to Canadians in order to gain supporters and members.

Bill C-24 also contains new disclosure requirements that make it easier to know who is donating to political parties and candidates. Democracy Watch (DW) recommends adding further provisions that would prohibit politicians and parties from having secret bank accounts and would require disclosure of all donations above $100. This would close a loophole that might allow a secret donation to a politician.

ELECTIONS CANADA

Ballot box and paper ballots in Canada.

- Democracy Watch: www.dwatch.ca
- Public Campaign: www.publicampaign.org
- Transparency International:
  www.transparency.org/toolkits
- *Yes! Magazine* (Fall 2003 issue is about reclaiming democracy): www.yesmagazine.org

DW also recommends prohibiting *all* donations from corporations, unions, and other groups. This is already the law in Quebec and Manitoba.

Surprisingly, these groundbreaking changes did not receive the widespread publicity they deserve. They will create a more level playing field for candidates for office and will make election funding more transparent and accessible for public scrutiny.

In Europe, campaign funding and TV advertising are both restricted.

The US movement for clean elections is a powerful campaign to separate corporate money from its influence on decision makers.[2] Several states have passed referendums mandating that an equal amount of public funds be available to candidates who raise small donations from many individuals, abide by strict spending limits, and agree not to take a dime of special interest money. This allows candidates to spend time with voters and creates equal opportunities for ideas and debate. When the clean candidates are elected, they are not obligated to those companies and individuals who financed their campaigns and are able to vote freely for such things as increased public health care, early childhood education, and social services. You can find information on the drive for clean election campaigns in the United States at the Public Campaign website.

People outside the United States often follow American elections closely because the outcome will affect everyone. They support the many campaigns by Americans who are committed to ensuring that their elections are clean, transparent, verifiable, and accurate. Those campaigns strive to achieve the following results:

- End the practice of gerrymandering, (resetting electoral boundaries to favor certain candidates).
- Ensure that voter registration includes all eligible voters.
- Safeguard advance and absentee ballots.
- Make ballot counting transparent and verifiable.
- Ensure that election laws are enforced without bias.

In Brazil, Transparency International runs a major campaign against corruption.[3] It works with newspapers, TV, and radio to teach people that corruption is not just an individual moral issue, but a systemic issue. To stop vote selling, group members used street theater, T-shirts, billboards, and buttons. To end corruption, they began to educate people on how to oppose it by the way they voted.

They learned that asking candidates about campaign financing was not as effective as exposing the sources of the candidate's funds. They also learned that the strategies they developed in-house to reach the public and get their message out were more effective than the professional PR campaigns. They don't say why that was true, but I suspect that we (the public) have developed sophisticated antennae to detect "spin" and respond to the authentic voice of ordinary people.

35

Ye shall know the truth, and the truth shall make thee mad.

— Aldous Huxley

Be the Wrench in the Works

Citizen Weapons Inspectors

When governments insisted that UN weapons inspectors go into Iraq and other countries to search for weapons of mass destruction, activists took up the task as well. In the United States, the United Kingdom, and other European countries, groups of citizens wearing blue jackets emblazoned with insignia declaring them to be Citizen Weapons Inspectors appeared at military bases where nuclear weapons were deployed. They would ask to be allowed to do a citizen inspection because they had heard rumors there might be weapons of mass destruction on that site. With television cameras rolling, they listened politely as the military police refused them entry — and then watched the exchange on the late news.

When I joined a weapons inspection team at Los Alamos, New Mexico, we were greeted respectfully, escorted to the main building, and told that we could not enter. Armed soldiers in camouflage gear stood at the ready on either side of us. The officer accepted our literature and we left, with a military van ahead of and behind us.

Then we held a press conference to describe the event and release information about radioactive contamination that had been found in the swampy area below the Los Alamos Laboratory, outside government property. There was excellent coverage of the visit, even in a community that is almost completely supportive of the local nuclear weapons facility.

Canadian MP Libby Davies visited the Trident submarine base in Bangor, Washington, as a Citizen Weapons Inspector and received major American TV coverage. She drew attention to the hypocrisy of demanding weapons inspections elsewhere, while nuclear weapons states like the United States and the former Soviet Union had more than 35,000 nuclear bombs themselves.

Citizen Weapons Inspectors at Los Alamos. Greg Mello and Amy Goodman of *Democracy Now.*

Citizen Weapons Inspectors choose between joining legal actions and stepping into nonviolent civil disobedience. Most participate in the kinds of actions that Libby Davies and the group I joined at Los Alamos do. Those who decide to do civil disobedience know that many who have been arrested for such actions as climbing fences into military bases have served years in jail, so this is not a choice anyone makes lightly.

Okinawa Peace Network

On the island of Okinawa, a similar campaign of nonviolent resistance that aims to close US bases is becoming a wrench in the works for the Japanese government. The bases occupy large sections of the island. When you stand on top of a hill looking down over the island, you get the feeling that the bases aren't on Okinawa so much as Okinawa is the space between the US bases.

There have been many crimes against women and girls, including rape and murder, since 1972, when Okinawa reverted to Japanese control. In 1995 a schoolgirl was abducted and raped by three marines, but the United States refused to allow the men to be tried in Japanese court. The anger of the population continues to fester as the US troops remain, and it seems

likely the Japanese government will ultimately be forced to yield to the local people.

IPPNW Students

Medical students in International Physicians for the Prevention of Nuclear War stop traffic in major cities to draw attention to the fact that despite the end of the Cold War, cities would be targeted in the event of a nuclear exchange. Their Target Campaign involves students all over the world. They place a huge red X on the pavement in the center of their city to mark the target, then wait to answer questions from passersby. Check out their website. It makes me want to start med school all over again.

- Citizen Weapons Inspections: www.motherearth.org/inspection/index_en.php
- International Physicians for the Prevention of Nuclear War (IPPNW) students: www.ippnw-students.org
- Okinawa Peace Network of Los Angeles: www.uchinanchu.org
- Philippine Women's Movement: mbeaw.org/resources/countries/philippineswomen.html
- *Webs of Power: Notes from the Global Uprising* by Starhawk, New Society Publishers, 2002

36

Walk the Talk

There is no glimpse of the light without walking the path. You can't get it from anyone else, nor can you give it to anyone. Just take whatever steps seem easiest for you, and as you take a few steps it will be easier for you to take a few more.

— Peace Pilgrim

Peace Pilgrim

Peace Pilgrim walked for 28 years. She wore a kangaroo shirt that said "25,000 miles walking for peace," but she walked many more miles than that. She was convinced that peace in the world would come only as we find peace in ourselves. She had no religious affiliation and carried all her worldly belongings in the pockets of her shirt. People met her in towns and cities across the United States, listened to her talks, and often tried to keep pace with her as she strode out onto the highway again.

"Take whatever steps seem easiest for you," she said, not expecting anyone else to walk 25,000 miles. Her little book *Steps Toward Inner Peace* tells of her meeting with a woman who said she wished she could do the kind of thing Peace Pilgrim was doing, but, unfortunately, she had to work. Peace asked why she had to work if she had no dependents. The woman replied that she had a large apartment filled with furniture she had inherited and that it was expensive to keep up. Peace said, "Ah, you are working to give your furniture a good home."

Peace brought an ancient message to a modern society: We can live on very little if we are able to release our attachment to material things. She was never ill through the decades of walking, even though she sometimes slept in ditches and under bridges. She rarely went hungry, but thought of hunger as fasting. I wish I had heard her speak. She died in 1981.

Her words have affected how I live, not because I have become an example of wisdom and self-sacrifice — I have not — but because my priorities have shifted. If I don't have to provide a good home for my furniture, I have a lot more time to think about what is worth doing.

Voices in the Wilderness

Voices in the Wilderness (VitW) was formed in 1996 to challenge the economic warfare the US government was waging against the people of Iraq. It has sent more than 70 delegations to take food and supplies into Iraq in violation of US law and the UN sanctions. Several members, including leader Kathy Kelly, have been imprisoned as a

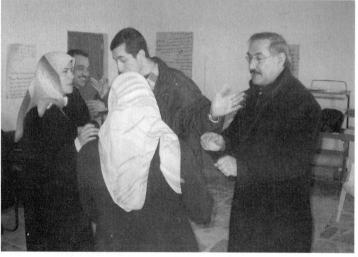

CHRISTIAN PEACEMAKER TEAMS

Muslim Peacemaker Team training session. They are role playing a "hassle line" with Team and police.

result. VitW members live with the Iraqi people and report on conditions under the US occupation from the inside.

The VitW website tells how we can support the group by educating ourselves and others, sponsoring an activist, or getting our own feet on the ground. The website reports that in Iraq in May 2005, a group of Shi'a Muslims traveled to Fallujah to help the Sunni Muslim population rebuild the city after it had been extensively bombed. This unprecedented action of solidarity is the work of Muslim Peacemaker Teams. Christian Peacemaker Teams have made working with Muslim Peacemaker Teams their highest priority in the region. After spending a day doing cleanup in Fallujah, the Sunnis and Shi'as attended a service together in the mosque. They said that they wanted to show unity in a tense time and counter the idea that Sunni–Shi'a sectarian violence is inevitable.

Ground Zero

Closer to home, in 1977 an intentional community called Ground Zero set down roots in Washington state adjacent to the Bangor Trident submarine base. The founders of the community were aware that the actions of thousands of people protesting against the Trident base, beginning in the mid-1970s, had alienated the military families who lived there. The military

families felt that their work was patriotic service and deserving of respect.

The people who formed Ground Zero realized that their protests against the base were perceived by the military families as a different kind of violence. They decided to walk the talk of peace. Nine people chose to settle in the area, where they could be a nonviolent presence. They try to live according to the Gandhian teaching that the enemy shares part of the truth, and the Christian teaching to love your enemy. They bought property adjacent to the base and have become part of the community (see Solution 38).

- Ground Zero Center for Nonviolent Action: www.gzcenter.org
- Muslim Peacemaker Teams in Iraq: www.cpt.org/iraq/iraq.php
- Peace Pilgrim site (Set up by her friends): www.peacepilgrim.org
- *Peace Pilgrim: Her Life and Work in Her Own Words*, compiled by some of her friends, Ocean Tree, 1994 (Also available on the Peace Pilgrim website)
- *Taking a Stand: A Guide to Peace Teams and Accompaniment Projects* by Elizabeth Boardman, New Society Publishers, 2005
- Voices in the Wilderness: www.vitw.org and www.vitw.org/archives/820

37

Bring Enemies to the Table

> Let me say, at the risk of seeming ridiculous, that the true revolutionary is guided by great feelings of love.
>
> — Ché Guevara

I was once on a radio talk show about nuclear disarmament when an irate listener phoned in and said, "Doctor, if you are so smart, why don't you go to the Soviet Union and chain yourself to a missile? They'll send you to the gulag and that's what you deserve."

After a pause to collect myself, I said, "I wish I had the kind of courage of the women of Greenham Common, who chain themselves to the fence of the US air base and get arrested [see Solution 15]. I don't have that courage, so I work the best way I know, and that is as a doctor. We think we are more likely to influence leaders when we are in the same room with them, and as doctors we often have access that perhaps others do not. We met with Soviet President Gorbachev and did influence his decision to meet with President Reagan to begin talks to reduce their nuclear arms."

The caller, to my great amazement, replied, "Oh, thanks a lot, doctor, and God bless you."

Many people believe they have good reasons for arguing against disarmament because they have come from a country where they were under the boot of the old Soviet Union, or because they fought in World War II. We need to listen to them because their fears are serious and justified.

- Interfaith Encounter Association: www.interfaith-encounter.org
- Nonviolence International (Mubarak Awad's organization): nonviolenceinternational.net

My experience with most people has been that if they know I accept the legitimacy of their arguments and acknowledge that I am also afraid of an oppressive government, we can dialogue. I tell them that what frightens me more than the threat of being conquered is the threat of nuclear annihilation. They almost always agree. Sometimes all I can do is plant a seed and trust.

There are many groups working to bring enemies to the table — too many to mention them all. In Israel, young adults from the Jewish, Muslim, and Christian faiths meet together in retreats organized by Interfaith Encounter Association and Nablus Youth Federation. The retreats are sponsored by the European Union, UNESCO, and the US embassy. Young adults aged 20 to 33 work in small dialogue groups with professional facilitation and translation. They talk about the challenges they face, particularly the religious issues such as dress codes, customs, traditions, and constraints. They often become deeply engaged by the topic of having a life that is modern yet still keeps their religious identity.

One of the students, Ali, is quoted on the Interfaith Encounter Association website saying, "For me to see the Jewish young adults ponder and argue how to conduct the prayer made me feel connected to them, as it reminds me of myself and my friends trying to find our ways in the older religious paths."

Eliran, who is Jewish, says, "The retreat changed many things for me. For the first time I can connect on a personal basis with Palestinian friends and find with them a common language

— the language of the heart." Eliran also mentioned the risks taken by the Palestinians, and the ten hours it took them to pass a checkpoint to get to the retreat.

In 1988, I heard Mubarak Awad speak about the nonviolent resistance work he was doing with Palestinians in Israel before he was expelled from the country. One of the most difficult initiatives was to invite Israelis to a shared meal with Palestinian farmers. The farmers agreed to host the meal because they were proud to show traditional Palestinian hospitality, but they reached a sticking point when they realized they were expected to sit down and eat together. Finally they agreed, and all managed to share the meal. It must have been as difficult for the Israelis to accept the hospitality as for the Palestinians to offer it.

In Montreal, a dialogue group began when people from the Jewish, Palestinian, and Christian communities of the city wanted to promote understanding and communication among the faiths. They meet to listen and share personal accounts and collective memories, and they have held an interfaith Passover *seder* where they read from the Koran, the Bible, and the Torah.[1] The group has grown from 40 in 2003 to more than 150 in 2005. Dialogue topics have included the effects of media on events and history, suicide bombings, and the separation wall. In 2005 they presented an art show titled "Meeting in the Middle" which

they described as an attempt to overcome their struggles both with others and with themselves. The brochure for the exhibition said "By letting go and moving beyond our communal and personal conflict, and by truly accepting the 'other' as an equal, we can hope to achieve peace."

LESLEY LEVY

Founders and Co-Presidents of the Montreal Dialogue Group, Nada Sefian, a Palestinian, and Ronit Yarosky, an Israeli/Canadian.

38

Demonstrate the Possible — Intentional Communities

> In separateness lies the world's great misery; in compassion lies the world's true strength.
>
> — Buddha

Intentional communities have a long and admirable history. As a result of religious persecution, many people fled Europe to settle in North America. The Amish, Hutterites, and Mennonites are pacifists who maintain communities apart from mainstream society in order to raise their families in their religious beliefs.

Oasis of Peace

Intentional communities have sprung up in improbable places like war zones. People determined to demonstrate that understanding and cooperation are possible even in difficult circumstances have founded communities with members from both sides of a conflict. In Israel, where there is ample reason for despair, *Neve Shalom/Wahat Al-Salam* (NS/WAS), which means "Oasis of Peace" in Hebrew and Arabic, is a community where Jews and Palestinian Arabs live and work cooperatively together.

The village is made up of 50 families. They receive financial and moral support from supporters outside the village and have been nominated four times for the Nobel Peace Prize. The residents of NS/WAS have built a primary school, the School For Peace, which is the only bilingual school in Israel. It provides conflict resolution encounter workshops for Palestinian and Jewish youth, university students, and adults. The Center for Spiritual Pluralism is a place for spiritual reflection on the issues that tear apart the societies of the Middle East and for discussion of how they might be resolved.

Doctors from NS/WAS traveled on foot through the mountains to deliver medicines to Nablus in the West Bank. On their website, they documented their harrowing journey, including being chased by a tank.

Peace Fleece is a US organization that supports *Neve Shalom/Wahat Al-Salam*, among other communities. The group was founded by US farmers who combined their wool with fleece from the former Soviet Union to make "Peace Fleece." Many years ago a friend knit me a toque using Peace Fleece, and I have followed the group with interest ever since. It is now selling a blend of wool from the flock of Abul Abed, who lives next to NS/WAS, mixed with wool from Maine. I buy Peace Fleece's beautiful knitting kits as gifts, knowing that I am supporting grassroots action to build understanding between enemies.

Nueva Esperanza

Another example of a community determined to live in nonviolence began in exile. During the war that engulfed El Salvador in the 1980s, a group of 104 people hid in a church basement for a year before they were able to escape to Nicaragua. They spent the next nine years as exiles, planning to found a special community when they returned home.

When they finally arrived back in El Salvador, they had only tents and plastic tools to dig latrines and wells. With the help of international solidarity groups, they built a cooperative known as Comunidad Nueva Esperanza, or Community of New Hope. The cooperative now has a school, small health and dental clinics, and artisan programs that teach embroidery and chicken farming. In 1993, members set up a new

- *The Cohousing Handbook: Building a Place for Community* by Chris ScottHanson and Kelly ScottHanson, New Society Publishers, 2004

- *Creating a Life Together: Practical Tools to Grow Ecovillages and Intentional Communities* by Diana Leafe Christian, New Society Publishers, 2002

- *EcoVillage at Ithaca: Pioneering a Sustainable Culture* by Liz Walker, New Society Publishers, 2005

- *Ecovillages* by Jan Martin Ban, New Society Publishers, 2005.

- Ground Zero: www.gzcenter.org

- *Neve Shalom/Wahat Al-Salam*: www.nswas.com

- Peace Fleece: www.peacefleece.com

- Voices on the Border supports Nueva Esperanza: www.votb.org/communities.html

model of an agricultural cooperative with the goal of legally defending the land while promoting sustainable agriculture and cattle production.

Ground Zero

The community of Ground Zero in Washington state (see Solution 36) formed around a commitment to living the nonviolence members believe is the only path to a peaceful world. They were, and are, committed to direct actions to oppose the Trident submarine system at Bangor. They have been arrested repeatedly for holding silent vigils and blocking the road into the base, where approximately 1,760 nuclear warheads are deployed.

Anne Hall blocking the road at Ground Zero to oppose the Trident Submarine base at Bangor WA.

The last three times the nonviolent activists were arrested, county prosecutors were not able to get a conviction against them. Sometimes they have been acquitted because the judge acknowledged that treaties signed by the United States take precedence over national law. In the most recent case, the charge was based on the intent of the protestors. The prosecutors claimed they intended to commit a criminal act. The accused took considerable time to describe their intention to prevent the possible use of nuclear weapons and to explain why they were personally willing to put themselves on the line to prevent such a catastrophe. Some recalled their childhood experiences, which led them to a commitment to justice and service. In the end, their intent to commit a criminal act was not at all clear, but their intent to prevent a much more serious crime against humanity was obvious. Since then, police have simply arrested and released the protestors without charge.

39

Aim for the Heart

Knowledge empowers people. If people know the rules, and are sensitized by art, humor and creativity, they are much more likely to accept change.

— Antanas Mockus,
former mayor of Bogotá, Colombia

Richard Horton is the distinguished editor of *The Lancet*, a prestigious medical journal from the UK. Recently I heard him speak about what produces a personal transformation from one worldview to another. He began by telling us it didn't happen from reading *The Lancet*!

Instead, he suggested that novels are far more likely to change our views because they draw us into the life of another and make us see the world from a new perspective. The emotional content of a story is often so compelling that we come to feel affection for a person or society we didn't know before.

For centuries, stories have been used by different cultures as a way to offer help and counsel to people in conflict or distress. One school counselor I know advised a child in trouble to ask herself what Laura in the book *Little House on the Prairie* would do in her situation. The child understood and knew her own answer immediately.

Documentaries that may transform our thinking:

- An Inconvenient Truth: www.climatecrisis.net
- *The Corporation*: www.thecorporation.com
- *Fahrenheit 911*: www.fahrenheit911.com
- *The Take*: www.nfb.ca/webextension/thetake
- *The End of Suburbia*: www.endofsuburbia.com

Animation:

- *When the Wind Blows* by Raymond Briggs: A book (Viking, 1982) and animated film about an elderly British couple following the government's instructions to protect themselves when a nuclear war occurs.

Street theater has a similar power to slip past our defenses and surprise us with new insights. Using exaggeration, comedy, and interaction to hold the interest of a passing audience, street actors bring issues to life. Sometimes they stir conflicting emotions about war, soldiers, victory, and defeat. When they show the effects of violence on innocent victims, they can move us to reevaluate our views of government policy.

There is a distinct rise in the popularity of documentary films today. Both the films and the audience are more sophisticated. Perhaps advertisers will note that viewers want material that is more thoughtful, challenging, and relevant than the contrived reality being offered in the mainstream. Documentary filmmakers often struggle to make a living because, until recently, the audience for their films has been small. We can support these artists by showing their films at local festivals, churches, and community gatherings, and by buying the DVDs to share. We can also ask that governments make more grants available for documentaries because they bring a deeper level of analysis than we get from regular news broadcasts.

Music reaches us at a level that bypasses our linear thinking and can bring complex feelings of sadness, joy, patriotism, or spirituality. During the Vietnam War era, musicians were a major influence that legitimized the antiwar movement. John Lennon's "Imagine" and "Give Peace a Chance" were more than just popular songs. They expressed the worldview of millions of young people. The antinuclear songs of Bob Dylan; Crosby, Stills and Nash; U2; Bruce

Cockburn, and countless others gave us a sense that we were not alone in our dread of nuclear war.

Recently Mayor Antanas Mockus of Bogotá used an inspired strategy of street theater and humor to change the mind-set of the city. Bogotá was "choked with violence, lawless traffic, corruption and gangs of street children who mugged and stole."[1] The mayor, a former mathematics professor who loved teaching, used creative methods to bring about change.

He hired 420 mimes to control traffic in the chaotic and dangerous streets. The city distributed 350,000 thumbs-up / thumbs-down cards for people to use to show their approval or disapproval of other people's actions. To show that the whole population had to conserve water during a severe drought, the mayor had a shower on television, carefully turning off the water while he soaped. Water consumption dropped 40 percent.

In response to the fear women felt when they had to go out at night, he launched a Night for Women and asked the men to stay at home to care for the children. Some 700,000 women went to the cafes and to free open-air concerts or strolled the central boulevard on the first of three Women's Nights. When they saw a man with a baby, they applauded. The city government found that people felt safe when there were women on the streets at night.

"In a society where human life has lost value," Mayor Mockus said, "there cannot be another priority than re-establishing respect for life as the main right and duty of citizens." In ten years, the homicide rate dropped from 80 to 22 per 100,000 inhabitants, and traffic deaths have dropped from 1,300 to about 600 per year.

Former Mayor of Bogotá, Antanas Mockus.

CHARLES NAILEN/THE HOYA

40

Learn to Attract Good Media

> If you don't like the news, go out
> and make it yourself.
> — Wes "Scoop" Nicker, quoted by
> The Ruckus Society

Many of us find it worrisome that a small number of corporate giants control so much of the media. This can't be good for a functioning democracy. At the same time, there are many ways to use media more effectively so our messages are more likely to be picked up. Various organizations have produced media kits and made them available on their websites. Some of the pointers they give can make the difference between a highly successful event and one that no one knows has happened.

Effective groups set up a media committee to build a strategy that will increase coverage of their work. My experience in planning a fundraising lecture may illustrate what a group committed to getting its message out can do.

Dr. Carlos Pazos (left) and Alberto Granado (seated) in front of a portrait of Che Guevara.

Getting Media Attention ... and a Full House

A group I was involved in had invited Dr. Carlos Pazos to give a lecture in Victoria, the city where I live. Carlos is a Cuban doctor who was a colleague and friend of Ché Guevara, the Argentinean revolutionary who fought alongside Fidel Castro in Cuba. Although Ché is well-known and still controversial, Carlos is not known at all.

We were lucky to have the help of a communications specialist, Bill Eisenhauer, who donated an hour of his time to teach us a little about attracting media. We asked Bill to tell us how to get a capacity audience for the benefit lecture. At first he laughed at the idea of 700 people coming to a lecture by an unknown Cuban doctor on a Tuesday night in winter. Then he gave us some pointers:

Before the event

- Pay attention to detail to make sure that the material you send out makes you look professional.
- Press releases are one page; event announcements are two sentences.
- Have at least three different people proofread everything you send out.
- Think of the needs of the media you are calling.
- Provide a hook for the story.
- Have a black-and-white photo of the speaker scanned and ready to send out.
- Send your information early.
- Involve as many diverse communities as possible in the event and give them tickets to sell.
- Poster all the places where your audience hangs out.
- Follow up contacts with a quick phone call.

- Institute for Media Policy and Civil Society (Tips for writing press releases): www.impacs.org
- *The Motorcycle Diaries* by Walter Salles: www.motorcyclediariesmovie.com
- The Ruckus Society (Media training manual): www.ruckus.org
- *The Troublemaker's Teaparty: A Field Guide to Effective Citizen Action* by Charles Dobson, New Society Publishers, 2003

- Help your speakers craft sound bites, and prepare them for likely interview questions.
- Practice interviews.

At the event

- Organize handout material and ask someone to display it and collect it afterward.
- Be sure to have membership and donation forms at your event. Have a receipt book, a name stamp for checks, and baskets for donations.
- Carry cell phones.
- Have a top-notch sound system managed by professionals.
- Get to the hall early enough to troubleshoot the slide projector. (Ours gave a computer technician half an hour of trouble and gave me heart palpitations.)
- Have fun.

We asked the university cinema to show *The Motorcycle Diaries* the weekend before our event, and we invited Carlos to introduce the film. The movie tells the story of Ché and his friend Alberto Granado when they were students. Alberto Granado, who is still living in Havana, sent a warm and touching letter to the city of Victoria with his greetings from Cuba and a photo.

We wrote and rewrote press releases and announcements for the community calendars at all the local newspapers, radio shows, and TV stations. They went out five weeks ahead of the event. If we had personal contacts, we phoned to give them a heads-up about the press release so they wouldn't miss it. We told them when Carlos would arrive so that they could arrange an interview. Two of the radio stations and three papers called back immediately to book interviews.

We had a professional design the poster, with the familiar image of Ché in the background. (Nonprofit organizations are permitted to use his image for events that are consistent with Ché's philosophy.) We made 2,400 small handbills and 250 posters and blitzed the campuses. (All our campus bulletin boards are stripped at the end of the month; check the policy where you are putting up posters.) Handbills turned out to be the most important tool.

We invited a local multicultural choir to sing Latin American music and featured the group on the poster because it is well-known in the city. The Latin American community in Victoria was vital to the success of the project; its members spread the word and volunteered to help.

We got half a page of coverage in the daily paper, with photos from *Motorcycle Diaries* and the one sent by Alberto. The local biweekly paper ran an interview and photo.

The result? The hall was packed to capacity with a young and welcoming audience. People donated generously to the benefit and also to the local Goods for Cuba group.

41

Seek God in Every Person

> Forgiveness is how you break the cycle of violence.
>
> — Azim Khamisa

Our newspapers regale us with the tragedies of innocent people targeted and killed in the Middle East and Afghanistan, to say nothing of North America, but they don't tell us of the many people who transcend grief and anger in response to their personal losses. Those stories of ordinary people are remarkably similar to the stories of legendary figures of our time, like Nelson Mandela. Mandela treated his prison guards with respect, and, in turn, he gained their respect and admiration.

Azim Khamisa

Tariq Khamisa was 20 when he was shot and killed by 14-year-old Tony Hicks during a botched robbery in San Diego. Tariq was delivering a pizza. Tariq's father, Azim Khamisa, felt he would never recover from his shock and grief, but nine months after losing his only son, he founded the Tariq Khamisa Foundation in order to turn his grief into positive action.[1] He began working with elementary and middle schools in San Diego to teach kids that they have the ability and responsibility to choose nonviolence.

From the beginning he felt that two people and their families were victimized by the tragedy — his son and the assailant, Tony Hicks. Azim is a Sufi Muslim whose faith encourages those who are bereaved, after 40 days, to channel their grief into compassionate deeds.

Azim met with Ples Felix, Tony's grandfather and guardian. Ples told Azim of his daily prayers and meditations for Tariq's family, and Azim told Ples of his. They now work together through the foundation, speaking to young people and helping them find the inner strength to resist the peer pressure that often leads to violence. In the video they have made, Azim actually gives his phone number and tells children to call him anytime, day or night, if they need help. He and Ples have spoken to thousands of school children in California and received many awards for their work.

A Journey through Dialogue

Daniel Pearl was an American journalist who was killed by his Muslim kidnappers in Pakistan in 2002. Just before he was killed, he said "I am Jewish." His father, Judea Pearl, has turned his profound grief into determination to build new relationships between faiths. He has written a book of reflections on his son's life and has

---

Five years after his son's death, Azim met Tony in prison.

It was a very healing time. I found him very likeable — well-mannered and remorseful. I told him that when he got out of prison there would be a job waiting for him at the Tariq Khamisa Foundation.

You do forgiveness for yourself, because it moves you on. The fact that it can also heal the perpetrator is the icing on the cake. Tony is studying in prison now, and I know that we will save him. In return, Tony will go on to save thousands of other children. I have recently written a letter to our governor to commute Tony's sentence.

— Azim Khamisa

TARIQ KHAMISA FOUNDATION

Ples Felix and Azim Khamisa.

joined Akbar Ahmed, a Muslim, in a speaking tour, addressing sold-out audiences all over the United States about interfaith understanding.[2] Their talks, "A Journey through Dialogue," bring a message people are very anxious to hear —

- Daniel Pearl Foundation: www.danielpearl.org
- The Forgiveness Project: www.theforgivenessproject.com
- The Tariq Khamisa Foundation: www.tkf.org
- Truth and Reconciliation Commission: www.doj.gov.za/trc
- United Religions International: www.uri.org

that there is a way to rise above the desire for revenge and give meaning to the death of a loved one.

Desmond Tutu

Archbishop Desmond Tutu has told extraordinary stories of forgiveness from the hearings of the Truth and Reconciliation Commission in South Africa.[3] In one case, four officers admitted to a hostile audience that they were responsible for the Bisho massacre. Suddenly one officer turned to the audience and begged for forgiveness. "Please forgive us, please. The burden of the Bisho massacre will be on our shoulders for the rest of our lives. Would you please receive my colleagues back into the community?" Tutu described the response as a demonstration of the "presence of grace." As angry as it had been, the audience broke out in incredible applause.

42

Become a Track II Diplomat

We are pointing our guns at someone we claim to be our countryman. You can do this for a time, but at some stage you must say something to him. Our trouble is we don't know what to say to him that will reach his heart. You have shown us the way.

— Assamese soldier speaking of Moral Rearmament (1970)

Track II diplomats are unofficial supporters of the peace process who work to build connections and trust between parties in conflict. Mennonites and Quakers are renowned for their quiet work in conflict zones, patiently going back and forth with messages in ways that officials cannot do. Many of their stories are not known because they commit to not publicizing the process. However, Dylan Mathews collected the stories of several Track II diplomats in his book *War Prevention Works*, and I've summarized several of them here.

Moral Rearmament

Dylan Mathews describes the influence a group called Moral Rearmament (MRA) had on a conflict in northeastern India. An American Lutheran pastor founded the Moral Rearmament movement in the UK in the 1920s. He believed that personal transformation is at the base of social change, so the group's approach to conflict is to lead both parties to a higher spiritual sensitivity that induces them to enter into genuine and deep dialogues marked by a sense of moral obligation.

In northeastern India after independence, violence between the indigenous hill people and the Assamese escalated when Assamese became the official language. The MRA in India invited leaders of the hill people to a dinner where they learned about how nonviolence can work and how MRA could help.

At the dinner, political leaders from many countries recounted their experiences of casting aside their hatred of the other in order to bring about reconciliation. The effect on Stanley Nichols-Roy, the leader of the hill people, was soon evident to the chief minister for Assam, who declared that he was then prepared to work with Nichols-Roy.

At the same time as leaders from both sides took on the task of resolving the issue of statehood for the hill people, MRA reached out to thousands of people, both the Assamese and the hill people, using morality plays and films to build tolerance, peace, and improved interclass relations. People watched the true stories of others who had resolved their conflicts without violence. They began to talk of reconciliation. In

M.W. Ashford

A medical exchange visit in Moscow under the ever-present bust of Lenin.

- American Friends Service Committee (Quakers): www.afsc.org
- The Community of Sant' Egidio: www.santegidio.org
- Moral Rearmament (Now Initiatives of Change, UK): www.uk.initiativesofchange.org
- *War Prevention Works: 50 Stories of People Resolving Conflict* by Dylan Mathews, Oxford Research Group, 2001

1970, the new state of Meghalaya (Abode of the Clouds) was formed. Many credited MRA with transforming the climate of Assam and abating the hate in the hills.

The Quakers

The Quakers have a history of going between warring parties and bearing communications from one side to the other. In 1968, for example, Adam Curle and John Volkmar did this during the Biafran war, when dissidents set up the republic of Biafra in southeastern Nigeria.

The practice of "disciplined listening" allows the Quakers to correct misperceptions that each side may hold about the other. They build trust by being neutral about the war and keeping their communication lines secret. Curle and Volkmar were able to carry a message to the Nigerians offering terms the Biafrans would accept but were unwilling to present for fear of looking weak. Sadly, despite all efforts of mediators, the war continued until 1970, when Biafra surrendered.

One remarkable outcome was the way Yakubu Gowon, Nigeria's leader, handled the end of the war. Instead of the expected violence and revenge, Gowon called for three days of prayer and declared an amnesty for all soldiers. His forces provided food and money to the Biafrans. Adam Curle recalls that "a wonderful spirit of reconciliation and brotherhood prevailed at all levels."

Community of Sant' Egidio

In 1968 in Rome, a group of young people formed the Community of Sant' Egidio, named for the tiny 16th-century restored convent in Rome where they met. They studied the Gospels and tried to put their message into practice in their own lives. They began by serving the poor in slums on the edge of Rome and setting up Schools for Peace for children. They provided humanitarian aid in many war zones and then began mediating between warring parties. They have become a community of 50,000 people in 70 countries, working to create solidarity between the Catholic church and people of different religions and beliefs.

During the war in Mozambique, members of the community brought leaders of the warring factions to Rome for dialogue. They met in the beautiful church of Sant' Egidio and were cared for by teams of volunteers. The Italian government supported the talks, and a British businessman, Tiny Rowland, provided his private jet and funding to ensure that the talks proceeded.

For two years the meetings continued and finally resulted in a comprehensive peace accord in 1992. It was said that the Community of Sant' Egidio provided the positive psychological space that permitted successful communication.

43

Lead by Example

> My life is my argument.
> — Albert Schweitzer

The world's great moral leaders, like Nelson Mandela, Archbishop Desmond Tutu, and the Dalai Lama, inspire us by their lives as much as by their teaching. Their influence is a source of strength for many people who are trying to live a life of peace. Each of us has met people who seem to live their life in ordinariness, but who bring a light of grace into ours.

I met such a person when I was in Seattle at a peace conference shortly after the attacks of September 11, 2001. A woman came to apologize that she would be leaving in the middle of my speech. She explained that she was on a roster set up by her Christian church and it was her turn to patrol the nearby mosque to ensure the safety of the people and the building. Christian churches maintained a 24-hour watch on the mosque. At the same time, they developed Christian-Muslim dialogues to ease the isolation of the Islamic community in Seattle.

- Dalai Lama and Tibetan Buddhism: www.dharamsalanet.com
- Desmond Tutu Foundation: www.tutu.org
- Interfaith Center on Corporate Responsibility: www.iccr.org
- Maha Ghosananda: www.buddhanet.net/masters
- *Pilgrim Voices: Citizens as Peacemakers* edited by E. Garcia (About the Philippines revolution), Quezon City: Ateneo de Manila University Press, 1994

Truth and Reconciliation Commissions

The first Truth and Reconciliation Commissions were set up in the late 1980s as dictators were toppled in Latin America, and more than 20 have been held now.[1] They came into the general public consciousness, however, after South Africa's brutal apartheid regime ended. Archbishop Desmond Tutu led the people in the process of truth and reconciliation, saying wryly that God must have a sense of humor because He had brought such a process to South Africans. From outside South Africa, it seemed impossible that a plan to bring together the perpetrators of horrific violence and the families of those who disappeared or died would be helpful.

Yet clearly it did help. Hearing the terrible stories of the suffering and death of their loved ones brought many families a sense of closure because they finally knew the truth (see Solution 41). Truth and reconciliation may not be sufficient in many cases, and people must see justice done before healing is possible, but it is a good first step.

Truth and Reconciliation Commissions are now commonly established in post-conflict situations, each one as painful and horrific as the previous one.[2] The lesson is always the same — war is not a noble endeavor. It invariably triggers the most degraded and brutal behavior imaginable. Yet the people who have disclosed their part in the brutal years of conflict and expressed their regret, and those who have reconciled with them in order to rebuild their societies, lead by example. In South Africa, the commission is only one dimension of solving the problems of a society staggering under the burden of poverty, unemployment, and HIV/AIDS, but the other problems could not be addressed without giving space for healing the hurt and rebuilding communities.

Investing Responsibly

We can lead by example through the choices we make when we invest our money, including pension funds and church investments. The Interfaith Center on Corporate Responsibility has been a leader of the corporate responsibility movement for over 30 years. It is an association of 275 faith-based institutional investors, with a combined portfolio of some $110 billion. Members take part in many shareholder actions involving major corporations and make their money talk. When a group of nuns addresses a shareholder meeting on the issue of corporate responsibility, it gets everyone's attention (see Solution 7).

Buddhists in War Zones

Buddhists demonstrate the nonviolent path by their actions in war zones. Three famous marches by Buddhist priests and nuns in Cambodia were led by Maha Ghosananda, known as the Gandhi of Cambodia. He led the third march through the most war-torn western province of Cambodia. The marchers were caught in the cross fire, and two peace members were killed. Nonetheless, they continued to walk, saying, "This violence is indeed the reason why we walk."

His Holiness the Dalai Lama, leader of the Tibetan Buddhists, works in exile with the community of Tibetans in India to restore Tibet to the Tibetan people, but he does so without rancor for the Chinese who have invaded his country. The refugee community in India is a model of people living the peace they profess. They follow the spiritual leadership of the Dalai Lama and say they are so imbued with his teachings that they can continue no matter what might happen to him.

RUSSELL DAVIDSON

Maha Ghosananda, known as the Gandhi of Cambodia.

44

Teach Nonviolent Resistance and Tolerance

Mubarak Awad taught nonviolent interventions to Palestinians in Israel (see Solution 37). One of the actions was to replant olive trees uprooted by Israeli bulldozers. Another was to challenge in the Israeli courts the practice of moving fences to reduce the size of Palestinian farms. The courts upheld the objections of the Palestinian farmers. Awad is the founder of Nonviolence International.

Some believe that the continuing use of violence by Palestinians has undermined the effectiveness of the nonviolent strategies. Gandhi demanded an absolute commitment to nonviolence in the struggle against the British in

Nonviolence takes a sustained discipline and planning. At this time in history, we hear a lot of Palestinians, especially those who were engaged in armed struggle, serious fighters, saying nonviolence is the way; teach us, we need to know more about it.

— Jonathan Kuttab, Palestinian lawyer and organizer

India. He was convinced that any violence by the Indians gave the British the justification they needed to increase their oppression. Recently, Gandhi's grandson, 70-year-old Arun Gandhi, has been teaching nonviolence to Palestinians.[1] He is convinced that had the Palestinians used nonviolence without exception, they would have justice by now.

In 2004, Arun Gandhi spoke in Ramallah to thousands of Palestinians, many of whom were already convinced of the value of nonviolent resistance. The next day, six buses of Israeli peace activists met with the Palestinians at Abu Dis, and 2,000 people marched with Arun Gandhi — Jews, Christians, and Muslims together.[2]

The groups are identified by their faith, yet their purpose is to join in nonviolent actions that cross the boundaries of their religious differences. Organizations that offer nonviolence training programs are often based in a specific faith and build on an individual's "soul-force," as Gandhi put it, but their programs are expressed in multi-faith actions.

My religion is based on truth and nonviolence. Truth is my God. Nonviolence is the means of realizing Him.

— Mohandas Gandhi

Arun Gandhi speaking at Abu Dis.

The Holy Land Trust in Bethlehem, a Palestinian organization, offers training programs in nonviolent resistance. The demand is so great that all its programs are oversubscribed. Organizers are greatly encouraged by the attendance of scores of former Fatah Brigade members who had fought for years in the al-Aqsa Intifada.[3]

The American Friends Service Committee (Quakers) trains international activists in nonviolent resistance so that they can join the Palestinian olive harvest.[4] They are not the only activists who arrive in Palestine in solidarity with the farmers. Busloads of Israelis, including Rabbis for Human Rights and Gush Shalom, pour into the fields and villages to join them and protect the Palestinians from Israeli soldiers and settlers.

Olive trees are of great importance to Palestinians. The oil is used in cooking and as an ingredient in soap. The branches are carved, and the pits used for fuel. Olive trees live hundreds of years and nourish many generations. They represent a sacred bond with the earth and are a significant symbol of peace and belonging. As Palestinian pastor Mitri Raheb says, "At times, when we feel as if the world must be coming to an end ... our only hopeful vision is to go out ...

and plant olive trees. If we don't plant any trees today, there will be nothing tomorrow. But if we plant a tree today, there will be shade for our children to play in. There will be oil to heal the wounds, and there will be olive branches to wave when peace arrives."[5]

The importance of Israeli support during the olive harvest cannot be overestimated. It brings a powerful message that not all Israelis support the occupation.

> **In nature there is fundamental unity running through all the diversity we see about us. Religions are given to mankind so as to accelerate the process of realization of fundamental unity**
> — **Mohandas Gandhi**

- American Friends Service Committee: www.afsc.org/israel-palestine/learn/ nonviolence-and-the-olive-harvest.htm
- Holy Land Trust: www.holylandtrust.org
- Nonviolence International: www.nonviolenceinternational.net
- World Council of Churches: www.eappi.org

45

*Live simply, serve others,
practice a spiritual discipline.*
— Bo Lozoff

Meditate, Provide Sanctuary, Pray

Meditate

Bo Lozoff is a wonderful teacher and author who has for many years been teaching prisoners to meditate. He and his wife, Sita, spent a couple of years on a yoga ashram in North Carolina. They frequently visited Sita's brother, who was in jail for smuggling marijuana. Bo pointed out that the ashram was so simple it was a lot like the prison, but he and Sita were living at the ashram by choice. He thought that if prisoners could learn to meditate, perhaps they could find spiritual freedom, even if they were incarcerated for life.

Lozoff calls prisoners to recognize that they are spiritual beings no matter what they have done, where they are living, or what the future holds. He does not charge for his teaching. He lives what he teaches, and he holds the prisoners accountable, while still supporting their search for spiritual meaning. I support his work through the Human Kindness Foundation. The funds donated pay for Lozoff's books to be sent to prisoners. Of his many books, my favorite is *We're All Doing Time: A Guide for Getting Free.*

Provide Sanctuary

With the pressure on the US armed forces, young Americans fear that there may be a return to the draft in that country. Several American soldiers have deserted and fled to Canada, where they have claimed refugee status. In the 1960s and 1970s, Canada received many young men who were escaping the draft for the Vietnam War. Most of them ended up staying in Canada. The current soldiers receive a mixed response because some Canadians support their right to refuse to serve in an illegal war, while others reject their plea on the grounds that they were not drafted but signed up voluntarily.

Nonetheless, many churches in Canada have taken up the cause of the young men and offered them sanctuary. So far the Canadian government has said that it will welcome Americans coming to Canada as it did during the Vietnam War. If the United States reinstates a draft, a new sanctuary movement will undoubtedly grow on both sides of the border.

Pray

In 1986 I went to the USSR with a group of Canadian doctors. We were guests of Soviet colleagues in International Physicians for the Prevention of Nuclear War. We traveled for two weeks, speaking to faculties and medical students about the threat of nuclear war and how doctors were speaking out about the dangers.

In Tbilisi, Georgia, we visited a monastery that had been established in AD 337, one of the first Christian outposts in the east. The building was old, and because the USSR was officially atheist, it was poorly maintained. The walls were covered with frescoes softened by centuries of candlelight, and the stone floor was worn down

- *We're All Doing Time* by Bo Lozoff, Human Kindness Foundation, 1985
- Human Kindness Foundation: www.humankindness.org

by untold numbers of feet. Around us were people lighting candles and praying, the church filled with silent activity.

I suddenly had an overwhelming sense of the presence of those very early Christians coming to bring a story that must have been truly revolutionary. The importance of their message of peace on earth and goodwill toward men seemed to have such immediacy that I turned to Sasha, our Russian colleague, and whispered, "I'm not Orthodox, so I've never lit a candle, but I wish I were because I would light one here." He listened, his eyes thoughtful. After a moment, he said, "I am sure you don't have to be Orthodox to light a candle for peace." He disappeared and returned with a handful of candles, which we lit in silence. He handed us the remaining few and said, "Please take these back and light them in churches in Canada with a prayer for peace. Tell the people where they came from and let the candles be a symbol of our common pursuit of peace on earth."

When I returned and asked the minister at my Anglican church if I could light one of the candles during a service, he suggested that the whole congregation join in. The church was packed for the service on the first Sunday of Advent. After I lit the Tbilisi candle, tapers were lit from it, and the light was passed to each person until the church was alight with 700 burning candles. A group of liturgical dancers

performed a sacred dance based on traditional Russian dances, while the choir sang Russian music. I said a prayer for Sasha and the congregation in Tbilisi, and also for us, that we might know to value and see God in every person.

Small brown candle from Soviet Georgia being lit in St. John's Anglican Church in Victoria, Canada, 1986.

GILLIAN DAVIDSON

46

Teach Barefoot Journalism

> Enlighten the people generally, and
> tyranny and oppressions of body
> and mind will vanish like evil
> spirits at the dawn of the day.
> — Thomas Jefferson

Peacebuilding has a new group of allies —
journalists! The flow of accurate and
balanced information is the lifeblood of healing
in societies torn by conflict and war. Stable
democratic government depends on an
informed public. Even amid the chaos of rival
armed factions fighting for position, reliable
information can cool tensions fueled by rumors
and propaganda.

The idea of media as a tool for peace is a new
concept, with levels of complexity depending on
the stage of conflict and the needs of the people.
It ranges from balanced reporting in conflict
zones to the production of soap operas and children's programs designed to build community
among diverse groups. Skilled reporters teach
local people how to produce newspapers or
radio and television programs to prevent conflict
or restore normal society.

In the context of ongoing fighting and insta-
bility, journalists teach the fundamentals of good,
independent reporting and involve people from
all ethnic and language groups. The principles of

objectivity, accuracy, and balance protect against
the destructive potential of media based in
biased and partisan reporting. Often what is
needed to defuse a damaging rumor is the correct information produced in several languages
simultaneously.

In Macedonia, a group of journalists from
different ethnic groups collaborated to produce
the same report in each of their languages.
When everyone knew the same facts, they could
begin to build trust.

There are many international organizations
that train journalists in conflict areas to use the
media to prevent an escalation of violence or to
contribute to post-conflict healing. These training sessions support the development of local
capacity for production so that the project will
be long-lived. Communication is a two-edged
sword; it can be used to promote hate or build
peace, and in the end it must be the local people
who maintain the objectivity and quality of the
material produced.

Where many people are poor and illiterate,
the best tool is radio because it is inexpensive to
set up a small transmitting station, most people
have access to radios, and wind-up radios eliminate the need for batteries. Radio was the obvious
choice for communicating in Somalia in 1991.

Somalia is an extreme example of a failed
state. It has no government and no infrastructure, which means there are no basic services
like electricity or garbage removal. It does have
more than its share of young men armed with
AK-47s. A government was elected in exile, but
has been unable to move back to Somalia

- HornAfrik (This website is not in English, but it is fascinating): www.hornafrik.com
- *The Power of the Media: A Handbook for Peacebuilders* by Ross Howard, Francis Rolt, Hans van de Veen and Julietter Verhoeven, www.impacs.org, 2003
- *Talk Mogadishu* by Judy Jackson: www.Bullfrogfilms.com

because of the continuing violence. Residents are afraid to go into the streets, and with no newspapers or radio stations, the only means of communication is cell phones.

In this dangerous milieu, three courageous Somali-Canadian men have established HornAfrik Media Network, a television and radio station that works with the BBC and Voice of America. They go to work in a jeep with four armed guards and have been attacked several times by warlords who disagreed with their comments. Their format is mainly local news and information that people have called in by cell phone, and they intersperse talk with music. They have a huge following because they are able to provide current information and talk shows.

A documentary film about these men, *Talk Mogadishu*, was made by a young Canadian woman, Judy Jackson. Her own story is as remarkable as the one she filmed. Even though she knew she risked being kidnapped for ransom, she managed to enter Mogadishu with a small crew, record the documentary in a few short days, and escape before her presence was noticed — quite a feat if you have red hair and white skin.

One of the stories related in *Talk Mogadishu* tells of a warlord who came to the station

threatening to kill the broadcasters. They were able to convince him of the value of the free spread of information and of the fact that HornAfrik is politically neutral. He finally decided not to kill them, but insisted that he be able to speak on the radio. They agreed, provided that he wait afterward to respond to phone calls from listeners. He was greatly shocked to hear the angry people (many of them women) who called in to demand that the warlords stop their violence and threats and get down to building a stable, democratic society.

HornAfrik interviews a warlord.

47

Support Journalism for Change

Understand the differences, act on
the commonalities.
— Search for Common Ground

In a country like Macedonia, where children of different ethnicities are segregated in their schools and communities, they only learn about each other from the stereotypes projected on TV or from people in their community who speak of other groups as the enemy. Yet the future belongs to all these children, and together they must somehow make a new life. Building a sustainable peace means reaching these children to change their knowledge, attitudes, and behaviors.

Search for Common Ground

Search for Common Ground is a not-for-profit organization that took on the challenge of using media to educate Macedonian children, working with the Sesame Workshop (producers of *Sesame Street*) to produce shows for 8 to 12 year olds. The show had to be entertaining so it would draw an audience away from the ethnic TV shows that promoted the opposite values, but its purpose was deeper than entertainment. It aimed to broaden the understanding between different ethnic groups so that they could build empathy with one another.

In the resulting TV series, *Nashe Maalo*, the children converse with an animated apartment building. The building itself is the wise teacher who listens when children get into conflict. Children have noticed that since the TV show began, there are fewer conflicts on the playgrounds. They say that if the kids on *Nashe Maalo* are able to solve this kind of problem, why shouldn't they do it the same way? They believe that they have learned new ways to solve problems that they will use for the rest of their lives.

Making shows that are both entertaining and transformative is a challenge for the writing and production teams. When it works well, the story is compelling and the message is woven seamlessly throughout.

In Sierra Leone, Common Ground set up Talking Drum Radio, with many different programs including a popular soap opera *Atunda Ayenda* ("Lost and Found"). When the theme song comes on, everyone stops to tune in their radio. The stories are about young people and how they got involved in the war. Subplots about topics like HIV/AIDS run through reflections on war and how to sustain peace.

Search for Common Ground has programs in 15 countries, and it does careful research to determine if the programs have led to positive social change. It has found convincing evidence that positive radio and television programs can successfully bring about intended outcomes.

BBC World Service

The BBC World Service uses the popular British radio soap opera *The Archers* as the model for radio dramas in countries recovering from war. In Afghanistan, the stories follow three fictional but typical Afghan villages. The characters may be returning refugees or families struggling to survive where the public infrastructure has been destroyed. The issues addressed range from conflict resolution to health, education, community development, landmine awareness, literacy promotion, and drug addiction.

In one episode, the UN special envoy at the time, Lakhdar Brahimi, played himself in a story

- BBC World Service: www.bbc.co.uk/worldservice
- Conflict and Peace Journalism Forum: www.conflictandpeace.org
- Conflict Resolution Information Source: www.crinfo.org/cgtjf/media_conflict_management.cfm
- Human Media: www.humanmedia.org
- Open Society Institute Network Media Program: www.soros.org/initiatives/media
- Radio Blue Sky (Established by the UN in Kosovo): www.hirondelle.org
- Search for Common Ground: www.sfcg.org
- Studio Ijambo in Burundi (Established to counter a recurrence of genocidal hate radio in Rwanda): www.sfcg.org
- United Nations Development Fund for Women: www.unifem.org

about the election of representatives to the *loya jirga* (Grand Assembly). In another episode, a man quit the mujahideen and became a de-miner.

A second strand of the BBC's work is educational feature programming that complements the messages and issues raised in the story lines of the soap. A third strand involves print media, including a cartoon magazine that provides further information for people with a low level of literacy.

In Uganda, the BBC radio soaps are called *Ngom Wa*, which means "Our Land." They feature a 15-year-old boy who confronts his past as a child soldier. In the refugee camps there is no traditional place where parents and children sit and talk in the evening. Instead, they listen to *Ngom Wa* on the radio. The program allows people to talk about reintegrating children who

have been kidnapped by warlords and forced to become the "wives" of warlords or to kill people, including their own families. In the mundane story of a child getting a flat tire on his bicycle, people can imagine normal life again and begin to overcome the brainwashing of the war.

The television series *Nashe Maalo* helps children in Macedonia learn to resolve conflicts.

SEARCH FOR COMMON GROUND

48

Learn and Teach Peace Journalism

For journalists who live and work on the front line, one careless word or one inaccurate detail can ignite a conflict. But equally, one clear balanced report can help to defuse tension and neutralise fear.
— Fiona Lloyd, Internews

When we read a report about a conflict, especially if the reporter is in a war zone, we often assume the report is objective and unbiased. Yet the reporter's choices about what to cover, how to frame the story, and what words to use all color how we understand the situation. When the reporter tells that story as if one side is to blame and the other side is the victim, the audience begins to think that military action may be justified. Often, under time pressures, a journalist will shorten a report and by so doing may polarize the discussion.

In times of conflict, the media become part of the conflict, whether or not that is their intention. In many cases, television coverage of a protest or conflict in a non-English-speaking country includes shots of people holding signs written in English. The action is set up for the cameras, and the coverage influences the outcome of the conflict.

Instead of this approach, Johan Galtung, the eminent peace scholar known for his theories of conflict transformation, calls for "peace journalism" that offers a more complex story with many more dimensions. Journalists can make a significant difference in a conflict if they persist in reporting the signs of progress toward peace from both sides. They can choose to interview people whose approach is to build bridges rather than destroy them. Often news reports imply that the only solution is victory for one side and defeat for the other. The reports do not discuss what happens after a ceasefire if the issues of the conflict remain unresolved.

Peace journalists seek out the causes of the conflict, including the deeper, often hidden, causes and the roles played by outside forces. They explore who stands to benefit from peace and who benefits from continuing destruction, such as companies providing weapons, ammunition, and materials for reconstruction. They ask different questions so that different answers emerge. Instead of asking their subjects where they disagree, they ask where they agree.

Johan Galtung suggests journalists ask "Who is working to prevent violence, and what are their visions of conflict outcomes, their methods and how can they be supported? Who is initiating genuine reconstruction, reconciliation and resolution, and who is only reaping benefits like reconstruction contracts?"[1]

Peace journalists find those people who have a different vision of the future than the political

RUSSELL DAVIDSON

Johan Galtung.

leaders are pushing, and they give coverage to alternative ideas. By focusing on the comments of moderates and those who support traditional ways of resolving conflict, the journalist can give credibility to new solutions.

Journalism in conflict zones is dangerous work. In the past decade, many hundreds of journalists have been killed in the course of their work; a large number of them were deliberately attacked because of their reporting.

A final piece of advice from those who practice peace journalism is to keep hope alive. Hope is fragile, but showing that small steps are working helps to give people courage to try one more time. The media can be central in informing the public that violent conflict is not inevitable and that, despite the ups and downs, people can build a sustainable peace.

- Find a radio station anywhere in the world: www.tvradioworld.com
- The Communications Initiative: www.comminit.com
- International Journalists Network: www.ijnet.org
- Internews: www.internews.org
- Media Diversity Institute (Builds peace and understanding among diverse groups): www.media-diversity.org
- Media for Peace, Colombia: www.mediosparalapaz.org
- Peace Journalism Training from Transcend: www.transcend.org

Mad Dogs and Englishmen

The following terms have all been used by the British press to report on the war in the Persian Gulf.

They have	**We have**
A war machine	Army, Navy and Air Force
Censorship	Reporting guidelines
Propaganda	Press briefings

They	**We**
Destroy	Take out
Destroy	Suppress
Attack	Eliminate
Kill	Neutralize
Kill	Decapitate
Cower in their foxholes	Dig in

They launch	**We launch**
Sneak missile attacks	First strikes
Without provocation	Pre-emptively

Their men are	**Our men are**
Troops	Boys
Hordes	Lads

They are	**Our boys are**
Brainwashed	Professional
Paper tigers	Lionhearted
Cowardly	Cautious
Desperate	Confident
Cornered	Heroes
Cannon fodder	Dare devils
Bastards of Baghdad	Young knights of the skies
Blindly obedient	Loyal
Mad dogs	Desert rats
Ruthless	Resolute
Fanatical	Brave

Their boys are motivated by	**Our boys are motivated by**
Fear of Saddam	Old-fashioned sense of duty

Their boys	**Our boys**
Cower in concrete bunkers	Fly into the jaws of hell

List compiled by Media Awareness Network (www.media-awareness.ca) and published in the *Guardian*, UK

49

Counter Hate Propaganda

A camera in the right hands at the right time at the right place can be more powerful than tanks and guns. Let the truth do the fighting.

— Peter Gabriel, Witness for Peace co-founder

Genocides do not happen out of a clear blue sky. They begin with the spread of hate propaganda through media like radio and television over a period of years. Organizations that monitor such hatred can predict that there will be a bloodbath if outside powers do not intervene.

Rwanda

In the case of Rwanda, Radio Milles Collines broadcast hate propaganda that foreshadowed the genocide there. The government-associated radio urged Hutus to kill the cockroaches (Tutsis) and even drew up lists of people to be killed. Many people believe that if Radio Milles Collines had been stopped, and other preventive actions taken, the genocide might have been averted.

As the horrifying slaughter began, international leaders refused to act, but a few strong individuals countered the hatred. Hundreds of Rwandans gathered in Hotel Milles Collines, operated by Sabina Airlines, for protection. When Hutu militants gave the temporary manager,

Paul Rusesabagina, 30 minutes to clear the hotel of people, he raced up onto the roof of the hotel and saw that it was surrounded by military forces. He and a number of the occupants used their cell phones to call influential foreigners for urgent help. One of the people they called was the director general of the French Foreign Office. Within half an hour, a colonel from the national police arrived and the siege was over.

The time for intervention was in the years before the genocide, when hatred and injustice cried out for action. We can only speculate what might have been possible if the hate radio had been blocked and replaced by media that focused on individuals who were working for understanding and justice.

The Space Bridge

During the Cold War, the war zone was the propaganda arena. The first "space bridge" between the US and the USSR was broadcast in 1982 and began to counter the negative images each side held of the other. The idea came from Steve

Studio in Ijambo in Burundi works to counter hate propaganda by building understanding.

Vosniak, co-founder of Apple Computers, and Joseph Goldin, a Soviet script writer, after a rock concert in California made use of giant TV screens to show the performance to the largest possible audience.

The space bridge linked 250,000 young people gathered for a festival outside Los Angeles with a Soviet audience in a studio in Ostankino. Popular journalists Phil Donahue and Vladimir Posner hosted the show. When the audiences saw each other on the screen and were able to wave and talk to each other, technology's great potential to bring the world closer together was clear.

Later space bridges connected scientists, journalists, public figures, and cosmonauts, who were able to discuss common questions. Search for Common Ground produced a bridge program showing Soviets and Americans grappling with the issue of how to deal with nuclear accidents. The program, *Chernobyl and Three Mile Island*, demonstrated to a mass audience that even highly contentious issues could be dealt with in ways that encouraged cooperative solutions.

Cambodia

Organizations working in Cambodia after that country's civil war learned many lessons about using the media to counter propaganda. UNTAC Radio, the voice of the United Nations Transitional Authority in Cambodia, is regarded as one of the successes in the 1992–1993 peace process. By that time the Khmer Rouge had been defeated, but it continued an insurgency even as the country prepared for its first election.

- "Bystanders to Genocide" by Samantha Power, *Atlantic Monthly*, September 2001: www.mtholyoke.edu/acad/intrel/power.htm
- A Rwandan Hero: Paul Rusesabagina: www.rwanda.net/english/whoswho/rusebagina/rusebagina.htm
- Search for Common Ground: www.sfcg.org
- Space bridge story: english.pravda.ru/world/2002/09/05/36059.html
- "UN Peacekeeping Missions: The Lessons from Cambodia" by Judy L. Ledgerwood, March 1994: www.seasite.niu.edu/khmer/Ledgerwood/PDFAsiaPacific.htm

Radio was the choice for communication because there was a low level of literacy and limited access to television coverage. Even though they had little formal education, people were very much aware of what was at stake and of the possibility of a new future for their country.

People were bombarded by Khmer Rouge radio programs claiming that millions of Vietnamese settlers and soldiers were overrunning Cambodia, and that only the Khmer Rouge could protect the Cambodians. On the other side, the government radio broadcast rhetoric of the glories of revolution. The people wanted to know that there would be real choice at the ballot box, and they needed reassurance that there would be no retaliation for voting.

UNTAC radio broadcast material from all political parties and, above all, assured the people that the ballots would be secret. At the same time UNTAC broadcasters stressed the significance of the elections, they also spoke openly about possible intimidation and human rights abuses. Some 96 percent of the eligible population registered, and on election day, 90 percent of those registered voted. Democracy in Cambodia is still fragile, but it is surviving and evolving.

50

Tell a New Story

> The state of media in Afghanistan today is not zero, it is minus zero ... It is critical that we extend that work to Afghanistan where much of what we think of as "journalism" has been destroyed.
>
> — Ahmed Rashid

When I find *Yes! Magazine* in my mailbox, I give a little inner cheer. A whole afternoon reading stories of people who have succeeded in changing the world, little by little, stretches ahead of me! The stories are an antidote to the poisonous mainstream media diet describing how humanity is failing in so many directions. Instead of all the accidents and murders, the natural disasters and the moral failures of politicians and CEOs, I read about people who like each other and who are building communities that encourage laughter, joy, and trust. *Yes!* features many American stories, but also covers international successes that give inspiring relief from the dangerous and frightening world shown hour after hour on TV.

Telling a new story seems to be as important in countries recovering from war as it is in North America. People respond to television and radio shows that offer a story line based in their reality but bring a new perspective of hope. They are ready to become absorbed by stories of people dealing with landmine injuries and health issues at the same time as they are dealing with an elderly parent or with their children making unwise choices. Sometimes the stories are fictitious, like the soap operas from Search for Common Ground (see Solution 47); sometimes the stories are interviews with real people who are taking positive actions for the common good.

In Afghanistan, Radio Sahar (Radio Dawn), a station managed by women, was set up with help from the Canadian media NGO IMPACS and its American counterpart, Internews.[1]

Afghan women learned to write and produce programs on such topics as health and women's rights. The station now broadcasts 14 hours a day.

The women who work at the station face many obstacles, even as their culture is beginning to change. They cannot stand alone on a street and cannot take a taxi without a male relative. One woman could not interview a policeman about a story because women cannot talk to strange men. Luckily her husband was willing to do it for her. The problems of equipment breakdown, short circuits, and lack of replacement parts are compounded by the continuing shortage of money.

Ismail Khan, the local governor in Herat, where the station is located, was notoriously ultra-conservative. He allowed the station to be set up, but on the day programming was to begin, the women waited tensely in case he rescinded his permission. The day the station opened, the Canadian ambassador flew in to attend, and Governor Khan joined him, thus giving his approval to the station.

The Afghan minister for Women's Affairs, Habiba Sarabi, felt that radio was the best tool to bring about social change for women because it is cheap, accessible, and does not require literacy skills. In the best of circumstances, it is difficult to discuss women's rights on radio, particularly the traditions of marriage dowries, forced marriage, and *khoonbahaw* (marrying a woman to a man from an opposing tribe to reconcile a conflict). The conservative element of the listening audience wasted no time in voicing its criticism.

- Internews:
  www.internews.org/regions/centralasia/afghanistan.htm
- Institute for Media Policy and Civil Society (IMPACS):
  www.impacs.org
- *Yes! Magazine*: www.yesmagazine.org

The women even get outraged phone calls when they play music that is not conservative enough, or if they make grammatical errors.

When she saw the problems for children living in extreme poverty, the Canadian trainer, Toni Mehrain, introduced a new project — teaching broadcast journalism to street children. The project would not only give them a skill that could provide employment; it would also give them hope.

As Mehrain anticipated, the children were shy and attentive. They were so cautious she realized they were terrified of making a mistake and losing this extraordinary opportunity. She told them that in the radio business, learning is a two-way street, and she expected to learn as much from them as they learned from her.

The children then relaxed and began developing their short programs. They were asked to spend five minutes on a story. Mehrain expected them to produce stories that might be told by a child anywhere — perhaps of a conflict with a sibling. Instead, one wrote of a working child being beaten by an adult, another of a child being kidnapped, and another of a child who wanted to attend school but had to work.

Radio is bringing a new story to Afghanistan — the story that women and children play an important role in the development of a strong, healthy society.

High school student and radio host Somia Neiabi in Herat.

SHAUNA SYLVESTER, IMPACS APRIL 2005

51

Meet Colleagues on the Other Side

> When an old culture is dying, the new is created by a few people who are not afraid to be insecure.
>
> — Rudolf Bahro, East German dissident and philosopher

When doctors from the west began to meet with Soviet doctors, they were called communists, and their Soviet counterparts were treated with suspicion in case they deviated from party ideology. Despite these obstacles, the doctors worked on joint research to let the world know the medical consequences of a nuclear attack. When Soviet doctors spoke on television to over 200 million people about the need to prevent nuclear war, their words were backed up by American colleagues giving the same message in the United States.

Doctors from all the nuclear weapons states, including India and Pakistan, continue to share research on the health effects of nuclear weapons and continue to issue joint statements to warn the public of the threat of nuclear war by accident, terrorism, or escalation of a regional conflict.

Teachers from the United States, Canada, and Europe traveled to the Soviet Union to meet with colleagues and learn from one another. Soviet children were excited to meet western visitors and speak English to them. In the mid-1980s, whole classes of students from the west traveled to the Soviet Union to meet students there and join in activities like hockey and figure skating. A class of young people from Quebec went to Moscow to meet a group of Soviet students who were studying French. Somewhat to the dismay of the teachers, not only did the students become close friends, but the Canadians taught their Russian friends to speak joual, a French-Canadian dialect that uses nonstandard pronunciation and grammar.

Peace Through Health

Peace Through Health is a new approach that uses health projects as the bridge to peace. One example of this method is a World Health Organization journal called *Bridges*, which is produced by Israeli and Palestinian doctors working together. The glossy public health journal is aimed at health professionals and informed laypeople. The first issue deals mainly with poverty and health inequity. It is the only WHO publication jointly produced by doctors on both sides of a conflict zone.

Another example of Peace Through Health is provided by Canadians from McMaster University in Hamilton, who are working with colleagues in Afghanistan to help children recover from the trauma of war. Child psychiatrist Joanna Santa Barbara uses soft hand-puppets, made by women in Hamilton, which are dressed as Afghan family members. The puppets perform in stories that are used to teach conflict resolution, reduce ethnic prejudice, support reconstruction and reconciliation, and help children talk about their traumatic experiences. Later, in schools, the teachers read the stories and the children animate them. In their free time, the children use the puppets to dramatize their own stories. More than 50 full sets of puppets have been sent to Afghanistan to be used by a wide range of people from military and government personnel to returning expatriates.

Joanna and her colleagues began their work teaching conflict resolution skills to children in an Afghan refugee camp in Peshawar, Pakistan, before the fall of the Taliban. There was such

- Bridges Journal: www.healthinforum.net
- International Physicians for the Prevention of Nuclear War: www.ippnw.org
- Peace Through Health: www.humanities.mcmaster.ca/peace-health
- Pugwash discussion of ethics for scientists and engineers: www.pugwash.org/reports/ees/corsica2004/corsica2004.htm

enthusiasm that the group was asked to teach their politicians. Perhaps that is something we could do in our own countries!

Pugwash

The organization Pugwash brings together scientists from around the world to discuss issues surrounding nuclear weapons. The organization was founded by Joseph Rotblat, who, along with Pugwash, won the Nobel Peace Prize in 1995 for his efforts to educate the world about the dangers of nuclear weapons. During World War II, when Joseph Rotblat learned that the Germans were not making an atomic bomb, he believed it was morally wrong for the Americans to continue with research to make atomic weapons, and he became the only scientist to leave the Manhattan project.

In 1957 he brought together 22 eminent scientists, including three from the Soviet Union, to talk about the dangers of nuclear weapons. In annual conferences, workshops, and other meetings, Pugwash scientists continue to address such issues as ballistic missile defense and new generations of nuclear weapons in an effort to build the political will needed to eliminate nuclear weapons. They have also drawn up a code of ethics for scientists and engineers who acknowledge that they are personally responsible for the way they use their training and that it is unethical to work on weapons of mass destruction.

> A campaign for abolition, based on moral principles, will be seen as a fanciful dream by many, but I trust not by this audience ... Arguments based on equity and morality may not cut ice with hardened politicians, but they may appeal to the common citizen.
>
> — Keynote Speech at IPPNW World Congress, Summit for Survival, Washington DC, May 4, 2002

PUGWASH CONFERENCES ON SCIENCE AND WORLD AFFAIRS

Sir Joseph Rotblat, 1908-2005.

52

Get the Facts Out

The fool persuades me with his reason; the wise man persuades me with my own.

— Aristotle

A civil-society organization can take the long view in pursuing truth and justice. It does not have to worry about a four-year election cycle. It can develop expertise and credibility that policy makers respect, and it can combine scientific studies with the social values of justice, protection of the environment, human rights, and peace.

Groups that work for the public good, rather than for profit or power, become trusted sources of information for all of us. Lawyers, physicists, engineers, religious leaders, and doctors can bring their special expertise to the issues of treaties, weapons, ethics, and the health effects of war. By getting the facts out to our policy makers, we are providing a service that is both useful and cost-effective. At UN conferences, documents from NGOs are highly valued, especially by diplomats from countries that do not make unbiased materials available.

Officials have often told me that what they most appreciate is a fact sheet on one page, not a long briefing paper. The longer papers are useful for staff assistants, but officials are not likely to read them. A fact sheet that makes a few coherent points and a clear recommendation for policy is likely to be taken seriously, especially if there is a credible reference for the information provided.

Translating the values of civil society into policy recommendations is not as easy as it sounds because you must explore the ramifications of each option before you choose the one that best expresses your values. When your recommendation includes the outcomes you have examined, your argument is more compelling and useful to the government.

I attended one government-sponsored public consultation on a foreign policy question. In small groups we addressed the issue in what were sometimes heated discussions. The leader continually asked us, "Right, so based on what you have concluded, what policy would you recommend to the government?" We found it amazingly difficult to be specific about the practical implementation of our views, and we began to be more sympathetic to the people we elect, who have to convert public opinion into policy.

We found that the more diverse the group studying the issue, the closer we came to developing actual policy recommendations. We needed the thoughtful input of the religious leaders, the perspective of women, and the knowledge of both political and physical scientists.

Getting the facts out applies to how we get clear information to the public as well as to the government. Sometimes I find myself thinking that if we could just get everyone into a lecture theater and show them the data, they would all agree and our problems would be solved. The

- *The Art of Teaching Adults: How to Become an Exceptional Instructor and Facilitator* by Peter Renner Training Associates, 1994.
- US Veterans for Peace: www.veteransforpeace.org
- Veterans Against Nuclear Arms: www.vana.ca

problem is that most of us don't change our behavior after listening passively to a lecture.

So much is now known about how adults learn, and how differently each of us responds to what we learn, that we can more effectively present information in a variety of ways to help people form their opinions. For example:

- People don't like being told what is good for them; in fact, they resist mightily when someone seems to be telling them what to do. On the other hand, if they are actively questioning and responding to a respected leader, they are more likely to accept new information.

- We will listen to new ideas when we feel safe and not threatened. That is more likely to happen in small groups where we can ask questions and feel sure no one will laugh or be angry because we have a different worldview.

- We like to be able to ask about what concerns us first and to have the discussion follow our needs.

- We want to be recognized as making a valuable contribution to the group.

- We need to know that after hearing new information, we can change our minds without losing face.

- We like to have small pieces of information, clearly presented with evidence for the statements.

- When we hear stories that reinforce the information, we are more likely to remember it.

- When we actually do something with a group of kindred spirits, we are more likely to continue in the new direction.

John, a doctor on an island near my home, was a member of Veterans Against Nuclear Arms (VANA). His next-door neighbor was also a veteran but refused to join VANA or walk with John on November 11 wearing the VANA white beret. After years of trying to persuade his neighbor, John gave up.

"All right," he said, "I won't ask you anymore. But just out of curiosity, why are you so against VANA?"

His neighbor then told of his years as a prisoner of the Japanese during World War II. John apologized for being self-righteous. His neighbor said the war was long past and it was now time for him to join VANA.

Veterans Against Nuclear Arms Joe Barber-Starkey and Gladys Kennedy.

PHIL ESMONDE

53

Support International Law — Hold Leaders Accountable

Civil society assumes that if a treaty is signed, we can be confident that the signatories will abide by its conditions. All international relations rely on an interlocking system of laws and treaties. When countries withdraw from treaties or block effective implementation of legal agreements, the entire foundation of international law is undermined.

The decision of the United States, the United Kingdom, and the coalition allies to attack Iraq in 2003 was illegal and based on deliberate misrepresentation of information. In 2005 it was revealed that the United States and United Kingdom had actually begun bombing Iraq's defense system in September 2002, six months

> Our moral authority is weakened when it appears that the US has a disregard for international agreements. If our nation appears to circumvent these obligations when it appears to be politically or militarily convenient, then we debase the very value that we have sacrificed so much to defend — the value of the rule of law. Our government must not seek clever ways to evade these agreements.
>
> — Robert J. Grey, president of the American Bar Association

before the much-publicized shock and awe bombing began.

With no international body prepared to address the illegal war, the war crimes, and crimes against humanity committed in the course of the war and the occupation, civil society took up that responsibility. A large group of experts, including prestigious international lawyers, academics, journalists, and numerous other authorities, initiated a World Tribunal on Iraq with more than 20 hearings in 15 cities around the world. Some of those involved included Richard Falk, professor of International Law at Santa Barbara University; Denis Halliday and Hans Von Sponek, who were both former assistants to the UN Secretary General; Arundhati Roy, author; David Krieger, director of the Nuclear Age Peace Foundation; and dozens of others.

The tribunal called hundreds of key witnesses to give testimony. Their findings are a powerful indictment of the US and UK governments, and of George W. Bush and Tony Blair personally. Although the tribunal does not have the power to enforce its findings, the documentation forms a clear historical record of the evidence against the leaders and personnel who perpetrated war crimes.

Richard Falk is convinced that the tribunal is a significant step in the development of

RUSSELL DAVIDSON

Richard Falk.

international law because it builds on the moral conscience of the millions of people who publicly marched against the war on Iraq on February 15, 2003. Civil society stepped into the vacuum to uphold the UN Charter and to take action on behalf of international law.

The UN Charter begins: "We the peoples of the United Nations determined to save succeeding generations from the scourge of war..."

The Charter speaks for the peoples, not for the nation-states. It is the peoples who have been constant in their call for an end to war and who have held leaders accountable for their actions. Professor Falk states, "When governments and the UN are silent, and fail to protect victims of aggression, tribunals of concerned citizens possess a law-making authority. Their unique contribution is to tell the truth as powerfully and fully as possible, and by such truthfulness to activate the conscience of humanity to resist."[1]

When the United States and United Kingdom, along with other coalition partners, bombed and occupied Iraq in 2003, they contravened the UN Charter, which expressly forbids member states from using force in international conflicts except in circumstances of self-defense strictly defined and under the authority of the Security Council. However powerful and invulnerable the US and UK leaders appear, the trials of Japanese and German leaders after World War II established the personal responsibility of leaders and personnel for war crimes and crimes against humanity.

Justice Robert Jackson, American prosecutor at the Nuremberg trials after World War II, stated, "If certain acts in violation of treaties are crimes, they are crimes whether the United States does them or Germany does them, and we are not prepared to lay down a rule of criminal conduct against others which we would not be willing to have invoked against us."[2]

The final statement of the World Tribunal on Iraq concluded: "We, the Jury of Conscience, hope that the specificity of these recommendations will lay the groundwork required for a world where the international institutions will be shaped and reshaped by the will of people and not by fear and self-interest, where journalists and intellectuals will not remain mute, where the will of the people of the world will be central, and human security will prevail over state security and corporate profits."[3]

- World Tribunal on Iraq: www.worldtribunal.org

54

Say It with Music

> If you sing, you have life... our life was so hard, had we not sung, we would have gone insane.
>
> — Lithuanian speaking about the Singing Revolution

In 1988 the Baltic countries of Lithuania, Latvia, and Estonia were still part of the Soviet Empire. People in all three countries began to protest against the Soviet occupation using the only means they could — singing. That year in Tallinn, Estonia, over 100,000 people gathered for a music festival of peaceful protest. Mass protest gatherings to sing of national identity and independence became known as the Singing Revolution. In August 1989 about two million people from Lithuania, Latvia, and Estonia stood on the Vilnius-Tallinn road, holding hands. The human chain stretched nearly 373 miles (600 kilometers). By 1991 the Soviet Union was reeling after a failed military coup and could no longer deny the demands of the Baltic States for independence. The Singing Revolution was finally over.

Musicians and poets are dangerous people if you happen to be a dictator. Creativity cannot be tolerated by a totalitarian state because it encourages people to dream of what might be. In the 1960s, the Beatles were a profoundly radical force in North America and Western Europe because they posed questions about conformity and patriotism. In 1964, if a male let his

- Aquarium: www.aquarium-web.com
- Plastic People of the Universe: www.furious.com/perfect/pulnoc.html
- Singing revolutions in Estonia, Latvia and Lithuania: www.en.wikipedia.org/wiki/Singing_Revolution

hair grow to cover his ears, it was cause for expulsion from high school. Within a few years, the Beatles made long hair acceptable, and they and other musicians were providing the soundtrack for the hippies, the antiwar movement, and the questioning of mainstream values.

The Soviet Union

The Beatles had an even more powerful impact in the Soviet Union and Eastern Europe, where rock music was a breath of fresh air. It was subversive not because it was protest music, but because it was free. Rock music brought with it a sense of a life that was different from the grey sameness of Soviet rule. In Leningrad, the rock band Aquarium was formed by a group of musicians who loved the Beatles and wondered why there was no comparable music about the lives and loves of young Soviets. They began to make that music themselves, playing in apartments packed with young people. They didn't amplify their music in case the neighbors called the authorities, but people taped the sessions and passed on the music hand to hand.

Aquarium became more and more popular despite the fact that it was dangerous to play in a prohibited band and dangerous to attend a concert. The authorities did not approve of the free lifestyle of band members, but it was proving impossible to keep music and western culture from spreading underground. By 1989, Aquarium was touring America, and the Soviet Union was in the whirlwind of change. The band's music began to reflect the new interest in religion and the search for personal meaning that was growing in Russia as the influence of the Communist Party waned.

Czechoslovakia

In Prague in the 1960s, rock music and all things American were enormously popular. The Soviets, however, decided that Czechoslovakia was becoming too free, and in 1968 they invaded and crushed the democracy movement. A month later the rock band Plastic People of the Universe was formed (see Solution 8). The band had a huge following and endured cycles of repression that culminated in band members being jailed in 1976. Their trial was seen as the hippies against the communist state. In 1977,

poets, writers, and professors rallied around the Plastic People and formed a human rights group. That group included poet Vaclav Havel, who would later become president of the Czech Republic. The group issued a famous human rights petition known as Charter 77. As a result, Havel was thrown in jail.

After the Plastic People members were released from jail, they continued to record, and eventually the Czech regime bowed to public pressure and allowed rock concerts. In November 1989, shortly after the Berlin Wall came down, Czech students began to gather daily in Wenceslas Square to protest police brutality. They were joined by playwrights, actors, musicians, and the entire Czech Philharmonic Orchestra until over 300,000 people were gathered. Music, theater and poetry had become tools to express public opposition to the communist regime. When Vaclav Havel stepped onto the stage at a Czech Philharmonic concert in mid-December, he was greeted by thunderous applause,and people could sense that the end of their oppression was very close. The so-called Velvet Revolution ended on December 29, when Havel was named president.

Canadian guitarist and singer Bruce Cockburn is a powerful voice in the campaign to ban landmines. Here he is with Cambodian musicians at Preah Vihear, Cambodia in 1999.

VIETNAM VETERANS OF AMERICA FOUNDATION

55

Give Peace a Dance

If I can't dance, I don't want to be part of your revolution.

— Emma Goldman

Emma Goldman was surely asking for more than dancing to be part of the revolution. I believe she was saying that everything that brings us love and joy is part of changing the world, and that we only really commit to something when it fills our need to create. Peacebuilding is a path of dancing, singing, laughing, hugging, painting, and just being ourselves. It is also a path of generosity and service, of tolerance and caring.

We may not succeed in ending war and violence in our lifetime, but we can make the path clearer to others by the way we live and how we use our gifts.

Give peace a dance, a symphony, painting, poem, art installation, rock concert, soccer game, marathon, banner, quilt, film, or commercial. Give peace legal advice, a health clinic, a loan, fund, or grant. We can each give our special expertise or professional skills in the service of building a culture of peace.

Artists have particular gifts that engage the public at a deep emotional level. I once heard a wise facilitator tell a strategic planning group that the reason creative people drive everyone else in a group crazy is that they just keep firing out new ideas. Before the group has caught up to them, they have another idea. "The interesting thing about them," he added, "is that they don't expect you to take up all the ideas, but they do expect you to take up one every so often; otherwise they move on." Dancers, musicians, and artists bring the creative expression that gives life to peace work.

"Give Peace a Dance" was the name of a community fundraising dance in support of our local peace walk in Victoria. Fundraising is an opportunity to build community with those who share our goals. Yes, it is work. It can also be fun and enriching in more ways than financial. We know the serious state of the planet, but that

Children's Peace Dance Flags.

WAHABA KARUNA, KARUNA ARTS, WWW.KARUNAARTS.COM

- Effective Meetings.com (Tips on organizing meetings): www.effectivemeetings.com
- Group Process Techniques: www.ncrtec.org/pd/lwtres/gpt.pdf
- *Leadership Strategies for Effective Group Process* by Nola-Kate Seymoar, available from www.enoughbloodshed.ca
- The Peace Company (Products and training for a more peaceful world): www.thepeacecompany.com
- Peace Choirs: www.peacechoirs.net
- Right to Play (Using sport to unite people): www.righttoplay.com
- Raffi Cavoukian's inspirational songs and sheet music: www.raffinews.com www.troubadourfoundation.org

doesn't mean we must always be earnest and somber as we work to make a better world.

Someone once said that after all the brainstorming and strategizing, everything degenerates into work and money. It costs money to build a movement, but it also takes a movement to raise the money. Building the movement is work, sustaining the movement is work, raising money is work — and all of it together is the movement.

Although working in groups to build peace is hard and often frustrating work, it is in groups that we are able to experience the joy of relationships, the satisfaction of expressing a collaborative idea, the rewards of producing transformation. Most of our work for peace is done through participation with like-minded others, and we enjoy it most when we do what we like the most.

One of the most useful articles I have read about working in groups was written by Nola-Kate Seymoar. She uses the tricycle as the metaphor for a successful group. The three wheels of the tricycle are the goal, the group process, and the personal satisfaction of each member.

To teach the metaphor to an audience, she invited Al, a football player, to demonstrate. First he rode onto the stage on a unicycle. She showed, by giving him a push, that if a group is purely goal-oriented, it is like Al on the unicycle — easy to push over, easy to turn off track, and not very well-balanced.

Then Al rode in on a bicycle. This time she found it harder to push him off course, but she was still able to make him wobble and then fall,

even though she is a small woman. She pointed out that the group that is goal-oriented and also concerned about how people work together is more stable than the first group, but it could be stronger.

Finally Al rode in on a giant tricycle. Nola-Kate tried her best to push him off course, to hold him back, or to tip him off, but he barreled straight across the stage. She concluded that the group that also cares about the personal satisfaction of each member is most likely to be strong, effective, and long-lived.

When the goal is as urgent as saving the planet from war or environmental catastrophe, the temptation is great to focus tightly on the goal and run over dissent and discomfort as if they were bumps in the road. If we recognize that our task will continue after our lifetime, we know our tricycle must be in good repair, and we must take time to ease over the bumps. The goal, then, must be to work so that the network will be sustained when we are gone. That means that dancing is as much a part of our group as marching.

56

Don't Build the War Machine

In the 20th century, war was seen to be good for business. Today, war may be good for military industries and for companies that reconstruct bombed countries, but for the rest of the economy, war is devastating. It removes public funding from the social needs of a society. Health care, education, public works, and social services all suffer cutbacks while the military budget increases. If we cut the military budget, there are plenty of exciting ideas for better ways to invest public money, and there are highly principled people willing to put their own jobs and future on the line to make them happen.

Many business leaders know that the US economy is suffering from the excessive military spending of the George W. Bush administration,

> Science and technology is not given. It was made by people like us. If it's not doing for us what we want, we have a right and a responsibility to change it. We need a clear view of what we want for science and technology and the courage to stand up and do something about it.
>
> — **Mike Cooley, British labor leader**, whose proposals to convert Lucas Aerospace to peaceful production won him a Right Livelihood Award in 1981

and they are taking action to oppose the war budget. Business Leaders for Sensible Priorities is an organization founded by Ben Cohen of Ben and Jerry's Ice Cream. The Business Leaders call for a reduction in Pentagon funding so that other urgent needs can be met.

The Oreo Cookie Show

Ben Cohen shows how the reduction would work by representing the US military budget with Oreo cookies. It's easier to picture the overstuffed Pentagon budget when you see it as a stack of cookies rather than as a graph. A stack of 40 Oreo cookies represents the annual military budget of $400 billion. Each cookie represents $10 billion, so Cohen says, "Just take five cookies a year off this pile. Use one cookie to rebuild our schools, one for alternative energy to eliminate our need for Mideast oil, and two to feed all of the six million starving kids around the world. Then take the last cookie, split it in half, and use half to provide health insurance and a quarter to provide Headstart for every kid that needs it. You can eat the other quarter cookie. But remember, that's $2.5 billion. Try not to choke!" (You can see the Oreo cookie show on the True

ANIMATION BY DAVE COUNTS, TRUE MAJORITY

Ben Cohen stacks Oreo cookies to show the benefits to children, education, and the environment if funds are moved from the Pentagon budget.

Majority website, and you can show it to your friends yourself.)

Skeptics ask how we can defend ourselves against our enemies if we cut military spending. Cohen points out that Russia spends fewer than seven cookies on the military, and China spends fewer than five — and they are our friends and trading partners! All the countries of the so-called Axis of Evil together spend less than one cookie. Cutting the budget as he suggests would not leave the United States vulnerable, but would provide a better life now, and a better future.

First we have to imagine how it would be if no children were homeless and hungry; if no one lost his or her job, home, and savings because of a catastrophic illness; and if no one missed the opportunity to study because of poverty. Then we have to imagine how we would make that dream a reality by using money from the military budget.

Lucas Aerospace

Many highly credible plans have been developed to transfer jobs from military to peaceful production so there would be increased employment. Almost any other sector creates more jobs than the military. The most famous example of a plan to convert a military industry was developed in the United Kingdom by Lucas Aerospace employees when they were threatened with unemployment in the 1970s.

- Business Leaders for Sensible Priorities: www.sensiblepriorities.org
- Coalition to Oppose the Arms Trade: www.coat.ncf.ca
- Military Conversion for Social Development report: www.bicc.de/publications/reports/report05/content.php
- Right Livelihood Awards: www.rightlivelihood.org
- Sekem (A company based on principles of serving human needs): www.sekem.com
- True Majority: www.truemajority.com

The workers joined together across union and factory lines to draw up a plan of 150 products that Lucas could make using its existing equipment and skilled staff. Their corporate plan included making kidney dialysis machines, heat pumps, a road-rail bus, and airships.

Although the plan was rejected by Lucas, it inspired other unions and factories in the United Kingdom and elsewhere. Most of the technical ideas have proven to be viable, and many have been manufactured.

Mike Cooley, one of the leaders of the Lucas plan, was fired in 1980 for spending too much time on union business and the concerns of society. He simply refocused his energy on developing innovative systems for employing people and founded the concept of human-centered systems. He received a Right Livelihood Award in 1981.

57

Support Cooperatives

> I am only one but still I am one. I can-
> not do everything, but still I can do
> something. I will not refuse to do
> the something I can do.
>
> — Helen Keller

As corporations downsize, the capitalist system reveals its lack of heart and conscience. People who thought they were secure for life find themselves unemployed late in their careers. The growth of consumerism is not only environmentally destructive; it is also soul destroying.

People are not simply hungry for enough money to buy food; they are hungry for more meaningful work and authentic community. The African word *ubuntu* means community in the deepest sense of people feeling a responsibility for others and for the Earth. *ubuntu* is the joyous statement that "I am what I am because of who we all are."

Free-market capitalism without any restrictions fosters competition without compassion. Communism also failed to produce just and equitable societies that nourished all their citizens. We are unlikely to end violence, terror, and war without taking a new path of mutual caring. The cooperative movement offers one model for people living and working in harmony with the Earth.

Triodos Bank

In Europe you can literally put your money where your heart is by using the Triodos Bank. Triodos was established in the Netherlands and now also operates in Belgium and the United Kingdom. It only lends to organizations with positive environmental, social, and cultural goals. It supports renewable energy initiatives, organic food and farming, social housing, Greenpeace, and grassroots economic development in the south.

Triodos says that banking should be for us and for the world we all share. That means that although Triodos does not make the level of profits the huge multinational banks do, it makes a sustainable profit and makes a difference at the same time.

Co-op Bank, UK

The Co-op Bank arose out of the UK cooperative movement that began more than 150 years ago. There has been a decline in co-ops as businesses, but the Co-op Bank got a new lease on life when it chose to focus on ethical investing. Using democratic decision-making, its members are able to shape the social responsibility of the bank. As a result, the Co-op Bank not only makes socially responsible investments, but also supports initiatives like a tree-planting campaign in national parks in Africa, the anti-landmines campaign, and a recent campaign for safer chemicals.

- Cooperative Bank: www.co-operativebank.co.uk
- Ethical Shopping: www.roughguides.com/storedetails.html?ProductID=541
- Ethical Shopping: www.thegoodshoppingguide.co.uk
- *Global Profit and Global Justice: Using Your Money to Change the World* by Deb Abbey, New Society Publishers, 2004
- Mondragon: www.mcc.es/ing/index.asp
- *The Mondragon Experiment*, BBC documentary, 1979. Available in most university libraries.
- Triodos Bank: www.triodos.co.uk

Mondragon

The town of Mondragon in the Basque region of Spain is famous for its democratic, worker-owned cooperatives. In 1956, a time of desperate hardship under the Franco regime, five engineers were encouraged by their priest to set up a cooperative foundry to make small paraffin stoves. The priest was inspired by the Rochdale cooperative in the United Kingdom.

As the cooperative began to earn money, the profits were turned back into new ventures. What is important about Mondragon is not its profitability, but its commitment to support all its members with employment or education. The structure avoids hierarchies that lead to some members having more power and money than others. Instead, management positions rotate, with new managers given extensive training for their four-year position. In the early days there was a set ratio of salaries throughout Mondragon, with the highest-paid person earning no more than five times the amount the lowest-paid person did. Today the ratio is still less than ten (compare this to the ratio in multinational corporations, where the highest-paid people earn 1,000 times more than the lowest-paid).[1]

Mondragon expanded into household appliances and became the major manufacturer of large appliances in Spain, as well as the largest cooperative in the world. Over the years it added a bank, schools, a university, health services, a research organization, and factories manufacturing a wide range of consumer goods.

All workers must loan a portion of their annual pay to the cooperative (they take it back if they leave). If there is a downturn in the economy, workers are not laid off, but are sent for further education or training. Each year, 10 percent of the profits are given to charity.

The town welcomes some 50,000 visitors annually. When I visited I was amazed that a manufacturing center could look like a university. It was nestled into a green valley, with no smokestacks or bleak, dingy buildings. Cycling and hiking trails wove through the parklike surroundings. The young tour guide told us that people usually stay for life or leave Mondragon after about two weeks because they either love the experience or find it intolerable. Perhaps that is an important insight into why some attempts to duplicate the Mondragon structure have not been successful.

Mondragon, Spain.

58

Support Democracy Movements

When he wrote this in *The Nation* in September 2004, Paul Rogat Loeb was referring to the sustained nonviolent opposition that finally defeated communist rule in Poland in 1989.[1] Over the past 30 years, new democracies have taken over from dictators in 60 countries.[2] More is known today than was known in 1989 about what is needed to support a popular nonviolent movement to bring regime change. Experts like Gene Sharp and Robert Helvey have studied successful actions in many countries and offer their expertise to dissident movements.

Dissent is now commonly supported by people outside a country. This support may include raising the profile of the dissident leaders in the foreign media because publicity affords them some measure of protection. Unions are often key players in resistance to oppression. Strikes, slowdowns, and sit-ins confront the government and disrupt "business as usual." In South Africa, for example, strikes, boycotts of white businesses, and withdrawal of foreign investment forced the apartheid regime to acknowledge that the economy was collapsing. The business community eventually became a central agent for change. The Rose Revolution in Georgia and the Orange Revolution in Ukraine were highly organized, sophisticated actions in which civil society took charge with financial and logistical support from outside the country.

George Soros's Open Societies Institute, and several American and European agencies, support democracy movements with expertise and funds. This outside involvement helps put the

As the Polish activists discovered, we gain something profound when we stand up for our beliefs, just as part of us dies when we know that something is wrong, yet do nothing. We could call this radical dignity. We don't have to tackle every issue, but if we remain silent in the face of cruelty, injustice, and oppression, we sacrifice part of our soul.

— Paul Rogat Loeb

government into the hands of the people and gives citizens responsibility for maintaining public participation in a functioning democracy. Accepting foreign nongovernmental intervention in a leadership struggle is fraught with risk because, unfortunately, no one can guarantee that the person who replaces a dictator will be wise and effective, and the interveners may have their own agenda. At the very least, the people begin with free, fair, monitored elections, backed by public expectations of transparency and an end to corruption. After that they face the same problems that all democracies face in keeping the system honest.

The struggle to establish labor unions under oppressive regimes is dangerous because often police or paramilitary forces threaten, kidnap, or murder labor organizers. Gene Bruskin, spokesman for U.S. Labor Against the War, notes that American unions have traditionally been very patriotic and have not taken up foreign policy issues.[3] Many union members are veterans, National Guard members, or have family serving in the armed forces.

Although unions lined up to support President Bush after September 11, 2001, the Patriot Act made many members nervous because they believed it could be used against unions. Union leaders began questioning the wisdom of the Iraq war for several reasons — a major one being that the Bush administration

- Albert Einstein Institute (Gene Sharp and Robert Helvey articles): www.aeinstein.org
- Common Dreams: www.commondreams.org
- *The Impossible will Take a Little While* by Paul Rogat Loeb, Basic Books, 2004
- Open Society Institute: www.soros.org
- Rose Revolution: www.en.wikipedia.org/wiki/Rose_Revolution
- *ScholarForum* (The fall 2004 issue of this Open Society publication is about the Rose Revolution): www.soros.org/initiatives/scholarship/ articles_publications/publications/sforum9_20050705
- U.S. Labor Against the War: www.uslaboragainstwar.org

has a strong anti-labor policy. Airport screeners had been in the process of unionizing before the attacks on the World Trade Buildings. The government then made them federal employees without union rights and threatened to intervene for security reasons if a West Coast labor dispute led to a strike by the International Longshoreman Workers Union.

Grassroots activists in diverse labor unions passed antiwar resolutions and organized U.S. Labor Against the War in January 2003, before the bombing of Iraq began.[4] The outspoken criticism of the war by military families and veterans helped reassure union members that supporting peace is patriotic and indicates support for the troops. U.S. Labor Against the War grew dramatically and by 2005 had 120 affiliated

organizations representing about two million people.

In a historic vote in July 2005, the AFL-CIO convention passed a resolution that applauded the bravery and courage of American soldiers in Iraq and called for their rapid return. The resolution addressed the needs of returning veterans and union members and emphasized the commitment of the AFL-CIO to support Iraqi trade unionists.

Iraqi trade unionists attended and spoke at the AFL-CIO convention about the lack of labor rights in Iraq under both Saddam Hussein and the occupation. Labor leaders in Iraq were, and continue to be, targeted for assassination.

U.S. Labor Against the War has established a fund to support Iraqi trade unions and accepts donations to the fund on their website.

DANIEL (DANYLO) SIKORSKYI

Orange Revolution Standoff at Odessa, Ukraine, 2004.

59

Don't Pay for War

Non-cooperation with evil is as much a responsibility as cooperation with good.

— Mahatma Gandhi

"War is big business" is a cliché that underlines the role of money in the perpetuation of the war system. World military spending in 2004 topped $1 trillion. The United States' military budget contributed 47 percent of that trillion dollars.[1] US military spending has increased rapidly between 2002 and 2004 because of the global war on terror. Most of the money is supplementary appropriations for military operations in Afghanistan and Iraq.

Don't Buy into the Military Mindset
Whole industries outside the defense manufacturers profit from the militarization of the planet.

- Ad agencies support the collaboration between the film industry and the Pentagon to produce films that glorify war as the ultimate testosterone adventure. *Top Gun* is a

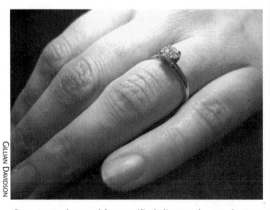

Consumer demand for certified diamonds can dry up the market for smuggled stones that fund conflict.

GILLIAN DAVIDSON

powerful recruiting tool, as are many of the endless stream of war movies.

- Computer and video games simulate combat to offer a virtual — and risk-free — experience of war to young males.

- Media networks present government press releases without independent investigation of their truth.

- Selective journalism offers a narrow range of opinions masked as balanced coverage.

All these industries sell war by building fear and by dehumanizing the enemy we are told is threatening us. The good news is that people are resisting propaganda and the control of information by producing alternative media sources that bypass the mainstream media (see Solution 48).

Don't Buy Conflict Resources
Sometimes we don't know that what we buy is financing war. Diamonds, for example, are marketed as a symbol of purity and love, but the diamond trade has funded bloody wars in Sierra Leone, Angola, Liberia, and the Democratic Republic of the Congo (DRC). Over 3.7 million people have died in those wars. The total world trade in diamonds is valued at nearly $12 billion a year.

A small organization called Global Witness began a campaign in 1998 to stop the sale of blood diamonds. They called on governments and corporations, especially De Beers, to certify that the source of their diamonds was legal and that their sale did not fund armed conflict. In

- Global Witness: www.globalwitness.org
- Global Witness's pledge against conflict diamonds: www.globalwitness.org/campaigns/diamonds/diamond_pledge.php
- Co-operative Bank (Ethics in Action): www.co-operativebank.co.uk
- Survival (An organization working to restore tribal rights to resources): www.survival-international.org

the beginning, De Beers was reluctant to become involved in the campaign against blood diamonds, but by 2003 it joined because it recognized that a consumer boycott would undermine the image of diamonds as a symbol of love.

Civil society, governments, and corporations developed the Kimberley Process to certify the origin of each diamond sold. It is difficult to track rough diamonds because miners of alluvial diamonds are mostly freelancers who make less than a dollar a day. Diamonds are small and easy to smuggle, so the miners are not likely to be motivated to comply with certification. "Until Africa's diamond diggers earn a fair wage, diamonds will always be a destabilizing factor in these countries," according to Ian Smillie from Partnership Africa Canada.

The Kimberley Process still faces technical and political obstacles. Many governments have not submitted the reports they have agreed to supply, and many do not allow independent monitoring of their reporting. On the other hand, diamond sellers are finding that consumers who demand certification for the diamonds they purchase make a significant impact.

Global Witness and other NGOs continue to demand an end to the illegal trade in diamonds and the abuse of human rights that accompanies the business. Supermodel Iman, a Somali, resigned from her role as the face of De Beers because of the company's practice of pushing the Kalahari bushmen off their land to make way for a diamond mine.

We need to let our governments know that we expect them to comply with the full intent of the Kimberley Process, not just the words. That means we expect them to close the loopholes in the mining and selling of rough diamonds.

Other resources that are illegally used to raise funds for war are gold, oil, rubber, tin, coltan, and timber. Coltan is a mineral found in the Democratic Republic of Congo that is essential to the manufacture of cell phones. Some development experts talk about the "resource curse," which refers to the fact that countries with the greatest wealth of natural resources are most likely to have armed groups fighting for control.

The obstacles to stopping the illegal trade in conflict resources reflect the weaknesses of the states involved. They need impartial justice and law enforcement systems; they need to be able to prevent bribery, repatriate stolen funds, and end money-laundering schemes involving foreign firms and the government. Weak states need help to establish functioning bureaucracies, with accountability built into the system, that might be able to track conflict resources and prevent their sale to fund war. They need the help of the rest of the world to support their reforms. As activists, we can question those who claim an armed conflict is the result of ethnic or religious differences and look instead for competition for a valued resource. And when we make recommendations for action to end a war, we must take into account the fuel that keeps it going. (For more on this, see Solution 60.)

60

Stop the Illegal Money Flow

> The basic test of economic justice is what happens to the most vulnerable groups in society.
>
> — World Council of Churches

Many conflicts begin as a result of one group's grievances against another. The conflict is often funded by the illegal sale of resources such as diamonds, timber, rare minerals, gold, or illegal drugs. As time passes, all too often the original grievances become secondary to control of the income from these illegal sales. That control becomes the purpose of the conflict.

Legitimate businesses must ensure that the products they import for sale are not from illegal trade that supports armed conflict — that is, they must not become part of the money-laundering cycle. Consumers can look for products whose origins are certified and call for more such designations.

Conflict Timber

Conflict timber is timber that has been illegally traded at some point by armed groups either to fund conflict or for personal gain. Conflict timber brings hundreds of millions of dollars in revenue that bypasses government and goes to buy arms. The chaos of warfare means the forests are poorly monitored, and when timber is stripped from the hillsides, it can lead to floods and landslides that make the area unsuitable for agriculture or habitation.

The importance of outside intervention to stop the trade in conflict timber is evident in the case of Global Witness in Cambodia.[1] In 1995, an undercover investigation by Global Witness revealed a multimillion-dollar trade in timber being shipped across the Cambodia/Thai border. Funding from Thai logging companies was supplying $10 to $20 million a month to the Khmer Rouge in its civil war against the Cambodian government.

When Global Witness released its findings, the Thai government was forced to close the border. By the end of 1996, the Khmer Rouge began to disintegrate due to lack of funds, and its troops defected to the government side. Ultimately the civil war in Cambodia ended in 1998. Global Witness has remained a key player in Cambodia because forest management continues to be a major problem. The Cambodian government has appointed Global Witness to act as an independent monitor of the forest sector. As in many other weak states, lack of transparency, poor governance, and corruption are obstacles to good forest management. Global Witness also works in Liberia, Cameroon, and the Democratic Republic of Congo on conflict resources.

Consumers should be aware that garden furniture from Vietnam is often made of timber illegally imported from Cambodia. The Forest Stewardship Council (FSC) identifies timber that does not come from the destruction of Cambodian forest. Garden furniture from Vietnam that is made from legal timber has an FSC logo.

- Forest Stewardship Council: www.fsc.org
- Friends of the Earth: www.foei.org
- Global Witness in Cambodia: www.globalwitness.org/campaigns/forests/cambodia
- UN Office on Drugs and Crime: www.unodc.org

(c) FSCA A.C.

The FSC logo indicates forests that have been certified in accordance with the rules of the Forest Stewardship Council.

Drug Trade

The arms trade and armed conflict are sustained by international crime, often using funds from the sale of illegal drugs. The international drug trade was worth $321 billion in 2004, and the cycle of crime supported by this trade includes the trafficking of women and children, as well as the illegal arms trade.

Criminals have to disguise their illegal profits in order to benefit from them. The process of moving their funds through what appear to be legitimate businesses is called money laundering. The UN estimates that the total amount of money laundered each year is between $500 billion and $1 trillion. The consequences of money laundering are bad for business, governance, and the rule of law. The UN Office on Drugs and Crime provides information on current international initiatives to combat money laundering.[2]

Money laundering empowers corruption and organized crime. Corrupt officials have to be able to launder bribes, kickbacks, and money siphoned from the public purse. Terrorist groups use money-laundering channels to get cash to buy weapons. To stop this corruption, the international finance system must find, freeze, and forfeit the money laundered.

Stopping the laundry cycle is becoming ever more difficult as transactions occur rapidly by computer, and the layers of transactions across borders obscure the trail of funds. Financial deregulation and the existence of countries willing to be havens for money laundering destabilize the legitimate movement of money internationally. The price to our societies is the breakdown of law; the degradation of communities where crime, prostitution, and drug dealing increase; and the increase of violence.

Most of the young people I meet seem not to be aware that buying illegal drugs supports the sale of women and children into prostitution, and facilitates the flow of arms to warlords in poor countries. Drug education should include more than just information about the effects on the body of ingesting mind-altering substances. It should also include details of the consequences of participating in this cycle of crime, enslavement, and death (see Solution 64).

61

Take a Stand

> Peace is not the product of a victory or a command. It has no finishing line, no final deadline, no fixed definition of achievement. Peace is a never-ending process, the work of many decisions.
>
> — Oscar Arias

Cities as Nuclear-Weapon-Free Zones

Many cities around the world have taken a stand by declaring themselves nuclear-weapon-free zones (NWFZ), even though some are in nuclear weapons states. The city of Arcata, California, is a powerful example of what cities can do for peace and disarmament. Not only did the city become a NWFZ, but it also established a NWFZ Commission with broad responsibilities that include assisting people in the smooth conversion of jobs and facilities affected by the new policy, educating the public regarding nuclear weapons, and collaborating with other NWFZs in the world. The commission reports that more than 250 cities worldwide and 75 Native American nations have declared themselves NWFZ.

Some ports refuse to allow nuclear-capable ships in their harbors. This includes some US cities, like Boston and New York, which refuse to admit US warships into their harbors! In 1975, the City of Kobe, Japan, declared itself free of nuclear weapons.[1] Before any warship can be admitted to the port, it must produce a certificate that declares it is not carrying nuclear weapons. Because the US Navy will neither confirm nor deny the presence of nuclear weapons, US warships are not admitted to Kobe. The city is able to enforce this policy because Japanese law gives cities jurisdiction over their ports. Although the United States requests that the policy be changed because of the war on terror, Kobe continues to refuse.

The mayor of Santa Fe, New Mexico, advocates that cities become nuclear weapons inspectors, despite the fact that New Mexico is host to two nuclear weapons labs, Sandia and Los Alamos.[2] It is also one of the poorest states in the United States.

Cities Boycott Nuclear Weapons Manufacturers

More than 20 years ago, Tacoma, Washington, banned city investment in, or purchases from, nuclear industries. The city of Arcata reviews its purchase orders to avoid buying non-nuclear materials from nuclear weapons contractors for any amount over $500. If the city purchasing agent can locate an alternative source for the items that charges less than 5 percent more, the nuclear weapons contractor is notified and is given 45 days to appeal.

The city has posted a list of the companies it boycotts and a long list of companies it is currently investigating.

Companies boycotted by Arcata, CA

Chrysler	IBM
General Electric	ITT
General Motors	Rockwell International
Hewlett Packard	Unisys

Peace Messenger Cities

The International Association of Peace Messenger Cities was established by the mayors of Hiroshima and Nagasaki in 1982 to recognize and encourage the role that cities can play in creating a culture of peace. The UN names Peace

- Find the cost to your US city of the war on Iraq: www.nationalpriorities.org
- Cities for Peace: www.ips-dc.org/citiesforpeace
- Cities for Progress: www.citiesforprogress.org
- City of Arcata: www.arcatacityhall.org/nukefree/index.html

Messenger Cities, and there are now almost 700 in 110 countries. New Haven, Connecticut, is a Peace Messenger City and became the first US sister city to a Vietnamese city. Its sister is Hue, Vietnam. New Haven also has a Peace Commission responsible for addressing violence, gun control, and other common urban issues. Other Peace Messenger Cities in the United States include Atlanta, San Francisco, and Concord.

Cities for Peace

Before the bombing of Iraq began in March 2003, 167 US cities passed resolutions opposing the US actions. Cities continue to call for an end to the war and the return of the troops from Iraq. The website of Cities for Peace keeps an updated list of US cities that have passed these resolutions. It also has a useful toolkit for activists that outlines ways to lobby your city council and suggests what you can do if the council won't address a resolution you propose.

Bradford, UK, has proclaimed itself a City for Peace. It has established many initiatives that help build peace in the city, ranging from a peace garden, peace awards, and a peace festival to campaigns for nuclear disarmament, combating racism, and challenging environmental abuse. The city pledges to promote justice, equality, and respect.

City Peace and Justice Committees

The City of Vancouver Peace and Justice Committee includes city councilors as well as leaders of peace and justice groups in the city. Its goals are to develop closer relationships with other cities working for peace and justice, to

work closely with peace and justice groups in the city, to collect and exchange information with other municipalities, to consider initiatives to reduce the possibility of war and ensure justice, and to establish Vancouver as a City of Peace and Justice. The work of the Peace and Justice Committee led to the World Peace Forum taking place in Vancouver in 2006.

Call your city hall and ask if your city is a nuclear-weapon-free zone and if it belongs to these international organizations. Find out if you have a city peace and justice committee. Then write a letter or speak to the council to encourage council members to take these steps.

Vancouver Canada is a Nuclear Weapon Free Zone and a Peace Messenger City.

62

Become a City of Peace

> Peace is an environment where conflicts are resolved without violence, where people are free, not exploited, living so they can grow to their full potential.
>
> — Gerard Vanderhaar,
> professor of religion and peace studies at
> Christian Brothers University in Memphis

Over 50 percent of the world's population lives in cities. Cities face, more immediately than nation-states, the crises of pollution, traffic, garbage, overcrowding, poverty, and disease. Add to this natural and human-made disasters, and you can understand why cities responded to a competition for 100-year sustainability plans. The competition, sponsored by the International Gas Union, had a profound impact on the participants because they found the 100-year view fundamentally changed their concept of sustainability, and they recognized that without peace, sustainability was impossible.

Suppose that more cities decided to take peace seriously and incorporate it into a 100-year plan for a sustainable city. What would that mean?

It would mean putting future generations at the forefront of their thinking and setting new priorities to build a decent society. It would mean considering justice as a fundamental criterion for policy makers. It would mean setting city policies to benefit the most vulnerable in the city and reduce the gap between rich and poor. Above all, perhaps, it would mean balancing the current emphasis on the rights of the individual with a focus on the good of our collective society.

Build economic justice: Over 100 years there should be time to restore the conscience of our communities and develop policies that reduce the income gap between the wealthy elite and the poor.

Care for the vulnerable: Early in a 100-year planning process, cities recognize their responsibility for the most vulnerable members of their communities — the poor and marginalized, minorities and women — and plan governance structures that engage them in solving common problems.

Provide quality social services: Surely it will not be 100 years before 45 million people in US cities have access to publicly funded health care. Quality education, daycare, and the social safety net can be publicly funded, and a progressive tax system can be implemented to cover the costs.

Provide for rights of minorities and women: When building a common future is a priority, policy decisions reflect a change in perspective. Cities see value in protecting workers against racial and gender discrimination, corporate greed, tax loopholes, and exploitation.

Build community programs that unite diverse groups: Cities planning for long-term sustainability strive for vibrant neighborhoods

Livable cities take a hundred year view. Jogger on Kitsilano beach, Vancouver Canada.

KA DAVIDSON PHOTOGRAPHY

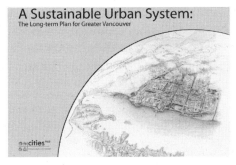

A Sustainable Urban System:
The Long-term Plan for Greater Vancouver

cities

Become a city of Peace.

- citiesPLUS 100-Year Plan for Greater Vancouver: www.citiesplus.ca
- Imagine Calgary: www.imaginecalgary.ca
- International Centre for Sustainable Cities: www.icsc.ca
- Planning for Long-term Urban Sustainability Network: www.plusnetwork.org

with amateur theater, community arts and music groups, and recreational facilities and parks. They design and support, through a broad tax base and incentives, neighborhoods with green buildings, green roofs, and community gardens that encourage food security as well as companionship. They provide inexpensive meeting space for nonprofit groups and give grants for multicultural projects and events that build bridges in society — like multiethnic festivals, art shows, and singing.

Deal effectively with the criminal drug trade: Healthy cities that are looking to the future recognize that they must deal with drug addiction and alcoholism, not simply to help individuals, but because the crime syndicates that control the drug trade destabilize our societies. Cities have reason to take real action on money laundering, corruption, and international crime.

Recognize service: Cities of the future need to build positive communities that engage citizens in hands-on volunteer work for the betterment of their community. Cities can move in that direction today if they recognize the value of community service by giving awards, especially to youth. Cities can offer scholarships to young people who provide volunteer hours during the summer holidays. Victor Frankl, the world-renowned psychiatrist who survived a Nazi death camp, said that service to others was the most powerful source of meaning in life, even for those who knew they faced imminent death.

Teach nonviolent conflict resolution: How can cities move to their ideal of peaceful, just, and sustainable communities? One course is to establish traditions of reconciliation and restorative justice. When all schools teach the principles of nonviolent communication and show how to work through problems, the community will have the language to address new situations.

Build participatory democracy: Over the past 20 years, the need for participatory multiparty processes has emerged as a common ground in the field of sustainable development. Sustainable cities encourage participatory democracy with town hall meetings and citizen input on round tables, inquiries, and forward-planning projects. They ensure that women, minorities, and the disenfranchised are represented, and that elections are fair and not influenced by big money.

Build tolerance for religious diversity: In the next 100 years, migration will change the mix of cultural, ethnic, and religious traditions in most cites. This offers an opportunity to create new ways to resolve conflict based on the ethical principles of the world's great religions.

Call your city hall and ask if the city has a 100-year plan. If it has one, and it seems to be on the right track to be sustainable, congratulate the mayor and council and find out where you can help. If it doesn't have one, call upon the council to develop a long-term plan. You can contribute to that plan using some of the ideas here, and join with others to give community input.

175

63

Become a Partner City — Adopt a Town

As we take a few of the million small steps to hope, we find others on the same road, bringing hope with them. After the bombing of Afghanistan and Iraq, people in many different countries began to build new relationships with communities that they had never heard of before.

Sister Cities

The Sister Cities movement began 50 years ago as a response to US president Dwight D. Eisenhower's call for people-to-people exchanges with cities outside the United States. The movement promotes peace through mutual respect and understanding, focusing on sustainable development, youth and education, arts and culture, humanitarian assistance, and economic growth programs. There are now more than 2,300 communities in 130 countries involved as Sister Cities.

The September 11, 2001, attacks in the United States led to a new initiative called "Sister Cities United for Peace and Friendship." This move to deepen relationships between Americans and non-Americans brought 33 percent more US communities into partnerships with towns and cities in the Middle East, and more individuals into the Coalition for Citizen Diplomacy, which organizes citizen exchanges.

The coalition uses person-to-person dialogues and exchanges to build understanding in both directions. It organizes community summits around the United States to help groups develop exchange programs, become host communities, and build dialogues. The summits involve youth, faith-based groups, government, educators, ethnic heritage groups, and the media.

The world has the answers to terrorism. They lie in a million small steps that lead people toward hope rather than misguided dogma and ideology. Surely we don't want to just sit here waiting for the next bomb to blow up.

— Jody Paterson,
Victoria Times Colonist, July 15, 2005

Adopt a Town

Three Canadian nonprofit societies founded a project called Adopt a Town, which connects Canadian cities with towns in Iraq and Afghanistan.[1] The director of the project is Yarub Al Shiraida, an Iraqi-Canadian who lives in Edmonton, Alberta.

One of the projects connects Calgary, Alberta, with Jurf Al-Sakhr, a district about 31 miles (50 kilometers) southwest of Baghdad that serves about 40,000 people. Jurf Al-Sakhr had a poor water supply and no facilities where children could play or where girls could go to school. The priorities for the Iraqis were a medical clinic, a water treatment plant, a medium-sized school for girls, a playground, and a small community center. They needed about US$365,000. The project touched a nerve with Calgarians, and at the request of the imam of the district, Adopt a Town developed an integrated community project. The Calgary city government, the local mosque and Moslem Council, and ordinary citizens are now involved in fundraising and education of both Iraqis and Canadians.

Adopt a Community

Many people outside the area ravaged by the tsunami of December 2004 responded by adopting a community in need. Many of the communities in Aceh or Sri Lanka had also suffered from long-term warfare. The small Australian town of Montville adopted a school in Sri Lanka, just inside the Tamil territory. The

- Adopt a Town: www.candil.ca/home/projects/adoptatown.php
- Coalition for Citizen Diplomacy: www.citizen-diplomacy.org/docs/CCD_Planning_A_Summit.pdf
- Multifaith Action Society of BC: www.multifaithaction.org
- Sister Cities: www.sister-cities.org

school was badly damaged, and only one toilet remained to serve 500 students and staff. The girls in the Montville school learned that older Tamil girls were likely to quit school if there were not private toilet cubicles. As unlikely as it sounds, providing toilets became an organizing goal for the Montville girls, and they raised $6,000 through a day-long soccer tournament and appeal. A letter exchange between schools is teaching Montville students about life in a developing country, the conflict between Tamils and Sinhalese, and the impact of a natural disaster. The Tamil students are learning that people outside their own culture care enough about them to dedicate themselves to a long-term partnership.

Community Links

The small municipality of Langford, BC, in Canada has an activist fire department. Volunteer firefighters traveled to New York a few days after September 11, taking funds raised in their community and offering help to the New York Fire Department. Their gesture of solidarity was warmly received in New York.

In 2003, the Langford fire department began to explore ways to help Afghan people get on their feet again. Together with the local Rotary club, it collected fire equipment valued at over $350,000 and took it to Kabul to help restore the fire department there. Three men traveled with the equipment and, with assistance from the Canadian military in Kabul, trained the Afghan firemen.

These are small steps, but they are multiplied in community after community where people are reaching across the divides of religion and ethnicity to build hope. You can adopt a community or a town through a local school or a women's or religious group. Supporting local interfaith connections is another way to build understanding.

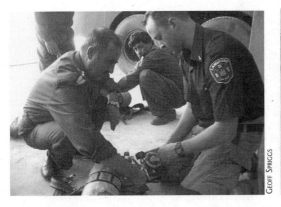

Langford Fire Chief Bob Beckett demonstrates donated firefighting equipment to an Afghan colleague.

S.A.F.E. Canadians Sending Afghanistan Firefighting Equipment is the project of the Langford Fire Department.

64

Try Something New

> Peace comes from being able to contribute the best that we have, and all that we are, toward creating a world that supports everyone. But it is also securing the space for others to contribute the best that they have and all that they are.
>
> — Hafsat Abiola, human rights and democracy advocate from Nigeria

Stubborn Peace

Some cities resist violence, even when confronted by injustice that caused other cities to riot. Ashutosh Varshney studied pairs of cities in India that do and do not riot in order to unravel the strengths of the non-rioters.[1] Varshney found that the non-rioting cities had many civic associations that united groups of people who might otherwise have faced tensions of race, religion, or ethnicity. They had business ties, reading clubs, mixed trade unions, professional associations, and recreational clubs. These links seemed to bind people to each other and make them less likely to rise up in anger against one another.

Transformative Thinking

Who would ever have guessed that Bogotá, Colombia, would be a world leader in urban transformation? The city of seven million people was certainly a leader in poverty, violent crime, traffic congestion, poor water stewardship, and pollution. Then the city elected a mayor, Enrique Penalosa, whose radical policies transformed Bogotá.

Ten years ago, the people who lived in Bogotá hated their city and its downward spiral into violence, drugs, and crime. What is more, they felt powerless to create a better future. The *New York Times* reports that now Bogotá is safer than Washington, DC, or Baltimore.[2]

Former mayor Penalosa noted that while 15 percent of the citizens had cars, 90 percent had children. He concluded, therefore, that the city should make children a priority, not cars. He said that improving public transportation is a sign of respect for the ordinary citizens who do not have cars. It is also a clear statement that the city values community and equality.

The city was committed to ensuring dignity for all citizens. It built housing for the poor, providing all public services for them. It built more than 1,000 parks and community spaces, which, in turn, encourages people to talk to each other, especially in poor areas. The mayor said that parks are a sign of true democracy, where all citizens, regardless of income, can meet as equals. The city built a network of paths and sidewalks for walking and cycling. All parks, libraries, and schools are accessible by public transit, bicycle, or foot.

© Project for Public Spaces, Inc. www.pps.org

Walking and cycling path, in Bogotá

To create a more egalitarian society, Bogotá made public transportation fast, comfortable, and convenient. By increasing the gasoline tax, the city was able to pay for the improved bus system. The buses are articulated and can hold up to 165 passengers. People pay as they enter the station rather than as they enter the bus. Platforms are at bus floor level so people can enter easily, and there are several doors down the side of the bus so that people can enter and leave without fighting through crowds. The mixture of express and local buses keeps traffic moving efficiently.

Every day, 40 percent of cars are restricted from circulating during rush hours, and 75 miles (120 kilometers) of roads are closed for seven hours every Sunday, when 1.5 million people come out to cycle, jog, and stroll. There is even a car-free day in February.

Mayor Penalosa's innovations were so successful that the mayors who followed him, Antanas Mockus (see Solution 39) and Luis Eduardo Garzon, have continued creative social policies. Garzon, the current mayor, is focused on fighting corruption, increasing transparency, improving health care and education, and initiating a new program to eliminate the drug trade. He opposes the US policies of the war on drugs and favors these alternative steps.

- Two articles on Bogotá's transformation: www.grist.org/news/maindish/2002/04/04/of/
- www.porelpaisquequeremos.com

- Stop the fumigation of coca plantations and instead manually remove the plants.
- Decriminalize the small growers and put in place a program to plant replacement crops that will provide them with a decent living.
- Deal with the international co-responsibility for the drug trade. Address money laundering, gun running, and international organized crime.
- Address drug use as a health issue. Personal drug use and possession would continue to be decriminalized "based on the constitutional principles of personal autonomy and free development of the personality."[3]

Decriminalizing drugs would require the support of the entire international community, but it might bring organized crime, the drug trade, and money laundering under control. The criminal syndicates divert close to a trillion dollars a year from the legal global economy. The present system to control drug trafficking doesn't work, and it promotes other brutal, destructive, illegal activity. It is time to move to a new strategy.

What we do locally to build strong, inclusive communities has a global impact. We can reduce our dependence on oil, reduce crime, improve our health, restore the green areas and waterways, and at the same time reduce violence and alienation. Let's get radical.

65

Join the Mayors' Campaign Against Nuclear Weapons

> The significant problems we face cannot be solved at the same level of thinking we were at when we created them.
>
> — Albert Einstein

Because our governments are not taking genuine action toward nuclear disarmament, cities are coming together to put pressure on nuclear weapons states. Dr. Tadatoshi Akiba, the mayor of Hiroshima, is an articulate spokesman who is asking mayors from all over the world to sign a declaration calling for the elimination of nuclear weapons. More than a thousand mayors have signed the declaration.

In May 2005, 167 representatives of cities, including 51 mayors, attended the Nuclear Non-Proliferation Treaty Review in New York. Mayor Akiba spoke to the General Assembly of the UN on behalf of cities. Cities are concerned because they would be the targets in the event of a nuclear war.

Even though the United States and Russia are now trading partners, they still have more than 4,000 missiles directed at each other's cities. If one were launched by accident, or by misinterpretation of a radar screen, millions of people would die as soon as it hit its target. Tens of thousands of missiles would immediately be launched in retaliation, and that exchange would almost certainly bring about nuclear winter and the end of life on Earth (see "What Is at Stake?" in the Introduction).

While far-sighted cities can anticipate, and create long-term plans for responding to, a variety of crises or disasters, they cannot prepare for a nuclear attack. Such an event would destroy the infrastructure of water, electricity, communications, hospitals, and transportation. No emergency plan could have an impact on the scale of destruction, the number of burn victims, or the radioactive cloud that would drift on the wind and produce black rain to fall on other cities downwind.

The Mayors for Peace will not be stopped by the inaction of the nuclear weapons states. They plan to press for negotiations similar to the Ottawa process that led to the banning of antipersonnel landmines (see Solution 30). Their ongoing campaign will last until our cities no longer face the threat of nuclear devastation.

The mayors pursue their goal through various conferences of mayors and municipalities, and they welcome suggestions for new initiatives that cities can take to advance their fight for the elimination of nuclear weapons. This is an ideal government/civil society project for local groups to join.

Action Plan

Go to the website of Mayors for Peace and check the list of mayors who have signed. If your mayor has signed, let him or her know that you appreciate the support for this initiative and suggest ways that your city might take another step, perhaps by becoming a nuclear-weapon-free zone or by posting signs on the roads entering your city that indicate its membership in Mayors for Peace.

If your mayor is not on the list, copy the covenant, program, and a registration form from

---

• Mayors for Peace: www.mayorsforpeace.org

the Mayors for Peace website and ask your city to join. When it comes time for the motion to be discussed, organize as many people as possible to call local councilors beforehand and attend the meeting to show their support.

If the city councilors vote in support of the covenant, your mayor will send a letter to the Conference Secretariat stating that your city supports the "Program to Promote Solidarity of Cities towards the Total Abolition of Nuclear Weapons" and would like to join Mayors for Peace (there is no charge). Shortly thereafter, the Secretariat will send a certificate confirming membership in Mayors for Peace.

Swedish doctor Christina Vigre Lundius with Tadatoshi Akiba, Mayor of Hiroshima.

Covenant of Mayors for Peace

In August, 1945, the first nuclear weapons ever used in human history caused an indescribable catastrophe for the cities of Hiroshima and Nagasaki. Even now a number of A-bomb survivors are still suffering physically, psychologically, and socially from various after-effects. Nevertheless, nuclear weapons have not been abolished; they continue to threaten human existence. Our goal is to maintain environments that enable citizens to lead safe, cultural lives, and to contribute to the attainment of lasting world peace. To this end, we pledge to make every effort to create an inter-city solidarity transcending national boundaries and ideological differences in order to achieve the total abolition of nuclear weapons and avert the recurrence of the Hiroshima and Nagasaki tragedies.

We agree to the intent of the "Program to Promote Solidarity of Cities towards the Total Abolition of Nuclear Weapons" proposed by Hiroshima and Nagasaki.

Signed

Officer

City

Date

66

Reduce the Gap Between Rich and Poor

A lan Greenspan's warning that the income gap is a destabilizing influence on democracy argues against unrestrained capitalism. The danger in allowing the free market to determine policy is that the financial bottom line does not have a conscience; people do. We form societies and nations to provide mutual protection and support. We expect governments to enact policies that ensure, at a minimum, that all people have access to food, shelter, education, basic health care, and the opportunity for gainful employment. However, the policies of the George W. Bush administration favor the flow of money to the wealthy, at the expense of the vast majority of Americans.

The anti-globalization movement opposes free-market capitalism because it does not protect the people from the ruthlessness of profit

> The income gap between the rich and the rest of the US population has become so wide, and is growing so fast, that it might eventually threaten the stability of democratic capitalism itself.
> — Alan Greenspan, chairman of the US Federal Reserve, quoted in the *Christian Science Monitor*, June 14, 2005

seeking without social and environmental constraints. In 2005, the people of France and the Netherlands rejected the constitution of the European Union because they did not believe that the EU could meld market-based competition with a compassionate welfare state.

> There are only two families in the world, as my grandmother used to say: the haves and the have-nots.
> — Sancho Panza in *Don Quixote de la Mancha* by Miguel de Cervantes

The gap between rich and poor is a major indicator of the state of human development in a country.[1] In general, countries with a very rich elite and a large population of poor people are less likely to be functioning democracies. In such countries, women are usually not represented in government, infant mortality rates tend to be higher, literacy levels are low, and life expectancy is poor. In the United States, inequality once seemed tolerable because America was the land of equal opportunity, but this is no longer so. Two decades ago, an American CEO earned 39 times as much as the average worker; today he pulls in 1,000 times as much.[2]

People in countries like Brazil, Argentina, Venezuela, and Bolivia, which have a large gap between rich and poor, are demanding governments that will address the injustice created by wealthy elites that exploit the resources of the country for their own

Quality of life and sense of well-being are better in countries with a minimal gap between rich and poor. (Copenhagen).

- Human Development Index: hdr.undp.org
- Peace Child (Human Development Index for children): www.peacechild.org

benefit. The populace was particularly angry at the attempt to privatize the water supply in Bolivia.

Venezuela has repeatedly re-elected a left-wing president, Hugo Chavez, despite opposition attempts to unseat him in a coup and through a referendum. Chavez has launched a series of initiatives that support local communities, bypassing the entrenched bureaucracy in education, health care, media, food production, and marketing.[3] Communities take ownership of the initiatives to provide services at the local level. Venezuela has oil revenues to support the reforms that Chavez is trying to implement, and his revolution is stimulating other Latin American countries to attempt similar reforms.

Reversing the impact of neoconservative policies will require action on many fronts:

- Remove the tax cuts for the wealthy and increase their share of taxation.
- Eliminate sales taxes except on luxury goods.
- Require employers to pay benefits to part-time workers.
- Ensure gender pay equity.
- Increase educational opportunities for marginalized youth.
- Increase affirmative action for employment of minorities in work above the base level.
- Increase social services for single parents, the unemployed, and the handicapped.
- Provide universal public health care.

- Provide affordable housing.
- Improve public transit by making it attractive, inexpensive, and convenient.
- Increase taxes on gasoline to discourage the use of cars and increase the use of public transit.
- Support alternative, sustainable energy sources, especially decentralized forms.
- Increase funding for preschool head-start programs and universal daycare.
- Provide school lunch programs, especially in inner cities.
- Support reform in the justice and penal systems to emphasize restorative justice and the reintegration of ex-prisoners into society.
- Provide sex education, family planning, AIDS prevention, and birth control free of charge.
- Promote values of community, sharing, and supporting one another, rather than advancing the individual above the collective.

If we think about what will make the world better for the seventh generation after us, we will have a better basis from which to evaluate political campaign promises so that we can use our vote to build that future. Perhaps the most important action we can take to promote the values of community is to talk about those values wherever we gather with friends and family. When adults include children as they talk about what is of greatest value to them, children learn to value those things as well.

67

Empower Women

After the genocide, women rolled up their sleeves and began making society work again.

— **Paul Kagame, president of Rwanda**

In most of the world, women play a subservient role to men. This domestic relationship is reflected by governments, where men are dominant at every level. This unbalanced structure of governance has institutionalized both the good and the bad dimensions of how men work in groups. Men tend to set up hierarchical structures that encourage competition for status and position, whereas women generally prefer to emphasize relationships and more level, inclusive organizational structures wherever possible. If necessary, women are often willing to sacrifice status in order to maintain a relationship.

A sign of progress came in ground-breaking elections in December 2005 and January 2006 when Harvard-educated Ellen Johnson-Sirleaf, became president of Liberia, and pediatrician Michelle Bachelet became president of Chile. They

Canadian High Commissioner, Lucie Edwards and Acharya Ramamurti at Mahila Shanti Sena event, 2005.

S HRAMBHARATI (PATNA, INDIA)

are the first women presidents in Africa and Chile. Bachelet promised to make half her cabinet women.

Deborah Tannen, a linguistics professor, videotaped both children and adults in her research into how men and women communicate differently and why we don't understand each other. Her insights into our most basic communications are valuable in understanding the consequences of governments that are dominated by men.

Her research into the interactions between pairs of little boys and pairs of little girls shows that gender differences in communication arise at a very young age. The boys sit side by side, not facing one another, while the girls sit face to face. The boys are quickly distracted, while the girls obediently complete their task. The men watching the children commented that the boys were wonderful and full of life, while the girls were too sweet and obedient. The women observers found the boys annoying because they couldn't stay on task, but they loved the girls because they did what they were told and paid attention to one another.

Tannen's insights help us understand everyday conflicts that seem to be hard-wired into our chromosomes. They are relevant today because almost all official discussions of peace, national security, disarmament, and arms control are among men. Scilla Elworthy, who has been nominated three times for the Nobel Peace Prize, founded the Oxford Research Group in order to identify the individuals who were making decisions regarding nuclear weapons. She found that of the hundreds of people who make those decisions, only a handful are women.

In other words, those people who make decisions about nuclear weapons tend to value status and position and are willing to rely on threat and coercion. They also find it more difficult to consider how to live together peacefully. What is needed is a balance that brings relationships and noncompetitive values into the mix. Without women at the table in greater numbers, we can only hope for the presence of men who are extraordinarily sensitive to relationships and who are able to work without always being one up on their peers. Unfortunately, such men do not usually gravitate to the top of competitive structures like governments.

The exceptional men — like Gandhi, Nelson Mandela, Julius Nyerere, and others — are remembered in history as great statesmen. Our world cannot rely on the chance appearance of a great statesman to save us. We must place more emphasis on the values that support working cooperatively, not competitively, if we are going to survive.

Governments can increase the meaningful participation of women by taking the following steps:

- Appointing women to 50 percent of the positions in key policy-making bodies.

- Asking senior decision makers to develop strategies to reach the 50 percent goal.

- Providing financing for women to attend global meetings and conferences.

- Nominating qualified women to serve on peacekeeping, peacemaking, and peacebuilding

- Oxford Research Group: www.oxfordresearchgroup.org.uk
- "Preparing for Peace: How Wars Could Be Prevented" by Scilla Elworthy, 2001: www.preparingforpeace.org/elworthy.htm
- Acharya Ramamurti's Mahatma Gandhi Lecture on Nonviolence: www.humanities.mcmaster.ca/gandhi/Lectures/2003-Ramamaurti.htm
- *You Just Don't Understand: Women and Men in Conversation* by Deborah Tannen, HarperCollins, 2001

commissions, as agreed in Security Council Resolution 1325 (see Solution 14).

- Including women leaders from NGOs in government delegations, especially those concerned with security, peace, and disarmament.

Tell your elected officials that women are not a special interest group: they are half the population. Women's issues are cross-cutting issues that run through all policy debates.

Indian women elected to positions on local councils are enthusiastic about training for their new roles.

Some of the trainees belonged to the lowest social castes. They were absolutely illiterate, and had never before worked with, or lived, in mixed groups. Let me tell you, Bihar's society is strictly purdah-observing. It should be no wonder to know that 45,000 women — few of them educated — were elected three years ago in a total of about 8.5 thousand panchayats (village councils) of Bihar. This is an indication of how women are fast becoming active members of the male-dominated Indian society.

— Acharya Ramamurti, 2003 Mahatma Gandhi Lecture on Nonviolence, Centre for Peace Studies, McMaster University, Canada

68

Reform the Democratic Process

Democracy can never be taken for granted. The fundamental requirements of free, open elections must be defended vigorously, as the contested results of the two most recent presidential elections in the United States have shown.

The Clean-Vote Chain

Keeping elections fair reminds me of the public heath task of keeping vaccines safe. Health care specialists speak of the "cold chain" that ensures vaccines are kept cool from the time they leave the manufacturer, through storage and transport, until they reach the patient. The same kind of protection is needed for democracy. Elections require a clean-vote chain that begins with how candidates are chosen, so that undue influence of money and power does not prevent fair selection. A clean-vote chain ensures that the processes of registering voters, producing ballots, voting, counting votes, and reporting results are all protected from illegal interference.

- Democracy Watch (International): www.democracywatch.org
- Fair Vote Canada (Includes information on alternative voting systems): www.fairvotecanada.org
- Kids Voting USA (Non-partisan classroom activities): www.kidsvotingusa.org
- League of Women Voters: www.lwv.org
- Project Vote: www.projectvote.org
- Rock the Vote (For young voters): www.rockthevote.com

My friends, I feel the winds of change blowing afresh today. This time they are the winds of democracy, of respect for individual dignity, and for the rule of law. I am convinced this process is irreversible. We must take heed of it, and respect the will of the people, who are insisting more and more that their votes be fairly counted, and their voices clearly heard.

— Kofi Annan, Secretary-General of the UN, speaking about Africa in 2000

American civil society is spearheading reforms that will provide safeguards to ensure a clean-vote chain. The joint requirements for transparency and accountability require an alert public that will persevere to prevent the subversion of democracy.

Maintaining or Reforming the System

We can learn from new democracies that had the choice of which electoral system to adopt as they emerged from dictatorships. Czechs and Kosovars chose the European system over the American because they wanted a parliamentary system with strict limits on campaigning. South Africans adopted a European model more suited to the social welfare state they planned.

Other dimensions of a functioning democracy are the justice system and the media. Democracy requires a fair and free judiciary that is not biased or partisan, and a law-enforcement system that is just and equitable. Democracy also requires a free flow of reliable information, and media sources that are held accountable to standards of truth. Because new legislation cannot guarantee a perfect system, civil society must be the watchdog that keeps the clean-vote chain functioning.

In the past, the American system of government appeared to bring economic benefits that made it the envy of newly emerging nations.

Today, according to journalist and political columnist George Monbiot, "In Sweden, you are three times more likely to rise out of the economic class into which you were born than you are in the US."[1]

Counting the Votes

Electoral reform includes how we decide who wins after we have counted the votes. There are several different ways that countries can weight the votes gained by each candidate. Using the same vote totals, a different person could be elected depending upon which system is used. It is now apparent that the systems used in North America and the United Kingdom are not nearly as likely to express the will of the voters as systems used elsewhere.

In the United States and Canada we use a system called "first past the post." In this system, the candidate who receives the most votes is elected. Most other democracies use a variation that gives weight to people's second choices. There are several alternative systems, one of which is the "single transferable vote." In this method, voters list their preferences in order, and after their first-choice votes are counted, the second and third preferences are given a partial weight that is added to the first-choice votes. This method avoids the split vote that can result when two popular candidates run against each other, split the vote, and allow a third candidate to be elected without gaining a majority of the total vote.

Another system is "proportional representation," in which small parties have an opportunity to win a seat in parliament if they

A graduate of YouthBuild addresses an audience at a political rally in Boston.

reach a threshold percentage of the vote. This is how the first Green Party candidates were elected in Germany.

Reclaiming democracy that has broken down should be easier than claiming democracy from a dictator, because the legal system is already in place to protect the clean-vote chain. Voters can ensure they don't lose the privileges they have, and children can be educated to cherish their legacy. Follow the clean-vote chain in your own community and help fix any damaged links — volunteer to register voters, drive voters to polling stations, be an observer of the voting process, take part in exit polling. Learn about initiatives in your community to change the voting system and participate in those discussions. We can reclaim democracy by joining the action.

69

Disarm Civilians

> It's legal to purchase a fully assembled Uzi machine gun in [the United States] but it's not legal to purchase a fully assembled low-watt radio transmitter.
>
> —Greg Ruggerio, editor and media analyst

The presence of large numbers of small arms in a civilian population increases the risk of injuries and death. In a post-conflict situation, it increases the risk that armed violence will recur. The global trade in small arms and light weapons includes handguns, hunting rifles, assault rifles, and machine guns, as well as rocket-propelled grenades and shoulder-fired missiles. The Worldwatch Institute reports that there are an estimated 639 million small arms in the world, including some 240 million military-style weapons.[1]

According to Worldwatch, hundreds of thousands of people are killed annually by small arms. After a conflict, the situation in a country will remain unstable until the troops are demobilized and reintegrated into society. Not only must the troops be disarmed, but weapons held by the rest of the population must also be collected and destroyed.

Guns are not limited to war zones, but they create war zones in many cities where their numbers are uncontrolled. Many countries have implemented gun buy-back programs to reduce the number of weapons, especially military assault-style weapons.[2]

El Salvador

After 11 years of war in El Salvador, there were an estimated 200,000 to 300,000 military-style weapons in the country. With social disintegration and a culture that accepted gun ownership, the government's gun buy-back program was not working. In 1995, therefore, a group of local businessmen and others created the Patriotic Movement Against Crime in El Salvador.

They approached the government, churches, and NGOs to set up a "goods for guns" program. Funds were raised from local businesses, but the program was so successful the money ran out. The president of El Salvador donated US$285,700 to keep it going. When that money ran out too, more was raised. The program was extensively publicized, and eventually 58,599 weapons, ammunition, and explosives were collected at a cost of $571,400. The program hasn't brought the end of gun violence, but it made a major dent in the supply of weapons and began the slow process of delegitimizing violence.

Australia

Australians were so horrified when a gunman in Port Arthur, Tasmania, killed 35 people in 1996 that they initiated a huge weapons-collection program. It lasted a year, had a budget of

The world's largest public gun destruction project took place in Rio de Janeiro in 2002.

- Coalition for Gun Control: www.guncontrol.ca
- *The Global Gun Epidemic From Saturday Night Specials to AK-47s* by Wendy Cukier and Victor W. Sidel, Praeger Security International, 2006
- International Action Network on Small Arms: www.iansa.org
- Worldwatch Institute: www.worldwatch.org

AUS$500 million, and collected over 643,725 weapons. The program was well promoted by the media and had strong public support. It was accompanied by education programs and tighter legislation. Five years later the homicide rate had fallen 50 percent overall and 57 percent among women.[3]

Brazil

In 2003, the Brazilian Congress prohibited civilians from carrying firearms in public, limiting this right to the armed forces, police, and security guards. Brazil implemented a gun buy-back program in July 2004. Close to 500,000 weapons were turned in and destroyed. In 2004, the number of gun deaths dropped by 8.2 percent — the first drop in 12 years. Brazil held a referendum in 2005 to ban the sale of firearms and ammunition. After an intense campaign by the pro-gun lobby, the referendum was defeated. Gun control advocates plan to press for another referendum in the future because the majority of Brazilians want action to reduce gun violence. They were simply not convinced that that particular referendum would be effective.[4]

United States

The United States has one of the highest rates of gun ownership, with an estimated 192 million legal firearms and an unknown number of illegal weapons. There have been more firearm buybacks in the United States — more than 80 — than anywhere else in the world.[5] In Oakland, CA, the first collection was held at a church in 1995. It was coordinated by the city of Oakland and supported by the police department, the local bar association, the Raiders football team, local law firms, and individuals. Guns were traded for Raiders tickets or used computers and computer training. The program was known as "Byte the Bullet," and some 500 people participated. Three hundred were given promissory notes when the prizes ran out. The police department then raised money to buy more computers to fulfill the pledges.

Canada

Canada passed gun registration legislation in 1995. There was vociferous opposition, but since then the numbers of homicides, robberies with firearms, and firearm injuries and deaths have all been dropping. A 2002 report from Statistics Canada showed the lowest rate of homicides since 1966, at 0.48 per 100,000.[6]

Gun control is an issue where opinions reflect gender differences, with women more likely to support it than men. The most effective action women can take is to educate the public about the effects of gun violence and the positive results of control measures in different countries. Writing letters to the editor of newspapers and drawing attention to progressive legislation elsewhere can raise awareness about ways to reduce gun violence.

70

Reduce Military Spending and Get Out of the Arms Trade

Dwight D. Eisenhower.

Until the latest of our world conflicts, the United States had no armaments industry. American makers of plowshares could, with time and as required, make swords as well. But now we can no longer risk emergency improvisation of national defense; we have been compelled to create a permanent armaments industry of vast proportions. Added to this, three and a half million men and women are directly engaged in the defense establishment. We annually spend on military security more than the net income of all United States corporations.

This conjunction of an immense military establishment and a large arms industry is new in the American experience. The total influence — economic, political, even spiritual — is felt in every city, every State house, every office of the Federal government. We recognize the imperative need for this development. Yet we must not fail to comprehend its grave implications. Our toil, resources and livelihood are all involved; so is the very structure of our society.

In the councils of government, we must guard against the acquisition of unwarranted influence, whether sought or unsought, by the military-industrial complex. The potential for the disastrous rise of misplaced power exists and will persist.

We must never let the weight of this combination endanger our liberties or democratic processes. We should take nothing for granted. Only an alert and knowledgeable citizenry can compel the proper meshing of the huge industrial and military machinery of defense with our peaceful methods and goals, so that security and liberty may prosper together.

— Dwight D. Eisenhower, January 17, 1961

When President Eisenhower made the famous statement above, he apparently planned to use the term "military-industrial-congressional complex," but deleted the word "congressional" before he spoke. Nonetheless, he recognized that the influence of military industries was so powerful that it threatened the very democracy that Congress was charged with defending. The rise of misplaced power has happened as he predicted, and some commentators

- Center for Defense Information: www.cdi.org
- Project Ploughshares: www.ploughshares.ca
- True Majority: www.truemajority.com

believe that it may be too late to restore the independence of Congress, even with a government that sees this as a priority.

Global military spending now exceeds $1 trillion a year, with the United States spending nearly half of that amount.[1] In other words, US military spending is almost as much as all the rest of the world combined. Does this vast expenditure make America more secure? The increase in military spending since September 11, 2001, has propelled the United States into a massive deficit that threatens the stability of the country and, indeed, the stability of the world.

Mercenaries have always been available as hired killers in wartime, but now the privatization of warfare is on a gigantic scale, with private soldiers, military support services, guards, and reconstruction firms on the public payroll. Their profits are in the tens of billions of dollars, but these mercenaries are not accountable to the public nor to international law. They blur the line between business and the military. Blatant conflicts of interest between decision makers and profiteers mean that making the case for war is an exercise in marketing rather than an explanation of foreign policy. The power of corporations like Halliburton, which serves the military, has become a seemingly insurmountable obstacle to achieving peace.

The diversion of funds from human needs to weaponry is tragic, and weapons production itself is an environmentally destructive process. The waste of resources, especially oil, is catching up with the world. The military are the world's greatest polluters and the greatest users of oil. The world is close to the peak of the global oil supply, and choosing to use this resource to fight wars to control the remaining supply is singularly short-sighted.

Our future depends on radical changes in the behavior of nation-states. These changes do not represent a utopian dream. They represent the reality of a world that cannot continue on its present path. Costa Rica eliminated its armed forces in 1949. There are now some 27 countries without armed forces, and Costa Rica is among the most successful of the developing countries because it freed its resources to meet human needs.

One of the most important actions we can take to make a better world is to write and phone our elected officials to press them to move money out of military budgets and into social programs, health care, education, and environmental restoration. True Majority gives you the facts you need about the Pentagon budget, and Project Ploughshares in Canada provides information about Canadian defense spending.

71

Hold Leaders Accountable to International Law

It took 17 years for Chileans to free themselves from the grip of Augusto Pinochet's military dictatorship (1973–1990), and it took another 15 years and the collaboration of the Spanish and UK governments to finally hold him accountable. In January 2005, after years of court battles and appeals, the Chilean Supreme Court upheld his indictment for kidnapping and murder.

Chileans had good reason to persevere in bringing Pinochet to justice. He was responsible for the assassination or "disappearance" of 3,197 people, and the torture of tens of thousands more (see Solution 8).[1] Human rights organizations kept thousands of files of evidence of torture, execution, and disappearances. Later

RUSSELL DAVIDSON

Judge Juan Guzmán.

Bringing down a dictator is like calling the customer care department of a major company and getting to talk to a human being. While obtaining justice for victims of a brutal regime can't really be compared to the goal of getting answers to your computer or prescription problems, these efforts do have one thing in common: they take perseverance.

— Daniela Ponce

their files became essential in the cases brought against Pinochet and his aides.

The underground networks of people in Chile sustained resistance to the regime, knowing all too well the consequences if they were caught. Their connections with important social institutions and human rights groups around the world made possible the many campaigns that undermined Pinochet's reputation abroad.

When Pinochet lost a leadership referendum in 1988, he granted himself amnesty and the position of senator for life. He used diplomatic immunity to evade prosecution in Chile or elsewhere. In 1996, however, a Spanish court indicted him for crimes against humanity, genocide, and international terrorism. Two years later, when Pinochet traveled to London, a Spanish judge petitioned British authorities to detain him. He was held for 500 days under house arrest before finally being sent back to Chile because a team of British doctors found him physically and mentally unfit to stand trial.

Chilean victims of imprisonment and torture were dismayed when Pinochet arrived at the Santiago airport, got out of his wheelchair, and, waving to his supporters, triumphantly walked away.[2] In 2002, however, Pinochet was seen in an hour-long interview on Miami TV. Following that exposure, Chilean judge Juan Guzmán saw that he was mentally sound. Guzmán interviewed Pinochet and declared him fit for trial.

Finally Pinochet was indicted for 10 specific acts of kidnapping and murder.

At the same time, Judge Sergio Muñoz was investigating the millions of dollars Pinochet had hidden in secret offshore bank accounts. Public outrage helped to ensure that Pinochet could not gain immunity from prosecution for any of his crimes.

The Pinochet trials have set new precedents in international law, including the first case in human rights law of a person arrested in one country being extradited to a second country for crimes committed in a third.

The international investigations and arrests give credence to the possibility that an international criminal court could bring war criminals to justice, even if their own country were reluctant to prosecute them (see Solution 78). Officials who have escaped prosecution in some South American countries are unable to travel abroad for fear of being arrested and extradited to a country that will put them on trial and possibly convict them.

As citizens, we can support investigative journalists and groups working to expose those people who are complicit in war crimes and crimes against humanity. In the context of the occupation of Iraq and Afghanistan, that means continuing to press for conviction of those responsible for illegal imprisonment and torture of captives. The investigation of prisoner abuse must be carried to the highest level, where orders were given. Continued public pressure is also essential to getting full disclosure of agreements made by British prime minister Tony Blair and American president George W. Bush before the bombing of Iraq. If they have contravened international law, they must be held accountable.

Governments often assume that the public will forget their misdeeds before the next election. It is up to us as citizens to ensure that we sustain our collective memory, especially if the actions of our leaders constitute war crimes. Justice and democracy depend upon an engaged public and support for international law.

> Though the mills of God grind slowly,
> Yet they grind exceeding small;
> Though with patience he stands waiting,
> With exactness grinds he all.
>
> — Henry Wadsworth Longfellow

- *A Force More Powerful* by Peter Ackerman and Jack Duvall, St. Martin's Press, 2000

72

Claim a Great Vision

> I suppose that human beings looking at it would say that arms are the most dangerous things that a dictator, a tyrant needs to fear. But in fact, no — it is when people decide they want to be free. Once they have made up their minds to that, there is nothing that will stop them.
>
> — Desmond Tutu

Great leaders rise above the obstacles of their time because they have a vision that extends further into the future than their personal term of office. When they seek to fulfill the most noble aspirations of human society, they bring their personal integrity to the fore. They consider the kind of society that might flourish in their land, the possibilities that might sustain people for many generations to come. Some nations have taken advantage of the crisis of regime change to bring new principles to the governance of their country. South Africa is one.

Violence and repression in South Africa pitted the white government against the black Africans in an explosive, brutal struggle, with terrorism, torture, rape, and murder on both sides. The world responded by rejecting the regime and its savagery. Consumers outside the country boycotted South African goods and demanded that their governments divest from South African funds and block South African exports. South African athletes were banned from international competition, and apartheid leaders were regarded as pariahs by the outside world.

- Human Development Index reports: hdr.undp.org/reports/global/2004
- Mont Fleur Scenarios (Available from the Global Business Network): www.gbn.com
- "The Literature of Nonviolent Resistance and Civilian Based Defense" by Bryan Caplan, *Humane Studies Review* 9, no.1

Within the country, nonviolent actions were an important part of the rebellion against apartheid. Boycotts, stay-aways, and strikes put pressure on white business owners and undermined confidence that the country could continue as it was. Both sides finally realized they could not overcome the other by force. When the government recognized that there was no future for the country if it continued on the existing path, F.W. de Klerk announced in the early months of 1990 that the time for negotiation had arrived. Nelson Mandela was released from prison and, amidst celebrations, the transition to democracy began.

Negotiations began in 1991, and it took two years to reach a deal. In that time, community networks and conflict-resolution projects spread throughout the country. Forums brought together diverse groups to talk about education, health, housing, and many other areas.

One such forum was the Mont Fleur project, backed by Royal Dutch Shell, that brought together 22 prominent South Africans from across the ideological spectrum to discuss futures based on different possible scenarios. The participants, who included politicians, activists, academics, and businessmen with right- and left-wing views, considered both the immediate and the distant future of the country. They met three times in three-day workshops and came up with four scenarios that were then developed and run as an insert in a national newspaper. Team members presented and discussed the scenarios with more than 50 groups. The scenarios were:

- **Ostrich**, in which a negotiated settlement to the crisis in South Africa is not achieved and the country's government continues to be nonrepresentative.
- **Lame Duck**, in which a settlement is achieved, but the transition to a new system is slow and indecisive.
- **Icarus**, in which transition is rapid, but the new government unwisely pursues unsustainable populist economic policies.
- **Flight of the Flamingoes**, in which the government's policies are sustainable and the country takes a path of inclusive growth and democracy. (Flamingoes characteristically take off slowly, fly high, and fly together.)

The vivid images of the scenarios provoked public debate and moved F.W. de Klerk to declare that he was not an ostrich. The public came to support the inclusive democracy represented by the flight of flamingoes.

South Africa's progress has been difficult, and although today it places above most other African countries on the Human Development Index (at number 119), it faces major challenges: poverty, extreme inequality in income, limited basic services, environmental degradation, and unemployment.

The rest of the world sees South Africa not just as a nation struggling to rise above its past, but as the home of two great leaders, Nelson Mandela and Archbishop Desmond Tutu. These two men will be remembered in history for bringing forgiveness and reconciliation to their country instead of a bloodbath.

South Africa's circumstances were extreme, but the scenarios sound quite similar to those created by cities developing 100-year plans (see Solution 62). Our nations must also think in a longer time frame than an election cycle if we are to address global warming, other environmental crises, and the destabilizing gap between rich and poor. As we consider different voting systems, we also need to establish a way for citizens to participate in the long-range decisions that must not change with every election.

Archbishop Desmond Tutu with the author at the Hague Appeal for Peace, 1999.

CHRISTA ROSSNER

73

Support Independent Media and Public Access to Mainstream Production

A military-industrial-media complex has grown huge while sitting on the windpipe of the First Amendment. And a media siege is normalizing the murderous functions of the warfare state. We are encouraged to see it as normality not madness.

— Norman Solomon, Institute for Public Accuracy

Allowing media conglomerates to own television, radio, and newspapers has led to a situation where a few companies control news broadcasting across the whole spectrum of sources, from print to TV, radio, and film. The same agenda is sold to us in movies and magazines, with commentators debating the fine points of war strategy, but not venturing to debate war itself. Whatever dissent there might be before a war begins disappears from all networks as soon as the first bombs fall. But the strategy is fraying at the edges. Bill Moyers' 2003 address on media reform was a powerful indictment of governmental secrecy, media conglomerates, and ideological influences coming together to paralyze democracy.[1]

Internet

Young people are leading the way out of dependence on TV networks by cutting the time they spend watching commercial TV. They are following issues on the Internet and taking action with organizations like MoveOn.org. They follow blogs (web logs — electronic newsletters) that give independent news reports and opinions, and they file their own comments and digital films online.

Communities are establishing blogs that give local community information all day long because their TV and radio stations don't have the resources to send people to every community event. It turns out that people are not interested in just blood and gore; they also want to know what is happening in their neighborhoods. As a result, broadcast stations are picking up materials from bloggers to add to their own coverage.

An innovative online newspaper in South Korea, *Ohmynews*, selects articles from about 250 to 300 submitted daily.[2] Some 30,000 reporters write occasional articles for the site. Although the pay is low, contributors say that they write for *Ohmynews* because it is democratizing communications.

Wikinews is another online news service that anyone can write for. As a nonprofit society, it takes only news, not opinion pieces. Articles must be written in a neutral form, with sources named. Anyone can correct spelling or facts. Guidelines for authors are posted on the site.

Well-known, credible, nonprofit organizations are adding web-casting or pod-casting to their sites. This means that you can watch interviews or events on the web and follow up through links to other sources. News can be posted from a variety of devices that send photos and text, as well as video.

Civil society is no longer constrained by what the market supports. Democratic communications have arrived.

Independent Broadcasting

Listening to a university or co-op radio is refreshing because you will hear irreverent commentary from diverse perspectives. You can

- Canadian Broadcasting Corporation: www.cbc.ca
- Democracy Now!: www.democracynow.org
- National Public Radio: www.npr.org
- Ohmynews: english.ohmynews.com/
- Public Broadcasting Service: www.pbs.org
- Public Radio International: www.pri.org
- The Real News: www.therealnews.com
- Wikinews: en.wikinews.org/wiki/Main_Page

listen to a real debate about global issues, often involving immigrants who correct the bias presented in the mainstream. Training young people in writing, production, and broadcasting is an excellent way to deepen the public discourse about issues that receive minimal and superficial coverage from the commercial stations.

Surveys show that public broadcasters are the most trusted source of information in the United States. (The military is the second-most-trusted source.) In Canada the CBC is the public broadcaster on TV and radio. Government support is essential to keep these networks alive and well, and their right to cover viewpoints not provided by commercial sources must be protected. These networks often play public broadcasts from Europe, Australia, or Africa during the night, adding a new slant to the news.

Now there is a new player on the field. The Real News is broadcasting online and on some cable channels without advertising or funding from corporations or government. It is supported by donations and membership. The Real News relies on some of the best journalists in the world to give balanced analysis of environmental, social, and foreign policy issues. Citizen journalists are invited to upload their own videotapes of news events, which will be vetted for quality and purchased if they meet The Real News' standards.

As a result, the priority for programming will be stories that are in the public interest, not necessarily in the interest of corporations or political leaders. We will get more critical thinking about who is behind an action, who benefits from a conflict, and who is working for change. We will get news that we want to know, rather than news that the sponsors want us to know.

RETURN TO KANDAHAR

Paul Jay of The Real News on location in Afghanistan.

74

Establish a Ministry of Peace

> The care of human life and happiness, and not their destruction, is the first and only legitimate object of good government.
>
> — Thomas Jefferson

There was once a Minister of Disarmament in the United Kingdom. It was during the term of Harold Wilson's Labour government from 1964 to 1970. Imagine having a minister responsible for advancing disarmament! Sadly, the Conservative government that succeeded Labour abolished the post.

Imagine if a country set up a Ministry of Peace at the cabinet level, with a budget of 2 percent of the defense budget. Such a small amount could fund major initiatives, both domestic and international, to reduce violence and prevent war. If it prevented one single war, it would save billions of dollars and thousands of lives.

The idea of a Ministry or Department of Peace is being advanced in five countries right now: the United States, the United Kingdom, Japan, Australia, and Canada. The idea has been brewing for years, but with the recent demonstrated successes of nonviolent conflict resolution at both the international and domestic levels, it may well be an idea whose time has come.

Why is it needed? The demonstrations on February 15, 2003 showed the global demand for nations to stop using war as a tool of foreign policy and to build a stable foundation for peace. Furthermore, the decade 2001 to 2010 has been named by the UN as the International Decade for a Culture of Peace and Nonviolence for the Children of the World. Civil society is calling on governments to implement a culture of peace by making it a central focus of government.

In the United States, Congressman Dennis Kucinich has introduced a bill proposing a Department of Peace at the cabinet level. The bill outlines a wide range of responsibilities for the Secretary of Peace and the Department, particularly the responsibility to provide the president, and the Departments of State, Defense, Education, and Justice with expertise and cutting-edge alternatives.

The bills proposed in the United Kingdom and Canada would also establish a Peace Commission that would include academic advisors and NGO experts to provide assistance to the government.

The three proposals raise similar issues that would be addressed by the Department of Peace. A few of these issues are listed below:

Saul Arbess and Penny Joy campaign for a Canadian Department of Peace.

- British Ministry for Peace proposal:
  www.ministryforpeace.org
- Canadian Working Group for a Department of Peace:
  www.departmentofpeacecanada.com
- US campaign for a Department of Peace:
  www.thepeacealliance.org

Domestic Violence Prevention

Support for programs to prevent violence in our societies, in particular:

- Protecting women, children, and the elderly.
- Addressing gang-related violence with programs for marginalized, alienated, and poorly educated youth so that they can be integrated into society.
- Building interfaith and interethnic bonds in communities.
- Reducing gun violence through legislation, education, and buy-back programs.
- Recommending policy to the attorney general on civil rights and labor law.
- Teaching violence prevention programs in communities and schools.
- Addressing violence in the media through education and advocacy.
- Establishing a youth service to train young people in conflict resolution and nonviolence during the transition years following high school.

International Responsibilities

- Advising the Secretary of State and the Secretary of Defense on all matters of national security including protection of human rights, prevention of armed conflict, and de-escalation and resolution of conflict.
- Training of civilian peacekeepers.
- Recommending steps to reduce weapons of mass destruction.
- Reporting on the international arms trade and its effect on national security.
- Advising on matters related to the UN Security Council.
- Addressing human security issues such as disputes related to religion or ethnicity, economy, trade, or resource scarcity.
- Supporting research and recommendations regarding the impact of media on conflict.
- Establishing a Peace Academy, patterned on military service academies, with a four-year program in all aspects of peacebuilding and peacekeeping, and a five-year postgraduate tour of duty in conflict resolution.
- Building public support for international law and the United Nations.

Politics should be the part-time profession of every American.

— Dwight D. Eisenhower

75

Give the Poor a Break

> If a free society cannot help the
> many who are poor, it cannot save
> the few who are rich.
>
> — John F. Kennedy

Millions of people watched the ten Live 8 celebrity concerts on stage and on world-wide television on July 2, 2005. Rock star Bob Geldof, who organized Live Aid for Ethiopian relief in 1985, again brought musicians together to wake up the world. This time Geldof put his weight behind the campaign "Make Poverty History."

War and poverty are locked together, especially in Africa, which has been the site of more wars in the past 40 years than any other continent. Africa is the focus of the campaign to end poverty because while conditions in Asia and Latin America have been improving, Africa has been left behind. Poverty has led to wars over resources, human rights, and self-determination, and war has brought deeper poverty, destruction, and disease. The countries with the most oil, diamonds, and other high-value resources have suffered the most wars and armed conflict.

The actions needed to bring Africa out of poverty are complex, but Geldof summarized them by saying that there's one plan: It's debt, trade, aid, and governance. It takes governments acting decisively to make it happen.

After the Live 8 concerts, critics said pop stars don't understand the complexity of the issues and shouldn't give oversimplified answers. Geldof was a member of the influential Commission for Africa that issued a very complex and thorough report in March 2005. The central message of the report is exactly what Geldof said: It is possible to end world poverty if the wealthy nations take appropriate action on debt, trade, aid, and good governance. What is of greater concern is that the G8 countries made pledges because the TV cameras were rolling, but when the lights went off, the pledges turned out to be insignificant.

Debt

- One hundred percent of the debt owed by sub-Saharan Africa must be cancelled.

- Restructuring set up by the International Monetary Fund and the World Bank must be stopped.

- African countries must have the right to choose what resources and services should be public and what private.

- Countries of the north must provide the help needed to build stable economies.

Trade

- Northern countries must stop subsidizing their agricultural products and then selling them in Africa below the cost of local production. The Commission for Africa points out that every cow in Europe receives almost $2 a day in subsidies, and those in Japan $4, while the average income in Africa is about $1 a day.

- Europe and North America must eliminate the trade barriers that prevent Africa from selling its exported goods to the northern markets.

- Africa must develop and diversify its exports.

- Commission for Africa Report: www.commissionforafrica.org
- Make Poverty History: www.makepovertyhistory.ca
- www.makepovertyhistory.org
- www.one.org
- Make Poverty History, children's campaign: www.unicef.org.uk/c8

- The international community must open negotiations on an international Arms Trade Treaty.

Aid

- Aid to the global south must not be tied to purchases from the donor country, particularly arms purchases.
- The aid given must not make a conflict situation worse.
- Aid must not fund megaprojects that provide more benefit to the donor than the recipient.
- Microbanking loans should be provided, especially to women. These loans, given directly to individuals, benefit small communities and ensure that funds are not siphoned off to corrupt officials.

Good Governance

When African countries gained their independence, many were taken over by dictators. However, in the past five years more than two-thirds of the countries in sub-Saharan Africa have held multiparty elections and succeeded in democratic change of leadership. One of the most serious problems is that, for decades, northern countries have funded dictators who looted the resources of African countries and sent the money to private Swiss bank accounts.

- To curb corruption, African politicians have agreed to an African Peer Review Mechanism to ensure transparency and accountability.

- Foreign banks must seize the private bank accounts of unscrupulous leaders, past and present, and repatriate the stolen funds.
- Outside governments must provide the assistance needed for African governments to establish justice systems, law enforcement, and transparent budget management.
- Governments must ratify the Anti-Corruption Treaty passed by the UN in 2003 and ratified by 27 countries, none of them from the G8.

Not to know is bad. Not to wish to know is worse.

— African proverb

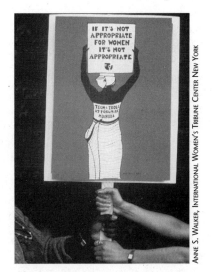

The timeless slogan of the Tech and Tools demonstrations at the UN End of the Decade for Women Conference, Nairobi, 1985.

ANNE S. WALKER, INTERNATIONAL WOMEN'S TRIBUNE CENTER NEW YORK

76

Support International Law and the United Nations

> Hope could not beat eternal
> without the United Nations.
> — Stephen Lewis

The existence of the United Nations is one of the greatest signs of hope in world history. In just over 50 years, it has transformed our view of how nations should act toward each other. We have high expectations for what it can do, and sometimes we forget that its only powers are the ones given to it by nation-states. Its failures are our failures.

When the US and UK governments planned to go to war in Iraq, they sought UN endorsement to give the war legitimacy. Secretary General Kofi Annan's statement that the war is illegal was an important declaration of the independence and neutrality of the UN.

The world has long accepted international law to govern such things as the use of airwaves, air traffic control, banking, passports, and the law of the sea, and the development of international law has progressed by leaps and bounds since the founding of the UN. International cooperation has proved effective in policing (through Interpol) and for disease control and immunization (through the World Health Organization). We share satellite communications systems, weather forecasting, and mail services. Treaties to protect the environment, endangered species, and cultural heritage sites are other successes of the UN.

International treaties related to peace and disarmament have succeeded in reducing the number of nuclear weapons from a high of 70,000 in the Cold War to about 30,000 today. This is not so impressive when you consider that it is still about the level it was in 1968, when negotiations opened for the Non-Proliferation Treaty.

We have a treaty to ban landmines, conventions on biological and chemical weapons, the Geneva Conventions, the Declaration of Human Rights, and the Convention on the Rights of the Child. Some of these treaties need ratification by key states, and some need verification protocols, but the fact they exist at all is no mean feat.

International law is our global conscience in written form. For that reason, global civil society must be at the table when decisions are made.

M.W. ASHFORD

Civil society's view of the United Nations General Assembly from the observer galleries.

- International Association of Lawyers Against Nuclear Arms: www.ialana.net
- International Campaign to Ban Landmines: www.icbl.org
- Lawyers' Committee on Nuclear Policy: www.lcnp.org
- Project Ploughshares: www.ploughshares.ca

Civil society wants nation-states to comply with the treaties they sign, and it wants the treaties written in such a way that there are no loopholes.

When the World Court gave its advisory opinion that nuclear weapons states have an obligation to work for nuclear disarmament (see Solution 79), it commented on Article VI of the Non-Proliferation Treaty. "Each of the Parties to the Treaty undertakes to pursue negotiations in good faith on effective measures relating to cessation of the nuclear arms race at an early date and to nuclear disarmament, and on a Treaty on general and complete disarmament under strict and effective international control." The court denied the existence of a loophole implying that nuclear disarmament didn't have to occur until there was general and complete disarmament. It said the states have a solemn treaty obligation to nuclear disarmament at an early date.

The World Court does not have a police force to back up its decisions, but the force of public opinion gives power to its judgments. In the 1980s, the court heard a complaint from Nicaragua that the United States was mining its harbors. It ruled against the United States. The US government stated that it did not recognize the jurisdiction of the court, but it stopped mining the harbors anyway.

When the final draft of the landmines treaty was being written in Norway, the United States wanted amendments that would ban landmines "except in times of war," and it wanted the right to leave US mines along the border between South and North Korea. Members of the NGOs gathered in Norway marched outside the conference with placards saying "No exceptions. No loopholes. No excuses." The delegations inside shared their views. The world held tight, and the treaty was written with no exceptions. Regrettably, it didn't include a ban on cluster bombs, which act like landmines, but otherwise it has proven to be a clear and concrete agreement.

A model convention for the elimination of nuclear weapons has been written by a group of international lawyers and filed with the UN. Now all we need is some nations with the political will to bring it to the floor for discussion.

Civil society is an important partner with the UN and an active participant in UN conferences, both officially and in the observer galleries. Civil society experts are able to set aside national interests and provide information of global importance.

77

Reform the UN

UN reform is necessary because today's world is so different from the post-war world of 1945. The UN must be able to respond to new power relations and new challenges to our very survival as a species. The nuclear arsenals, the ability of one nation to maintain a safe distance while causing total destruction to another nation, and the existence of weapons that contaminate vast areas with radioactive waste are only a few of the new dimensions of war. In addition, the targeting of civilians, especially women and children, has peeled away any remaining veneer of honor from the pursuit of war.

The World Federalists have been staunch supporters of the UN for decades, and their policy papers are highly respected. In their recommendations for UN reform, they suggest that four principles need to be applied:

- The pre-eminence of international law
- Equal representation of nation-states

- Empower the UN: www.empowertheun.org
- Parliamentarians for Global Action: www.pgaction.org
- *Responsibility to Protect*: www.iciss.ca/report-en.asp
- United Nations Association USA: www.unausa.org
- United Nations Association Canada: www.unac.org
- World Federalist Movement: www.wfm.org
- World Federation of UN Associations: www.wfuna.org

The United Nations has helped bring about over 170 peace settlements, including those that ended the Iran-Iraq war in 1988; led to the withdrawal of Soviet troops from Afghanistan in 1988; and brought the El Salvador civil war to a close in 1992. The 60 UN peacekeeping missions since 1948 have helped countries maintain ceasefires, conduct free and fair elections, and monitor troop withdrawals in numerous global hotspots, including ongoing missions in the Middle East, Haiti, Kosovo, Sudan, and Liberia, among others.

— Hilary French, Worldwatch Institute, Global Security Brief, 2005[1]

- Accountability
- Transparency

They point out that the General Assembly is the UN's most democratic body and should have corresponding authority.

Many international policies are decided by diverse bodies within the UN system, and their decisions are often contradictory. The General Assembly is the appropriate body to resolve differences involving poverty eradication, trade agreements, environmental protection, human rights standards, labor rights, and social development. The World Federalists suggest that the General Assembly's mandate should extend to the coordination of overall policy, including that of the International Monetary Fund, the World Bank, and the World Trade Organization.

The Security Council was set up with five permanent members, Britain, China, France, Russia, and the United States. All have nuclear weapons, and all have a veto. Granting the veto was necessary in order to draw the great powers into the organization. The council has often been unable to act to prevent war because one or more of these nations have threatened to veto actions deemed not in their narrow national interest. Ironically, criticism of the UN for being nothing but a debating group arose when the Security Council did not approve the US-led coalition's bombing of Iraq — that is, when the UN was fulfilling its mandate by acting to prevent war. Its goal is not to facilitate illegal acts of war, but to stop them.

A more democratic Security Council would have equal representation from all regions of the world and more transparent decision-making procedures. The report of the International Commission on Intervention and State Sovereignty, *Responsibility to Protect*, calls for the UN to intervene in cases of genocide and large-scale human rights abuses.

The report points out that when the Security Council fails to maintain international peace and security, the General Assembly is empowered to act under a "Uniting for Peace" resolution. This resolution stipulates that "if the Security Council ... fails to exercise its primary responsibility ... the General Assembly shall consider the matter immediately with a view to making appropriate recommendations to Members for collective measures to maintain and restore international peace and security." Despite countless examples of inaction by the council, this resolution has been used only ten times.

The sticking point is that the General Assembly is unable to force the most powerful nations to comply with international law. As civil society's influence and ability to exert moral pressure on the major powers grows, however, it may become part of the solution, ending the attitude of exceptionalism that leads some of the powerful nations to disregard international law.

For decades, civil society organizations have advocated the creation of a UN Parliamentary Assembly, a consultative assembly that would be made up of representatives elected by national parliaments or directly by citizens. The purpose would be to increase the accountability and transparency of international decision making and to give a voice to people who are not represented by their national government.[2]

As citizens, we can become more aware of, and contribute to, the discussions and evolving ideas about UN reform by joining a local UN Association or the World Federalists. Universities and colleges often have speakers and seminars on UN reform.

Global Action to Prevent War conference on the creation of a United Nations Emergency Peace Service, Cuenca, Spain, February 2005.

78

Join the International Criminal Court

Truthfully, most of us thought the ICC was more likely to be established in 2098 rather than 1998.

— Bill Pace

When you stand facing the flags in front of the UN building, the UN Church Center (777 UN Plaza), where civil society hangs out in New York, is on the right, behind you. I think of it as being behind the UN, like a cheering section, but it may really be in front of the UN. The 12th-story meeting room of 777 has hosted many historic meetings of NGOs, but perhaps the most significant was a small gathering on February 10, 1995. The World Federalist Movement invited a group to talk about setting up a coalition to advocate for an International Criminal Court.

The ICC was to be a permanent international institution with jurisdiction over individuals who commit genocide, war crimes, or crimes against humanity. It would replace ad hoc tribunals such as the International Criminal Tribunal for the Former Yugoslavia. Unlike the World Court at the Hague, the ICC would not hear cases between nation-states, but would address criminal behavior of individuals and would only hear cases that national courts were unwilling or unable to hear. Although there are national laws and several multilateral treaties, there has never been a permanent enforcement mechanism with jurisdiction over individuals, regardless of their position.

The Coalition for an International Criminal Court (CICC) began with three staff. Ten years later, there are 2,000 organizations in the coalition, and probably 200 of those groups have full- or part-time staff focusing on the ICC every day.[1]

One of the people who was there on February 10, 1995, was William J. Butler, presi-

dent of the American Association of the International Commission of Jurists. He had doubts that the project would ever succeed. "I never thought an ICC would happen in my lifetime," he recalls.

Over the next year, the NGOs met with like-minded governments that were interested in an international criminal court. By 1997 there was a fairly clear vision of what an ICC would look like and how it would function. The NGOs encouraged governments to organize a diplomatic conference to negotiate the ICC Treaty. In Rome, for five long weeks in June and July 1998, NGOs and diplomats slogged through the seemingly endless discussions to come up with wording that would pass a vote. Just three years after the first meeting, the ICC Statute was adopted and the treaty was opened for signing.

The United States was reluctant to join the treaty, but after an intense NGO campaign, President Clinton signed on December 31, 2000, the last day it was open for signatures, Iran and Israel signed the same day, the last of 139 signatories. The treaty entered into force on April 11, 2002, when the 60th country ratified it. The goal of NGOs working to create the ICC is to have universal ratification by all of the countries that have signed. So far, 99 have ratified.

International lawyers and jurists say that the International Criminal Court is one of the greatest advances in international law in the last hundred years.

Unfortunately, when President George W. Bush took office, he removed the United States' signature from the treaty. Later the United States

- Coalition for an International Criminal Court: www.iccnow.org
- International Criminal Court: www.icc-cpi.int
- World Federalist Movement: www.wfm.org

demanded that countries sign bilateral immunity agreements or lose their US aid. The agreements would mean that Americans would not be prosecuted by the court.

The first cases brought before the court involved the Democratic Republic of Congo and Uganda. In July 2005 the court issued its first arrest warrants for leaders of the Lord's Resistance Army in Uganda.

Despite US hostility to the court, on March 31, 2005, the ICC reached another milestone when the Security Council passed a resolution referring ongoing violence in Sudan's Darfur region to the court.[2] The United States insisted

on a clause exempting Americans from prosecution, but refrained from using its veto to prevent the referral. The US clearly recognized the need for intervention in Darfur and the possibility that investigations by the court would stop the genocide occurring there.

The French ambassador to the UN, Jean-Marc De La Sablière, commented that the Security Council resolution also marks a turning point, "for it sends the same message beyond Darfur to the perpetrators of crimes against humanity and war crimes, who until now have all too often escaped justice. The Security Council will remain vigilant to ensure that there is no impunity."[3]

UNITED NATIONS

Bill Pace, WFM Executive Director and Nicola Reindorp, Head of Oxfam International, New York.

79

Work with Civil Society and the World Court

> Never doubt that a small group of thoughtful, committed citizens can change the world: Indeed it's the only thing that ever has.
>
> — Margaret Mead

A small group of thoughtful, committed citizens brought about the first great triumph of civil society at the UN when they persuaded the General Assembly to refer the question of the legality of nuclear weapons to the World Court. (The World Court deals with issues involving nation-states, while the International Criminal Court deals with individuals accused of committing war crimes or crimes against humanity.)

The World Court Project began in 1986 when it occurred to Harold Evans, a retired magistrate in New Zealand, that nuclear weapons must be illegal under existing international law. To make the point, he realized that the World Court would have to rule on their legality, but a person cannot ask a question of the court; only a nation or a UN agency can do so. Evans was soon joined by groups of doctors, lawyers, and experienced activists in New Zealand who began an international campaign to get the question to the court.

Doctors from New Zealand brought a resolution to the World Congress of the International Physicians for the Prevention of Nuclear War (IPPNW) in 1988. It called for IPPNW to support the World Court Project. I was chairing the meeting and I remember that the resolution passed unanimously. To my embarrassment, I also remember thinking it was a harebrained idea to think that we could ever influence the UN to ask the World Court for an opinion. I could not have been more wrong.

IPPNW and the International Alliance of Lawyers Against Nuclear Arms (IALANA) began by lobbying the World Health Assembly (WHA) to ask whether, on health grounds, the use of nuclear weapons would be illegal. The WHA had already issued a statement, in 1983, which said that "nuclear weapons constitute the greatest immediate threat to the health and welfare of mankind" and "prevention is the only answer to the risk of nuclear war."

New Zealanders Kate Dewes and Alyn Ware led the project through the UN, working with nations of the Non-Aligned Movement to put a resolution before the UN General Assembly. Teams of activists met with national missions

WORLD COURT PROJECT

Photo of the Japanese delegation with Keith Mothersson, the "father of the Declarations of Personal Conscience" and the boxes of millions of declarations to be deposited with the International Court of Justice at the Hague.

at the UN in Geneva and New York; doctors and lawyers met with their own governments at home. Ambassadors told us the nuclear states were frantic. They sent envoys to various capitals, threatening to cut aid and trade to countries supporting the initiative.

A second path was started using a clause from the Hague Convention of 1899. The convention banned certain weapons, but one diplomat at the time was concerned that a new weapon that should be banned might be developed later, and he added a clause stating that in the case of weapons not covered by specific international agreements, the principles of humanity and the dictates of the public conscience applied. The question for the World Court Project was "How could you show the court the dictates of the public conscience?"

Organizers called for individuals to send declarations of conscience to the UK organizers. One declaration said, "It is my conscientious belief that nuclear weapons are abhorrent and should be banned under international law, and I request that the International Court of Justice give an advisory opinion on their legality." More than four million declarations, three million from Japan alone, were deposited as evidence with the court.

The UN General Assembly agreed to ask the court if the threat or use of nuclear weapons would be illegal. The court called for briefs and held hearings in which nations presented their viewpoint. The mayors of Hiroshima and Nagasaki showed giant photographs of the destruction of their cities and the suffering of the people. The court's attention was riveted on the mayors, and the quiet weeping of survivors of the bomb, who were present at the hearing.

On July 8, 1996, the World Court decided that "a threat or use of nuclear weapons would generally be contrary to the rules of international law...and in particular the principles and rules of humanitarian law." It also unanimously agreed that "there exists an obligation to pursue in good faith and bring to a conclusion negotiations leading to nuclear disarmament in all its aspects under strict and effective international control."

The opinion of the court has been profoundly useful to nations and civil society. It is frequently cited in the preamble to UN disarmament resolutions. Activists have used it successfully as a defense in cases of civil disobedience because their actions are in defense of international law, and international law supersedes national law in most countries (see Solution 15).

- International Association of Lawyers Against Nuclear Arms: www.ialana.net
- International Physicians for the Prevention of Nuclear War: www.ippnw.org
- New Zealand Disarmament and Security Centre: www.disarmsecure.org

80

Eliminate Nuclear Weapons

The recent upsurge of young people's interest in nuclear disarmament has brought about a generational shift in the antinuclear movement. Suddenly we have students traveling around the world, rallying their peers against nuclear weapons. They meet with government officials and with the press. When an international student website posted photos of the Target Project in Germany (in which individuals mark a huge red X on a downtown crosswalk to show that it is a target for a nuclear missile — see Solution 35), Target Projects appeared in countries on the other side of the world. The website became a colorful ongoing news show of youth against nuclear weapons.

Any use of nuclear weapons, by accident or design, risks human casualties and economic dislocation on a catastrophic scale. Stopping the proliferation of such weapons — and their potential use, by either State or non-State actors — must remain an urgent priority for collective security.

— "A More Secure World: Our Shared Responsibility" by the Secretary General's High-Level Panel On Threats, Challenges and Change

The UN conferences on disarmament are being monitored by 2,000 NGOs that send representatives to New York to observe and network. National government delegations meet with their own NGOs and find themselves on the same side. The reports that go back to national capitals describe the pressure that civil society brings to bear on these issues, and it certainly helps that the activities of young people dispel the sense that this is a white-haired movement. The vast majority of countries in the world have renounced weapons of mass destruction by joining the Nuclear Non-Proliferation Treaty and the conventions prohibiting chemical and biological weapons.

The most exciting development in nuclear disarmament happened in 2000, at the review conference of the Non-Proliferation Treaty (NPT). President Bill Clinton of the United States wanted a final document at the end of the review but was reluctant to commit his country to serious steps to disarmament. The smaller nations and the middle powers were determined that if there wasn't a meaningful final document, there would be nothing.

Medical students mark a target on the pavement to raise awareness of nuclear weapons.

LAUREN GILES

- Abolition 2000: www.abolition2000.org
- Center for Defense Information: www.cdi.org
- International Association of Lawyers Against Nuclear Arms: www.ialana.net
- International Physicians for the Prevention of Nuclear War: www.ippnw.org
- "A More Secure World: Our Shared Responsibility" (Report of the Secretary General's High-Level Panel on Threats, Challenges and Change): www.un.org/secureworld/
- Reaching Critical Will: www.reachingcriticalwill.org
- Thirteen Steps: www.reachingcriticalwill.org/legal/npt/13point.html

In all-night sessions, negotiators finally agreed on acceptable wording. At last the world had a clear statement of the 13 steps it needs to take to eliminate nuclear weapons. All of the nuclear weapons states signed, including the US. (You can see the 13 steps on the "Reaching Critical Will" website.)

The 13 steps included:

- Bringing the Comprehensive Test Ban Treaty into force, and stopping all tests in the meantime.
- Negotiating a treaty to control fissile materials.
- Breaking the roadblocks at the Conference on Disarmament in Geneva.
- Agreeing that nuclear weapons treaties are irreversible.
- Abolishing nuclear weapons.

Champagne corks popped all over the world as governments and civil society toasted the new era for the Earth.

Unfortunately, when George W. Bush took office, he reversed the final statement of the NPT and halted progress. Nonetheless, the rest of the world is determined to stay with what we know can be achieved. We now know that it is possible to reach the end of the nuclear era if the US government is onside. We also know where the other countries stand and what they were willing to sign. The other nuclear weapons states have not renounced their agreement to the 13 steps.

The sticking point is that the US government is reversing its agreements on treaties that it has signed. The world will not tolerate one state setting itself above the law, while at the same time demanding that others comply with it. States are beginning to work together to advance arms control and disarmament agendas in alternate ways. The result of the US government's efforts to weaken the UN is that other nations are strengthening their commitments to make the UN work. At the same time, American civil society is pressing its government to respect international law and support the UN.

We know that people in every country want nuclear disarmament. Poll after poll shows that more than 70 percent of the public, including citizens of the United States, want an end to nuclear weapons. The World Court has stated that the nuclear weapons states have a solemn treaty obligation to get rid of their nuclear arsenals. Civil society is determined to see it happen.

Add your voice to one of the civil society groups listed above and help build momentum for the abolition of nuclear weapons.

81

Eliminate Chemical Weapons

Our human situation no longer permits us to make armed dichotomies between those who are good and those who are evil, those who are right and those who are wrong. The first blow dealt to the enemy's children will sign the death warrant of our own.

— Margaret Mead

The 20th century saw the use of three kinds of weapons that can sign the death warrant of the user as well as the victim: nuclear, biological, and chemical. Significant advances have been made in the control and elimination of biological and chemical agents.

Chemical weapons have a long history, dating back to the Peloponnesian war in 429 BC. According to the Monterey Institute, chemical weapons have been used in battle by Germany, Britain, the United States, Italy, Japan, Egypt, and Iraq.[1] The common agents include mustard gas and lewisite, which are blistering agents that burn and destroy exposed skin and lungs; phosgene and chlorine, choking agents; and sarin and VX nerve gases that cause respiratory failure and death.

During World War I some 125,000 tons of toxic chemicals were used, causing 1.3 million casualties, of which over 90,000 were fatal. The international community found the use of these agents so abhorrent that they were banned under the 1928 Geneva Protocol. Unfortunately, the ban didn't forbid stockpiling the chemicals, and there were no enforcement measures. Many countries that had signed the protocol went on producing and stockpiling the chemicals.

In 1989 I visited the Japanese Poison Gas Museum on Okunoshima Island. I went with experts on chemical weapons who had spoken at the World Congress of IPPNW in Hiroshima, Japan. The volunteer curator told us that the Japanese manufactured several poison gases, and more than 6,000 tons of mustard gas were produced at the facility between 1929 and 1945. Toward the end of the war, young people from Okunoshima were pressed into service at the factory. Nearly a thousand, some as young as 14, and many of them girls, were given the most dangerous work of storing the filled shells and cleaning up the factory floors. Many suffered lifelong illnesses afterward.

Soldiers were given a shorter period of required military service if they served at the facility. The curator was one of those who survived. He was told that the gas was for defensive purposes and that the Japanese would never use it. After the war, when he heard it had been

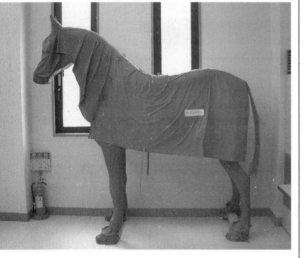

Museum exhibit of a reconstructed horse in protective oil cloth as used at the chemical weapons facility on Okunoshima Island, Japan, in WWII.

MR. IZUMI, THE CITY OFFICER OF TAKEHARA IN CHARGE OF THE MUSEUM used in Manchuria, he was overwhelmed with remorse and committed himself to educating people about poison gas so that it would never be made again. He told us of the numbers of workers who died or developed chronic illnesses, especially lung disease, as a result of their work, despite being shielded by protective clothing, with their heads covered by gas masks.

Chinese historians say that over 10,000 people were killed in 2,000 attacks between 1931 and 1945. Japan is only now beginning to confront its wartime past and acknowledge the atrocities committed by its troops.

Aum Shinrikyo, a Japanese doomsday cult, used sarin gas in 1995 in the Tokyo subway, killing 12 and injuring 5,000 people. While knowledge of the chemical process to produce such agents is widespread, it is difficult to use the gas as a weapon because of its unpredictability.

International pressure to ban chemical weapons grew after Iraq used chemical weapons against its own Kurdish population in 1988. UN negotiations finally produced the Chemical Weapons Convention, which entered into force in 1997. It is the first disarmament treaty that provides for the elimination of an entire category of weapons of mass destruction.

Some countries claim that they need chemical or biological weapons as a deterrent to nuclear weapons states. Establishing the Middle East as a zone free of all weapons of mass destruction would be a helpful step toward security for all.

In the United States and Canada, the best protection against possible chemical weapons use by terrorists is to strengthen the capacities of the emergency responders (police and ambulance) and to ensure that the public health system is functioning effectively.

- International Physicians for the Prevention of Nuclear War: www.ippnw.org
- Physicians for Social Responsibility: www.psr.org

82

Strengthen the Biological Weapons Convention

With all my heart, I believe that the world's present system of sovereign nations can only lead to barbarism, war and inhumanity, and that only world law can assure progress towards a civilized peaceful community.

— Albert Einstein

> The Geneva Conventions mandate appropriate training for the entire military; they go still further, however, calling for an effort to educate the general population about their principles. These obligations, together with bigger questions about what America stands for at home and abroad, invite reflection. Americans must ask what more we can do in our political life and educational system to nurture a knowledge and appreciation of the humanitarian ideals of the Geneva Conventions, and the call to pay greater respect to human life and the dignity of the human person they imply.
>
> — Steven C. Welsh,
> Center for Defense Information[1]

Biological weapons have been called the poor man's A-bomb because of their capacity to cause massive global devastation. Biological weapons like anthrax, plague, and tularemia were produced and deployed by the US and USSR during the Cold War. The British tested anthrax on Gruinard Island, off the coast of Scotland, and were unable to decontaminate the island until the late 1980s.

The Biological Weapons Convention

The Biological Weapons Convention (BWC), signed in 1975, prohibited the development, production, and stockpiling of biological weapons. It has been signed and ratified by 146 countries. Because the treaty lacked adequate verification requirements, the international

community spent six years hammering out agreements to strengthen verification and compliance measures. To the world's dismay, the United States derailed the entire process in 2001.

The US pharmaceutical industry claimed that the inspections would compromise the industry's trade secrets, and it is believed their pressure led the Bush administration to withdraw its support. It has also been alleged that the US military wishes to pursue new defensive bio-weapons programs, in violation of the BWC. It is almost impossible to separate biological weapons research that claims to be defensive from that which is offensive.

The best way to bring biological weapons under control and to eliminate them is to support the rule of law, sign the protocols to strengthen verification and transparency, and permit onsite and random, unscheduled inspections. No countries should pursue further research into biological weapons, even if the research is labeled defensive. The United States should increase the budget for the Cooperative Threat Reduction Program, which provides American funding to help Russia and the former Soviet states secure and destroy their stockpiles of biological weapons so that they do not fall into the hands of terrorists.

Smallpox

The most serious threat is that smallpox might be used by an enemy or terrorist. Smallpox was eradicated in the 1970s as the result of a global vaccination campaign. The last two cultures were stored in Atlanta and Moscow, with plans

- Institute for Energy and Environmental Research: www.ieer.org
- Physicians for Social Responsibility: www.psr.org

to destroy them later. There are now suspicions that cultures have been obtained by other countries, threatening the possibility of a worldwide pandemic if they are released.

Physicians for Social Responsibility (PSR) has examined the question of whether huge numbers of Americans should be immunized against smallpox. The question is not straightforward, because smallpox immunization carries certain risks. As many as 40 people out of every million vaccinated will face life-threatening reactions, and one or two will die. The risk is higher now because of the large number of people with compromised immune systems. Some have HIV/AIDS, others have eczematous skin rashes or various autoimmune diseases. Many hospitals and health workers have rejected participation in the first round of vaccinations.

PSR supports those who have decided to opt out of participation. The organization encourages the use of specific guidelines that have been developed by the Grady Memorial Hospital in Atlanta to refine protocols that would allow for the rapid inoculation of smallpox vaccine should an outbreak occur.

PSR also points out that the widespread poverty and poor nutrition in the United States, combined with the fact that 45 million people do not have access to health care, make an ideal environment for the spread of an infectious disease. Those without health care may not seek medical attention until they have spread the disease extensively.

The best way for us to protect ourselves from an epidemic is to ensure that hospitals and public health programs are well-funded and efficient, that all people have access to affordable health care, and that programs are established to provide for the basic nutritional needs of the whole population.

Langford fire fighters practice in hazardous materials outfits.

LANGFORD FIRE DEPARTMENT, 2005

83

Oppose Ballistic Missile Defense

The development and deployment of missile defenses has not only been elusive, but has proven to be one of the most divisive issues of the past generation.

— Congressional Research Service[1]

When it first appeared that the US government wanted Canada to support ballistic missile defense (BMD), Canadians let their government know in no uncertain terms that they did not want Canada to participate or give moral support. It turns out that, due to Canada's responsibilities in joint North American defense,

Don't Blow It campaign of Physicians for Global Survival.

the country is enmeshed anyway, but the public opposition continues unabated. The new minority government elected in Canada in January 2006 supports joining the American missile defense program, but will likely face difficulties passing such a resolution.

Proponents of BMD describe it as a system in which a missile fired from the ground or a ship shoots down another missile. For decades, scientists have ridiculed the idea of a scheme that amounts to shooting a bullet with a bullet. They have stated clearly that the system cannot defy the laws of physics. It just won't work. According to the Pentagon's own test evaluator and the US General Accounting Office, there is to date no convincing evidence that BMD works.

Both China and Russia are likely to increase their nuclear arsenals in order to be able to overwhelm an American missile defense system. The system is designed to intercept isolated missiles, not multiple missiles and decoys. Scientists who are critics of the system say that any nation with the technological ability to launch missiles would be capable of launching inexpensive but effective decoys that would overwhelm it.

Ernie Regehr, senior analyst with Project Ploughshares in Canada, has been a member of Canada's official delegation to the Non-Proliferation Treaty review conferences and frequently works as a consultant to government. He says some Canadians want to join BMD because they believe the system will protect Canadians. They also believe it will help the country gain access to industrial contracts and

- Center for Defense Information: www.cdi.org
- Project Ploughshares: www.ploughshares.ca
- Union of Concerned Scientists (Video on BMD): www.ucsusa.org/global_security/missile_defense/countermeasures-video.html

achieve more amiable relations with Washington.[2]

To counter these arguments in favor of BMD, Regehr points out that Canada would not be protected by such a system. It is designed with limited capacity and is intended only to protect against "rogue" states such as Iran and North Korea, not against China and Russia. The Canadian government believes that Iran and North Korea can most effectively be dealt with by arms control diplomacy.

Proponents argue that BMD could protect North America if a Russian or Chinese missile were launched accidentally, thus preventing an accidental nuclear war. Regehr's reply is that China has only about 20 missiles capable of reaching North America, and because they use liquid fuel, launch preparation takes several days. Furthermore, their nuclear warheads are believed to be stored separately from the missiles, so an accidental launch from China is not an issue.

The possibility of an accidental launch by Russia is a more serious threat, but the most effective way to prevent such an accident was outlined in the final document of the Non-Proliferation Treaty review in 2000. The 13 practical steps in this document commit states to "concrete agreed measures to further reduce the operational status of nuclear weapons" (see Solution 80).

One step the United States and Russia should take immediately to prevent an "accidental"

nuclear holocaust is to take nuclear weapons off a "launch on warning" (LOW) setting. No LOW is the most important immediate step to make the world safer (see Solution 92).

> If Canada really were to negotiate with the US for BMD involvement beyond that already in place through NORAD, it would presumably be in pursuit of protection from a missile defence system that is specifically not designed to provide protection from the threat that exists and that has no demonstrated capacity against a threat that does not yet exist.
>
> — Ernie Regehr

Regehr suggests several long-term steps that would address the missile threat better than BMD:

- Prevent the further spread of missiles by working with the Missile Technology Control Regime.
- Prevent the weaponization of space by working with the UN's Geneva Conference on Disarmament (see Solution 84).
- Prevent nuclear proliferation by supporting the International Atomic Energy Agency (IAEA) and the Non-Proliferation Treaty review conferences.

84

End the Paralysis of the Conference on Disarmament in Geneva

The Conference on Disarmament (CD) in Geneva is the body designated to hold discussions on disarmament, including the elimination of nuclear weapons. Unfortunately, the CD has been paralyzed for six years because the United States and China refuse to agree to a Program of Work. It has been wiggling its toes for the past two years, but it hasn't started walking yet.

In the quote above, Pierre Pettigrew is referring to the possibility that discussions on disarmament might have to move outside the CD in order to advance. The landmines treaty was negotiated outside the CD through the Ottawa process, which brought together like-minded states to draw up and sign a treaty to ban landmines. To take such a step again would undermine the credibility of the CD as the official forum for disarmament negotiations, and thus would also undermine the UN.

The CD is at a stalemate because China and Russia wanted to negotiate Prevention of an Arms Race in Outer Space (PAROS). The United States opposes PAROS, saying that there is no arms race in outer space. Instead, the US wanted to negotiate a Fissile Materials Cut-off Treaty (FMCT). No work could begin on either issue until the conference agreed to a Program for Work. (Civil society organizations consider PAROS to be an urgent issue that must be addressed *before* countries begin to station weapons in space.) Finally, in 2003, China agreed to a program of discussions only (for PAROS) and dropped its demand for negotiations. Russia followed suit. The United States did not support a program of discussions, and the CD continued to be paralyzed.

> The Conference on Disarmament remains our preferred forum to take this work [disarmament] forward, but if it is unable to include this subject in a Program of Work and start implementing it soon, we and others will have to look elsewhere.
> — Pierre Pettigrew, Canada's Minister of Foreign Affairs, March 2005[1]

However, as I said, the toes are wiggling. The CD president called for a series of informal discussions on several issues, including the cessation of the nuclear arms race, nuclear disarmament, prevention of nuclear war, PAROS, negative security assurances (nuclear weapons states agreeing not to use nuclear weapons against a non-nuclear state), new types of weapons of mass destruction, a comprehensive program of disarmament, and transparency in armaments.

States began presenting statements, called non-papers, that laid the groundwork for the eventual negotiation of a space weapons ban,

> Russia is pursuing a steady course of prevention of an arms race in outer space. Let us recall that as far back as 1983, the Soviet Union assumed an obligation not to be the first in placing any kind of anti-satellite weapons in outer space. We remain committed to this obligation up to the present day. Moreover, we shall not be the first to place any weapons in outer space. We call on all nations with an outer space potential to follow our suit, which will make it possible to maintain a peaceful status of outer space. We are confident that this will benefit all the nations with no exception.
>
> — Anton Vassiliev, Russian deputy permanent representative in Geneva[3]

- Acronym Institute: www.acronym.org.uk
- Federation of American Scientists: www.fas.org/nuke/control/paros/index.html
- Project Ploughshares: www.ploughshares.ca
- Reaching Critical Will: www.reachingcriticalwill.org

including defining the terms for such a treaty and debating the options for verifying the ban. Ambassador Hu Xiaodi of China said that if we sit on our hands, outer space will be made into the fourth medium of warfare, after land, sea, and air.[2]

An arms race in outer space would not only destabilize international relations, but would also threaten the satellites that many countries use for global positioning systems (GPS), communications, and weather forecasting. There is already a problem with space debris that endangers these satellites because very small objects, which move quickly in space, can be disproportionately destructive. If a weapon destroyed a satellite, it would not only cut off communications for a part of the Earth, but would also add more debris.

The possibility of new technologies such as lasers being used from outer space is also of great concern.

There are two things that we can do as activists to press for action at the CD:

- Expose this deliberate tactic to obstruct discussions at the CD by publicly demanding that nations agree to a Program of Work and stop holding the CD hostage.
- Support initiatives to work outside the CD while it is stalled and to return to the CD as soon as the program is set.

This is a good topic to raise with elected officials and professionals in the foreign service so that they know we are fed up with inaction at the CD.

The empty Council Chamber in the Palais de Nations in Geneva.

> The objective must not only be to prevent the placement of weapons in space, but to prevent space from becoming a theatre of armed conflict. The consequences of space combat, from the generation of space debris to undermining the security of the communications, commercial, scientific, and other uses of space that terrestrial society now relies on, are truly immeasurable.
>
> — Ernie Regehr, Project Ploughshares[4]

> Space is our final frontier. It has always captured our imagination. What a tragedy it would be if space became one big weapons arsenal and the scene of a new arms race. In 1967, the United Nations agreed that weapons of mass destruction must not be based in space. The time has come to extend this ban to all weapons.
>
> — Paul Martin,
> Canadian Prime Minister, 2004[5]

85

Expand Nuclear-Weapon Free Zones

The Cuban missile crisis of 1962 was a turning point for me because I discovered that even in Edmonton, Alberta, I was not safe from a nuclear missile attack. I was a new teacher and my husband was a resident at the University Hospital. We outfitted our Volkswagen bug for sleeping and kept it packed with survival gear, planning to drive to the mountains in the event of a nuclear attack. We didn't talk about how I would get from my high school to the hospital. We knew Whyte Avenue would be jammed with cars and I would be stuck on the road.

My father was on the Civil Defence Committee. He told us there would be people stationed all along the highway, handing out soup to people fleeing the city. We didn't talk about the obvious idiocy of the city's plan, or of our helplessness and dread.

In Latin America, the crisis must have been vastly more immediate. People there realized it made no difference that they were not directly involved in the conflict between the superpowers; a nuclear exchange would destroy them anyway. The Mexican ambassador, Alphonso Garcia Robles, met with a number of diplomats

- Agency for the Prohibition of Nuclear Weapons in Latin America and the Caribbean: www.opanal.org
- Arms Control Organization: www.armscontrol.org/factsheets/nwfz.asp
- Parliamentary Network for Nuclear Disarmament: www.gsinstitute.org

This splendid and innovating idea of Latin America and the Caribbean had a great deal of opposition at the beginning, and especially it encountered many skeptics. Thirty years ago Latin America and the Caribbean were considered a group of Quixotes fighting against imaginary windmills. We do not fight against imaginary figures. On the contrary, we have succeeded in becoming the first shield for the world, protecting mankind from the most destructive weapons known.

— Agency for the Prohibition of Nuclear Weapons in Latin America and the Caribbean (OPANAL)

to draft a declaration that proclaimed the Prohibition of Nuclear Weapons in Latin America. Eighteen states signed the Treaty of Tlatelolco in 1967, agreeing not to manufacture, acquire, possess, or test nuclear weapons.

They wanted to demonstrate that governments have the political will to put aside their own interests and their differences for the good of the international community. They acknowledged that militarily denuclearized zones are not a goal in themselves, but rather a means for achieving general and complete disarmament at a later stage. They also declared the need for states to restrain themselves because nuclear proliferation would make disarmament very much more difficult. In 1975, the nuclear weapons states signed additional protocols agreeing not to use nuclear weapons against the Tlatelolco countries. By 2002, all 33 states in Latin America, including Cuba, had signed and ratified the Treaty of Tlatelolco.

The Treaty of Rarotonga (1985) made the South Pacific a nuclear-weapon-free zone (NWFZ), Mongolia declared itself a nuclear-weapon-free state in 1992, and the Treaty of

Bangkok (1995) brought in Southeast Asia. African countries have signed the Treaty of Pelindaba (1996), and the five countries of Central Asia — Kazakhstan, Kyrgyzstan, Tajikistan, Turkmenistan, and Uzbekistan — completed a draft treaty in February 2005, but have not yet signed it. Treaties are under consideration in the Middle East and the Korean Peninsula. The Antarctic Treaty of 1959 prohibits any military activity on that continent. In all, the zones include more than 100 states. That is more than half the 191 states in the international community.

The nuclear weapons states have not yet agreed to sign the protocols promising that they will not use nuclear weapons against the Central Asian countries planning to form a NWFZ. Tsutomu Ishiguri, the UN facilitator of the Central Asian talks, said, "The nuclear weapons states in general don't like nuclear weapon free zones because — if I really simplify it — they have to make a commitment not to threaten to use nuclear weapons."[1]

The nuclear weapons states' reluctance to sign the protocols indicates that they take the commitment they are making seriously. They continue to suggest that if a nuclear weapons state were attacked, it would be justified in responding with nuclear weapons. The NWFZ nations reply that such a response would be against international law because it would not be proportional. There is no comparison between a conventional attack and a nuclear response.

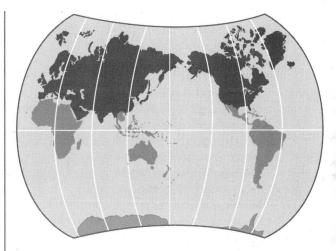

The light grey areas represent Nuclear Weapon Free Zones. More than 50% of the land on Earth is free of nuclear weapons (99% of all land south of the equator).

The NWFZ states plan to convene a meeting of like-minded states to discuss new options for bringing about nuclear disarmament in the face of the failure of the 2005 review of the Non-Proliferation Treaty. They hope to strengthen the NWFZ treaties and encourage more states to join.

We can write to the heads of all the nuclear weapons states, urging them to give security assurances that they will not use nuclear weapons against states in a NWFZ. We can ask our cities, states, and provinces to become NWFZ, and we can urge our national governments to work for the elimination of nuclear weapons.

86

Act Early

Again and again we hear that armed conflict might have been prevented if only people had acted earlier. So why don't they? The short answer is "They do, now." One of the major problems was that a detailed, credible analysis of a brewing conflict didn't get out to those who could make a meaningful intervention soon enough. Now it does, and people are acting earlier.

In January 1993, two men were seated together on a flight out of Sarajevo. Mort Abramowitz was president of the Carnegie Endowment for International Peace, and Mark Malloch Brown became head of the UN Development Program and is now Kofi Annan's chef de cabinet. Sarajevo was in the grip of a bloody siege, and the international community was dithering about the Balkans in the face of the worst bloodshed since World War II. The two men debated why it had been so difficult to get the world to respond to Bosnia and other conflicts.

They got the idea of forming an independent organization that

The events of the last few days [the Asian Tsunami] have rammed home to us messages that should long ago have been loud and clear, but on which as an international community we have been lamentably slow to act:

- that the world of 2005 is very different from that of 1945;
- that the security threats we face reach far beyond states waging aggressive war;
- that they involve human security as much as state security;
- that they are interdependent and affect us all;
- that we have a shared responsibility to deal with them; and
- that we need fundamental and far-reaching changes to both our policies and our institutions if we are to exercise that responsibility effectively.

— Gareth Evans, president of the International Crisis Group, January 15, 2005

would serve as the world's eyes and ears on the ground in countries in conflict and that would, at the same time, press for immediate action. The International Crisis Group was founded in 1995.[1] In ten years it has become one of the most authoritative and credible sources of information about conflicts all over the world. It has experts in the field reporting frequently to update governments, NGOs, and the media about what is happening and what is behind the visible events.

Nicholas Hinton became Crisis Group's first president until his tragically early death. He had run Save the Children UK for ten years and expanded its operating budget seven-fold during that period. As he once declared, the best way to get things done was to "wear a dark suit and think radical thoughts."[2] Former Australian foreign minister Gareth Evans has been president of Crisis Group since 2001 and has helped it grow nearly six-fold, with a budget of over $12 million a year and more than 110 full-time staff people.

Gareth Evans, President of the International Crisis Group.

CRISIS GROUP

- International Crisis Group: www.crisisgroup.org
- Transnational Foundation for Peace and Future Research: www.transnational.org

The present chairman is former European commissioner for external relations, Chris Patten.

Crisis Group doesn't hesitate to speak truth to governments, and as a result, some of its leaders are *personae non gratae* in certain countries. They call on governments to take action in situations that are evolving rapidly, and often they step on toes. As one senior European foreign minister complained, "What you are trying to do is to get us to give you a golden stick with which to beat us over the head, in order to get us to do what we've already decided we do not want to."[3]

Its reports have become a trusted source of information for many involved in peacemaking, peacekeeping, and peacebuilding efforts, particularly from the perspective of governments and the UN. George Soros financed the first field project in the Balkans with a million-dollar grant. It works now across five continents in over 50 different areas of actual or threatened deadly conflict. In 2003 it provided substantial support to the Israelis and Palestinians, who were working on what would become the Geneva Accords (see Solution 89).

Other groups provide highly credible analyses of deadly conflict from the perspective of civil society and professionals in the field of conflict transformation. One excellent source is Transnational Foundation.

Those of us who advocate nonviolent resolution of conflict are often asked, "Well, what would you do now about the war in ...?" We find ourselves in the same situation as a doctor in the intensive care unit who is asked, "What are you going to do now?" for a patient who has been a heavy smoker and drinker for 40 years and whose heart and lungs can no longer respond to an illness. In both cases, the best treatment would have been to take action many years earlier, and in both cases the answer is to do the best we can under the circumstances. Knowing as much as possible about what professionals are recommending, from both a governmental and an NGO perspective, helps clarify the options still available. A Global Emergency Response Force that could complete the whole picture and connect the various groups acting to resolve a crisis without violence would be useful in strengthening a broad spectrum of response (see Solution 100).

Together in a remarkably short time, you have made the International Crisis Group a global voice of conscience, and a genuine force for peace. You have made the international community better able to anticipate and understand conflict, if not actually prevent it. You have stepped in when others couldn't; you have spoken out where others have remained silent; and you have challenged all States to live up to ... their responsibility to protect. Your mediation work — and your leadership in early warning and conflict prevention — have been enormously important. So has your intellectual contribution to finding new approaches to long-standing conflicts. Your well researched and carefully argued reports have greatly helped us in understanding the origins and complexities of the conflict in which we become involved — often at short notice.

— UN Secretary General Kofi Annan,
October 5, 2002[4]

87

Prevent Terrorist Attacks

Terrorism is the war of the poor
and war is the terrorism of the
rich.

— Peter Ustinov

The war of the poor may mean terrorist attacks against an invader or it may mean suicide bombings away from the country of origin. The terrorism that really concerns the United States and its allies is that which might take place in their own countries — like the slaughter of children and families in a market or on a subway. Preventing that terrorism means looking at the root causes and motivation that lead people to take such savage action, even at the cost of their own lives. Studying the causes and motivation does not justify the terrorist act any more than studying the bacteria that cause pneumonia justifies the disease. Responding to such terrorism is a multidimensional challenge to communities, especially where minorities are not well assimilated.

Police Action

The British government, responding to the bombings of the London transit system on July 7, 2005, showed what it had learned through decades of experience countering the IRA. First, the apprehension of the attackers is a police task that requires sophisticated intelligence and the surveillance of public spaces. The skill and rapid reaction of Scotland Yard led to the quick arrests of a core group and a network of others who supported the bombings with technical skills and money. Unfortunately, it also led to the killing of an innocent man on the subway two weeks later. The man was a 27-year-old Brazilian who emerged from a house that was under police surveillance and walked to the tube station. He was pursued by plainclothes policemen,

apparently because he was wearing a bulky overcoat that might have hidden explosives. When the man ran, the police caught and shot him. The case raised serious concerns about police policies related to young men whose race or ethnicity raise suspicions, particularly because the police shoot to kill if they fear the suspect may be a suicide bomber.

Build Mutual Respect and Community Action

Soon after the London bombing suspects were shown on TV, the British prime minister made a statement emphasizing that the government recognized that the majority of Muslims were against terrorism and suicide bombings. Within days, several members of the government met with leaders of the Islamic community to develop a joint approach to prevent further violence.

A few months later, in early 2006, many European papers published caricatures of the prophet Muhammad. This caused an eruption of anti-western violence in Muslim countries, and the Danish and Norwegian embassies in Syria were set on fire.

The newspaper publishers claimed to be defending freedom of expression, but in Norway, a Christian newspaper that had published the cartoons apologized to the Muslim community a month later. The editor, Vebjoern Selbekk, said that he had not foreseen the pain and anger they would cause among Muslims.

"I reach out personally to the Muslim community to say that I am sorry that their religious feelings were violated by what we did," he said.

- Oxford Research Group: www.oxfordresearchgroup.org.uk
- Peace Direct: www.peacedirect.org

"It is also only right for me to admit that I, as the editor, did not understand how offensive it was to publish the copies."

Selbekk made the apology in a news conference, accompanied by the leader of the Islamic Council in Norway, Mohammed Hamdan. The editor praised the Islamic community in Norway for insisting on dialogue, not violence, in response to the cartoons. Hamdan stressed that Islam values forgiveness, and that Selbekk, who had received scores of death threats, was now under his protection. "Selbekk has children the same age as my own. I want my children and his children to grow up together, and live in peace and friendship," Hamdan said.[1]

Begin a Dialogue

An amazing story from Yemen appeared in the *Christian Science Monitor*.[2] Judge Hamud al-Hitar and four other Islamic scholars challenged Yemen's Al Qaeda prisoners to a Koranic duel. They said that if the prisoners could convince them that the Koran justified their ideas, the scholars would join them in their struggle. But if the scholars convinced the young men they were wrong, then they must renounce violence. The scholars succeeded. The young men have completely given up violence and have been released from prison. Now 364 prisoners have gone through the dialogue process and have been released from prison. None have re-offended.

In our own communities we can build dialogues with people of other faiths and cultures so that we have a foundation of goodwill that will help bridge conflicts that may arise. Conflict is inevitable in human relations, but it can be managed without violence if there is already a level of trust.

Editor of Magazinet, Vebjorn Selbekk.

88

Take a New Approach to Terrorism

Mohammad Sidique Khan made a videotaped statement before he committed the suicide bombing in London that killed six people and injured 120 in July 2005. In the tape he gave his reasons: "Until you stop the bombing, gassing, imprisonment, and torture of my people we will not stop this fight ... We are at war and I am a soldier." He spoke of avenging his Muslim brothers. His words aroused fury in Britain because people disagreed with his justification for killing and injuring so many people.

What is important, however, is not that his words justify the act to us, but that they justified it to him. We must ask what to do to prevent other young people from acting on the same feelings of anger, humiliation, and powerlessness.

A letter from Michael Jay, the British Foreign Office's top official, to Prime Minister Tony Blair a year before the London bombings showed that British foreign policy was a recurring negative theme in discussions of the Muslim community,

International terrorist groups prey on weak states for sanctuary. Their recruitment is aided by grievances nurtured by poverty, foreign occupation and the absence of human rights and democracy; by religious and other intolerance; and by civil violence — a witch's brew common to those areas where civil war and regional conflict intersect.

— "A More Secure World: Our Shared Responsibility" by the Secretary General's High-Level Panel On Threats, Challenges and Change

especially in the context of the Middle East peace process and Iraq. "British foreign policy and the perception of its negative effect on Muslims plays a significant role in creating a feeling of anger and impotence among especially the younger generation of British Muslims."[1] He also mentioned feelings of discrimination, disadvantage, and exclusion in the British Muslim community.

If a nation's foreign policy supports international law and the public good, it can easily be defended. The problem is that the bombing and occupation of Iraq are illegal, and their justification was based on a series of untruths and misrepresentations. The Geneva Conventions set standards for the treatment of prisoners of war. They prohibit imprisonment and torture of detainees. Unfortunately the conventions have not been applied to the prisoners held in Iraq, Guantanamo Bay, and Afghanistan. In Guantanamo, many prisoners have attempted suicide. They are held indefinitely without charges, without access to lawyers, and without regular visits by the Red Cross. Many are being tube fed because they are refusing food or water. The atrocities that took place in Abu Ghraib Prison in Iraq brought suffering and death to prisoners, disgrace to American forces, and widespread anger among Muslims.

HTTP://ALBUISSONSTAMPS.HEINDORFFHUS.DK

M. PIERRE ALBUISSON (FRANCE)

CONVENTIONS DE GENEVE

1949 - 1999 MONACO 4,40

Commemorative stamp.

- Demos: www.demos.co.uk
- "A More Secure World: Our Shared Responsibility" (Report of the Secretary General's High-Level Panel on Threats, Challenges and Change): www.un.org/secureworld/
- Not in Our Name: www.notinourname.net

One of the results of this inhumane treatment of prisoners is the loss of respect for the Western justice system that has evolved over centuries to ensure the fair, impartial treatment of all people before the law.

The illegal bombing and occupation of Iraq and the abuse of detainees may not be the root cause of the terrorist bombings, and they certainly do not justify these actions, but they often drive alienated young people to act. The deliberate humiliation of prisoners, including Saddam Hussein, contributes to the simmering resentment of Muslims in many countries.

Professionals know how important it is to show respect to both sides in a negotiation if you want to end hostilities. They are careful to use respectful language and to avoid giving ultimatums or making demeaning statements. Respect for international law would go a long way toward reducing the anger of the Islamic world — and it is the right direction in any case.

Terrorism does not disappear with increased repression and military attacks. On the other hand, we have seen countless examples of the end of terrorism when injustices were addressed and people given an opportunity to participate in society as equals.

> **Don't tell me it's impossible. Look at Northern Ireland .... Centuries were put to bed and a new day has dawned.**
> **— Bill Clinton, referring to the Good Friday Agreement in Northern Ireland**

Children in Pyong Yang day care centre.

Children in Kabul Afghanistan.

The world has a responsibility to protect children in all countries so that they are not threatened by violence and do not grow up to threaten violence against others.

89

Deal with the Grievances and Injustices

Longstanding grievances can fester for generations, repeatedly surfacing to provide fuel for violence and the pretext for war. Governments are reluctant to acknowledge injustice, past or present, because redress will likely be expensive and cost them political support.

Globally, we can see that separatists are gradually shifting from using armed violence and terrorism to using the political process. This shift has been far from smooth in Northern Ireland or the Basque region of Spain, but public support for an end to violence keeps drawing the process back to the ballot box. On the other hand, no agreement or peace accord will last if it does not deal with the grievances that have fed the hostilities.

Israel/Palestine

Resolving the Middle East conflict may not resolve other conflicts, but not resolving it means that terror and injustice between Israelis and Palestinians can continue to be used to inflame hatred between Muslims and Jews elsewhere.

In 2001, civil society took up the task that governments were unable to complete. The ongoing suicide bombings, the clashes over the wall Israel is building along its border to keep Arabs out, and the dismantling of Jewish settlements hide from view the steady ongoing progress toward resolution of the longstanding issues.

The Geneva Initiative (GI) brought together influential and experienced negotiators and professionals, both Israeli and Palestinian, to forge an agreement. Many had participated in past international resolutions and peace proposals including the Quartet Road Map, the Clinton parameters, the Bush vision, the Arab Peace Initiative, and others. The project was led by Yossi Beilin on the Israeli side and Yasser Abed Rabo on the Palestinian side.

GI teams met hundreds of times over two years before producing a model agreement in 2003. Knowing that both sides would have to give up some things to gain others, they arrived at a plan that both Israelis and Palestinians on the teams could support. They demonstrated that, contrary to official rhetoric, there were people who would negotiate on both sides and that a plan was possible.

The Swiss government supported the process and hosted the ceremony to make the Geneva Accord public. In addition to Jewish and Palestinian delegations, the ceremony included world leaders and Nobel Peace Prize winners. The release of the Geneva Accord has been celebrated as a milestone to peace.

The Geneva Initiative did not stop there. Team members set out to engage the populations on both sides in discussions. Previous proposals did not address some longstanding grievances, and the steps to a final resolution were not spelled out. The GI teams recognized that before formal negotiations between governments could be successful, the public needed to be prepared. They stressed the need for a negotiated settlement and a comprehensive end game to the conflict. The proposals have been widely recognized, including by

• Geneva Accord: www.geneva-accord.org

former Israeli prime minister Ariel Sharon, as a way to move Israeli policy toward disengagement.

The GI strategy is to show that the people will support their governments if they seek peace. GI also wants to gain international recognition and support for the process and the peace plan in order to reduce external tensions that contribute to the conflict.

Polls have shown a steady increase in support for the tenets of the Geneva Accord (with the exception of the proposals for Jerusalem, which are still not well received on either side). In 2005, polls in Israel indicated 58 percent of the people would support permanent status discussions with Palestinians.

Since the death of Yasser Arafat, there has been an increase in Palestinian support for a two-state solution with 1967 borders and no massive return of refugees.[1] In 2003, only 39 percent of Palestinians supported such an agreement, while in 2005, 54 percent supported it. There has also been a significant rise in support for reconciliation between their peoples since Mahmoud Abbas took power.

On the proposal for the mutual recognition of the Jewish and Palestinian states, the support from Palestinians has risen from 57 percent in 2003 to 63 percent in 2005.

On the Israeli side, support has increased from 65 percent to 70 percent over the same period.

Knowing that there is support on both sides for steps to resolve longstanding grievances means that both Palestinians and Israelis can take more moderate positions. The election victory of Hamas brings new challenges, but paradoxically offers the possibility of new diplomatic openings because all factions are represented in the discussions. Furthermore, when hardliners negotiate, the public often assumes that they can get the best possible deal — an assumption they may not grant to leaders seen to be soft.

Jews and Arabs demonstrate together in Haifa against mortgage policies that lead to the eviction of poor people from their homes, 2006.

90

End Bombing and Occupation

The army is a poor school for democracy.

— Pierre Trudeau, former Canadian prime minister

Cindy Sheehan rose to fame in August 2005 when she began camping outside President George W. Bush's ranch in Crawford, Texas. Sheehan's 24-year-old son, Casey, was killed in Iraq, and she requested a meeting with the president so she could ask him "What noble purpose did my son die for?" Her vigil in Texas galvanized the antiwar movement in the United States, as thousands joined her protest. Support for bringing the troops back mushroomed, despite Americans' preoccupation with Hurricanes Katrina and Rita. Some 300,000 people marched in Washington, DC, on September 24, 2005, to call for an end to the war in Iraq.

Sheehan's question peeled away the false glory of war. In both Afghanistan and Iraq the supposedly noble reasons for war turned out to be based on misinformation and unacknowledged motives. Osama bin Laden was not captured in Afghanistan, there were no weapons of mass destruction found in Iraq, and there was no connection between Saddam Hussein and 9/11 or Al Qaeda. Polls showed that Americans were skeptical that armed occupation would build democracy in Iraq.

The problem is that two members of the Security Council have blatantly broken international law and disregarded the UN, but the rest of the Security Council has taken no action. Obviously council members cannot enforce the rule of law against two of the most powerful nations in the world. If they moved to censure the actions of those members, a cycle of tit-for-tat censuring might follow, or the organization would deteriorate into something even less effective.

Nations could, however, refer the question of the legality of military interventions to the World Court. This would establish whether US and UK leaders have initiated illegal actions that amount to war crimes or crimes against humanity.

In June 2005, the German Administrative Court issued its findings in the case of a military officer who was demoted from major to captain because he refused to work on a software program that might support the war on Iraq. He believed that the war was illegal, and he refused his orders as a matter of conscience. The court acquitted him and also gave a judgment that the war and occupation of Iraq are not legal under international law, and neither was Germany's agreement to allow the use of its airspace for bombers.[1]

When national governments do not act, the force of public opinion can expose this unacceptable behavior. The World Tribunal on Iraq was one step in this direction (see Solution 53). Public pressure on other governments can demonstrate the strength of opposition to the continuation of military occupation.

The situation in Iraq is changing daily. The following conclusions are based on the situation in February 2006.

- The insurgency is increasing, not decreasing.

- It seems unlikely that the permanent US bases under construction will be viable over the long term because Iraqis are so determined to end the occupation.

- A constitution that does not provide for fair distribution of resources and power to Shiites, Sunnis, and Kurds will not bring stability.

Political columnist Arianna Huffington and Gold Star Families for Peace mother Cindy Sheehan, Los Angeles, September 2005.

- A constitution developed over time, with extensive input and consent from the Iraqi people, could be a first step in a healing process. In South Africa, over one million responses from the public were received as the constitution was drafted.

- The withdrawal of occupying troops may temporarily worsen the conflict among the Iraqi factions, but the country is already at war. Without the occupation, the Iraqis might begin their own negotiations toward a democratic government.

- When occupying forces are withdrawn, the new context may allow the UN to become involved as a neutral agent.

- Iraq has become a magnet for extremists, and thus contributes to the rise of terrorism outside Iraq.

- Baath party members were not all supporters of Saddam Hussein, and the country needs their participation in the bureaucracy and the government.

- The hundreds of thousands of small arms left unguarded after the fall of Saddam Hussein pose a huge threat to the development of a new democratic system. A program to buy back weapons from civilians should be established as soon as possible.

- The reconstruction of Iraq under Iraqi control can provide employment and stability for Iraqis. Foreign companies taking the work and the profits from Iraq will contribute to more conflict.

- The US economic conditions that impose free-market globalization on Iraq's economy and undermine the strength of Iraq's local businesses must be ended.[2]

- Other Islamic countries can support efforts to reconcile the factions in Iraq. In fact, there are likely quiet diplomatic efforts underway already, in anticipation of an end to the occupation.

- The role of third parties will be important as Iraq must reconstruct its infrastructure and establish justice, education, and health care systems.

- Women have a major role to play in the resolution of conflicts between factions and in the reconstruction of the country and its government.

There is no easy solution to the quagmire in Iraq, but ending the occupation is a necessary precondition for change. Public pressure in the United States is the best means to achieve this end. Increasing numbers of protest marches supporting withdrawal of troops are reflected in the number of elected officials beginning to take the same position. People in other countries can write to their governments to support a UN call for an end to the occupation.

- Gold Star Families for Peace (Cindy Sheehan's website): www.gsfp.org
- World Tribunal on Iraq: www.worldtribunal.org

91

Declare Zones of Peace

I am more aware than ever of the great role you have played and the work you do in my country where everyday horror is greater than fiction, just as I am convinced that I owe my life to you, and that of my family, too.

— Osiris Bayter, Colombian human rights worker, speaking of a Peace Brigades volunteer

The Philippines

After Philippine president Ferdinand Marcos was overthrown, Corazon Aquino took office. When fighting continued to flare up in areas of the country, peace activists formed the Coalition for Peace (CFP) and the Multisectoral

WITNESS FOR PEACE

"Michael and Colombian Child": Witness for Peace volunteer with a Colombian child from the war-torn Catatumbo region of Colombia.

Peace Advocates (MPA). They tried to meet with the government, but the officials would not give them the time of day. Instead, the CfP and MPA decided to build a "third party" that would work for peace between the government and the guerrillas. They began to meet with aboriginals and peasants who were caught in the crossfire.[1]

First the army would come and execute those villagers it claimed were collaborating with the guerrillas. Then the guerrillas would come and execute villagers they accused of collaborating with the army. The strategy the villagers developed was to draw a map of their village with a circle around it. They took the map to both groups. "This area is a zone of peace," they said. "Do not enter this area carrying weapons."

Surprisingly, the army and the guerrillas respected the zones of peace. Soon there were ten zones of peace throughout the region. The Coalition for Peace found that where aboriginal traditional community structures were in place, or where strong church-based social structures had been formed, the zones of peace were usually able to survive. In other places, villagers could not resist the armed groups.

Colombia

Eduardo Marino from Colombia attended a peace conference in the Philippines and took the idea of zones of peace back to his community. In an area known as La Indie, the peasants were caught between the army, the paramilitary groups supported by the government, and the guerrillas. The farmers were being summarily

- Global Partnership for the Prevention of Armed Conflict: www.euconflict.org
- Peace Brigades: www.peacebrigades.org/colombia.html
- Witness for Peace: www.witnessforpeace.org

executed, exactly as the Filipino people had been. They were told by the army: "You have only these choices: join us, join the guerrillas, leave the area forever, or die."

The farmers devised another choice. They went to each group and asked, "Who are you fighting for?" Each group responded by saying, "We are fighting for you." The farmers were unequivocal. They said, "You have been fighting for us for 15 years, yet the only victims of this conflict have been ourselves. We ask you to stop fighting for us. We want to stay on the land and work for a living in a safe environment for our children."

Periodically, peace was established in the region so that the farmers were able to grow and market their crops, but still the murders continued. San Jose de Apartado, in the war-torn state of Uraba in northwestern Colombia, had a horrendous history of purges, which drove 10,000 people to flee to the south. Graffiti sprayed on the walls of deserted homes left no doubt as to the fate of anyone who dared to return. "Worm, you will soon be full of worms," read one message.

There are powerful interests at play in Uraba — it is an important site for the banana industry, coal, and possibly oil, as well as a smuggling route for arms and narcotics. Drug barons have become property owners, and the government does not respond to the murders.

In 1997, the inhabitants of 28 refugee settlements centered around San Jose decided to declare themselves a Communidad de Paz in the middle of a war zone.[2] Witness for Peace, Peace Brigades, the Fellowship of Reconciliation, and other accompaniment organizations are working with the community (see Solution 5). Although 150 people have been killed in the past eight years, the community is convinced that the international presence is preventing much worse carnage.

> **The death sentence against each and every one of us has not been carried out only because we have had Peace Brigades International accompaniment.**
> — **Colombian activist, 1995**

Peace Brigades and other organizations are calling on the US government to stop supporting the Colombian military with arms and money and to ensure a transparent, impartial investigation of these murders, with those responsible prosecuted by civilian authorities.

Members of the community are refusing to leave because they are determined to live with justice and peace in their own area. You can support the community through Witness for Peace.

92

End Launch on Warning

> I had a funny feeling in my gut. I didn't want to make a mistake. I made a decision. That's it.
>
> — Colonel Stanislav Petrov

On September 26, 1983, Lieutenant Colonel Stanislav Petrov disobeyed orders and saved the world from a nuclear holocaust.[1] Just after midnight, the 44-year-old Petrov was commander on duty in an early warning bunker south of Moscow. It was a time of high tension between the Americans and the Soviets. The Americans were about to deploy Pershing missiles in Europe in response to the Soviet deployment of SS-20 ballistic missiles. The Soviets were worried that a planned NATO exercise in Europe might be a cover for a preemptive strike. As well, just three and a half weeks earlier the Soviets had shot down Korean Air Flight 7, killing all 269 people on board.

Suddenly the klaxon alarm went off. The computer displays indicated that a missile was headed toward the Soviet Union from Malmstrom Air Force Base in Montana. Petrov knew his orders were to forward the warning of an attack immediately to the Politburo so that Soviet missiles would be launched in retaliation. He knew that this massive response would trigger the launch of thousands more US missiles. He knew that the ensuing nuclear disaster would cause millions of deaths, nuclear winter, and mass starvation on the whole planet.

Petrov, knowing that the new satellites had been rushed into service, waited to see if the signal was an error. Then, to his horror, another missile was detected, and another, until five missiles appeared to be headed toward the Soviet Union. His control board was flashing CTAPT (START), and the klaxons were deafening. The minister of defense and others in the Soviet General Staff had also received the alarms and were calling Petrov. He had less than ten minutes to make a decision. He reasoned that no one would start a war with only five missiles, and despite pressure from the minister, he decided to take no action.

Five minutes after the alarm started, Petrov was certain it was an error. Later, experts speculated that it was caused by sunlight reflecting off high-altitude clouds over Malmstrom and shining into the sensors on the satellite. A global war was averted.

RUSSELL DAVIDSON

Lt. Col Stanislav Petrov.

• Association of World Citizens: www.worldcitizens.org

Petrov was investigated by the military, and although he was not punished, he was transferred to a less sensitive post and eventually he resigned from the military. On May 24, 2004, he was given the World Citizen Award and $1,000 from the San Francisco-based Association of World Citizens.

Computer errors and misinterpretations have brought the world close to disaster over 20 times. If the presidents of the United States and Russia took their missiles off Launch on Warning (LOW) settings and instead implemented a system of Retaliatory Launch Only on Detonation (RLOAD), the risk of an accidental nuclear holocaust would drop to zero.[2]

If RLOAD had been in place when Colonel Petrov was on duty, the leaders would have been alerted when the klaxon alarms went off, but no missiles would have been launched until they received confirmation of a nuclear explosion. If there were no explosion, there would be no unwarranted retaliatory launch and no nuclear war.

If an explosion had occurred, nuclear war would have begun. The Soviets could have launched their remaining missiles within minutes of the first explosion.

Whether the Soviets had LOW or RLOAD, the Americans would still have faced mutually assured destruction if they initiated an attack. If the Americans also chose to set their missiles on RLOAD, the risk on both sides would drop to zero. Choosing RLOAD is simply a matter of the president giving the order to stop LOW and go to RLOAD. It could be done this week.

Many people advocate de-alerting nuclear weapons by separating the warheads from the missiles so that it takes time to prepare them for launch. This is desirable, but it requires an agreement between the adversarial countries and a verification scheme. Such an agreement is not likely in the next several years. In the meantime, we can't base our survival on the hopes that Colonel Petrovs will always be on duty in both countries.

93

End War on Public Health

When I visited Auschwitz I was horrified.
And when I visited Iraq, I thought to
myself, "What will we tell our children in
fifty years when they ask what we did
when the people in Iraq were dying?"
— Mairead Maguire, Nobel Peace Prize Laureate

War is not over when the last bomb is dropped. When civil infrastructure is destroyed, the result is essentially a war on public health. Infrastructure includes water treatment plants, electricity grids, sewage disposal plants, communications systems, and food distribution systems. Other essential structures include hospitals, bridges, and food processing plants. Sanctions that prevent the repair and maintenance of infrastructure are a continuation of war.

Current war strategies include the precision bombing of these key components of civil infrastructure. The people who die in these bombings are called "collateral damage," but their deaths are not an unexpected consequence, and it is well-known that the destruction of infrastructure causes further deaths. However, the illnesses and deaths that result from infrastructure breakdowns often don't show up until months or years later, so they may not be attributed to the war.

When safe water is not available, the weakest members of a community (babies, the elderly, and the ill) die of diarrhea, hepatitis, cholera, typhoid, and other waterborne diseases. The Pentagon was aware before the destruction of water purification

Iraqi mother holds up her baby who is hospitalized for diarrhea and malnutrition.

plants, and before imposition of sanctions that prohibited the importing of chlorine for water purification, that the result would be the spread of these serious waterborne diseases.[1]

The breakdown of health routines during a conflict hits children hard. Many do not receive immunizations against common childhood diseases. When children are malnourished, diseases like measles become life-threatening. Many children in refugee camps or conflict zones die of pneumonia or of diarrhea associated with measles. Hepatitis A, tuberculosis, and brucellosis are common in areas of overcrowding, poor sanitation, and poor nutrition.

Shortages of food, medicine, and basic supplies quickly become a crisis when people can no longer cross a river because a bridge has been bombed. Countries like Afghanistan are struggling to rebuild their infrastructure after decades of war and deprivation. The winter brings the most serious hardships. The effects of cold are felt throughout the society, but they disproportionately affect the elderly, the sick and disabled, and the very young. In industrialized countries, even under the best of circumstances, the death rate increases by 20 to 35 percent in winter. Daily caloric requirements increase 1 percent for every degree the temperature drops below 68°F (20°C). When weakened people must go out into the cold to search for food or fuel, they are susceptible to respiratory and cardiovascular disease as well as death from exposure.[2]

Bombing industrial sites also causes longlasting contamination with poisonous chemicals. In Kosovo, NATO bombing caused

- Disengaging Responsibly from Iraq: www.scn.org/ccpi/INOCshortPosition9Sep04.html
- Global Policy Forum: www.globalpolicy.org/security/sanction/indexone.htm
- Voices in the Wilderness: www.vitw.org

thousand of tonnes of extremely toxic materials to be released into the river and soil ecosystems. The region already had serious problems with toxic waste, which were made much worse by the bombing.

The Geneva Conventions, which were designed to protect civilian populations from indiscriminate suffering and death, forbid war on civil infrastructure. In order to prevent this kind of destruction, the United Nations must restore the conventions to the highest priority in international law. If humanitarian interventions are planned through the UN or unilaterally, they must do more good than harm. This means that bombing, attacks by rockets, and any other destruction of civil infrastructure must be explicitly forbidden.

Countries must not impose sanctions that affect the health of a population. The 12 years of sanctions on Iraq resulted in over a million deaths, about half of them children. No political objective can justify that suffering. Sanctions that targeted the leaders and their families — freezing their bank accounts or stopping their international travel — would have been much better alternatives to general sanctions. One of the reasons the United States and other allied countries give for their attacks on a nation's infrastructure, or for the sanctions they impose so infrastructure cannot be repaired, is that the resulting suffering may cause the people to rise up and overthrow their leader. This strategy did not succeed in Serbia, Iraq, North Korea, or Cuba, and punishing a population in order to depose a dictator is a callous and cynical form of coercion.

Leaders who cause large numbers of civilian deaths through bombing or sanctions should be prosecuted at the International Criminal Court. Now that precedents have been established to indict people accused of war crimes or crimes against humanity in a second country (see Solutions 71 and 78), those guilty of such crimes will be unable to travel freely for fear of arrest. The day is soon coming when leaders will hesitate to commit war crimes because they know that they will be held personally responsible and not granted immunity whether they stay in their own country or try to flee to another.

An important role for civil society is to raise awareness that precision bombing does not protect civilians because it destroys the public health infrastructure, and that general sanctions cause suffering to the population but do not usually cause regime change.

Communications building, Baghdad.

GERRI HAYNES

94

Protect Children in War-Affected Areas

Ali Ismail Abbas

I saw his picture.
War is a twelve-year- old boy
With no arms, brown eyes.

— Daniel Amoss

Ali Ismail Abbas is an Iraqi boy who lost his arms and his entire family in an American rocket attack while they were sleeping. He was flown to the United Kingdom for treatment and prosthetic limbs. Daniel Amoss's poem about him was awarded first place in the under-12-years category of the 2003 Barbara Mandigo Kelly Peace Poetry competition of the Nuclear Age Peace Foundation.

Children should not be the victims of violence that is used by adults for political purposes. Sadly, they are often the first casualties. According to War Child, a network of organizations across the world that work to help children affected by war, 1.5 million children have died in wars in the last decade alone. Four million have been disabled, and a further ten million have been traumatized.

UNICEF credits the Coalition to Stop the Use of Child Soldiers with bringing the scale of the conscription and abduction of children in war zones to the attention of the world. The Coalition was formed in 1998 by a large group of organizations that include Amnesty International, Save the Children, and Human Rights Watch. They work closely with the International Committee of the Red Cross and with UNICEF. When the world learned of the

Sri Lankan child soldiers released with help of Nonviolent Peaceforce

Mel Duncan (edited)

Last summer, a group of mothers whose sons had been kidnapped during a temple festival came to one of our teams and said that they had had enough, that they wanted to go after their children. Very quickly, we were able to determine where the children were being held and trained in the jungles, and we accompanied the mothers there. Mothers met with the leadership of the Tamil Tigers who were running the camp. Those local leaders were quite surprised to see this group of mothers, accompanied by a team of a dozen or so international peace keepers from eight different countries. So they sent for their superiors, who came in. In the afternoon, we were able to have UNICEF join us, on the pretense that there were mothers out in the hot jungle and they needed biscuits and tea. Throughout the afternoon, the mothers negotiated directly with the military leadership. By late afternoon the children, 28 boys, were released to their mothers, with bus fare, to go home.

— Mel Duncan is the executive director of Nonviolent Peaceforce[1]

TOM BOTTOLENE/CIRCLEVISION.ORG

Mel Duncan, Founder of Nonviolent Peaceforce.

- Coalition to Stop the Use of Child Soldiers: www.child-soldiers.org
- Nuclear Age Peace Foundation: www.wagingpeace.org
- *State of the World's Children*: www.unicef.org/publications
- War Child: www.warchild.org

use of child soldiers in the wars in Mozambique and Uganda, the practice seemed a horrendous aberration. Now it is clear that it is happening in many countries at war, particularly in Africa and Asia.

Children are often abducted, forced to witness violence, and then forced to participate in it. Sometimes they are forced to hack another child to death when that child has tried to escape. Often they are the lookouts or runners. Girl children are frequently raped and forced to be sexual slaves for military forces. The prevalence of HIV/AIDS means that the girls often contract the disease and then, if they become pregnant, transmit it to their infants.

The situation of children in war is grim, even if they are not conscripted. They suffer overwhelming fear and dread, malnutrition, the loss of family members, loss of stability, and, most importantly, they suffer the loss of childhood. The psychological trauma of being a witness to the savagery of warfare may never heal, even if the armed conflict eventually ends.

In El Salvador in 1985, Dr. James Grant, then director of UNICEF, recognized that children in war zones were not being immunized.[2] He met with the government to ask for a three-day ceasefire so that he could bring in health teams to immunize the children and women under 40. The government said they could not have a ceasefire because they did not recognize the guerrilla army,

but they would not fire any weapons for those three days. With this nonagreement in hand, Grant flew to meet the rebel leaders. They refused to recognize the government, but agreed to hold their fire for three "days of tranquility." Some 20,000 health workers immunized 250,000 small children against polio, measles, diphtheria, tetanus, and whooping cough. The process was repeated for six years. As time went by, it was possible to negotiate the days of tranquility with both parties in the same room. One government member admitted that the ceasefires had changed the context and permitted both groups to consider an eventual end to hostilities.

Susan Granada, a Nonviolent Peaceforce Field Team member from the Philippines talks with refugees in a camp near Jaffna, Sri Lanka.

95

Comply with National and International Law Regarding Prisoners

At the end of World War II, the scale of the atrocities perpetrated by the Nazis and Japanese against defenseless civilians and prisoners so shook the world that leaders agreed to a set of principles to outlaw behavior that is unacceptable even in the chaos of war.

In 1949, the Geneva Conventions became the basis of modern international humanitarian law. The conventions have been signed and ratified by 188 states. By accepting them, states commit themselves to the humane treatment of noncombatants and prisoners of war, with the expectation that their own people will be treated humanely by their adversaries.

Additional protocols from 1997, and other humanitarian treaties, supplement the 1949 conventions and give details about the medical and humanitarian care that must be made available to all who require medical care, regardless of whether they are combatants, prisoners, or civilians. Medical units must be respected and protected at all times and must not be the object of attack.

All military personnel are required to receive training in the Geneva Conventions and humanitarian law. Contractors who are combatants in war must also be held responsible to the same laws.

The Conventions state:

"**Prisoners of war must at all times be humanely treated. Any unlawful act or omission by the Detaining Power causing death or seriously endangering the health of a prisoner of war in**

The detention facility at Guantanamo Bay has become the gulag of our times ... When the most powerful country in the world thumbs its nose at the rule of law and human rights, it grants a licence to others to commit abuse with impunity and audacity.

— Amnesty International Report 2005

its custody is prohibited ... prisoners of war must at all times be protected, particularly against acts of violence or intimidation and against insults and public curiosity."

"No physical or mental torture, nor any other form of coercion, may be inflicted on prisoners of war to secure from them information of any kind whatever."

Prisoners have the right to be visited by the Red Cross or the Red Crescent Society, to practice their religious faith, and, among many other rights, to send and receive mail.

On March 31, 1999, three American soldiers were captured in Yugoslavia close to the Macedonian border. The soldiers were shown on Serb TV with cuts and bruises on their faces, but they otherwise appeared healthy. The United States accused Yugoslavia of denying the soldiers their rights under the Geneva Conventions, which recognize the right of the International Committee of the Red Cross (ICRC) to visit prisoners of war. On April 26, the president of the ICRC, Cornelio Sommaruga, was able to visit with the prisoners, hand over mail from their families, and receive mail in return. The ICRC

- Center for Defense Information: www.cdi.org
- Geneva Conventions:
  www.unhchr.ch/html/menu3/b/91.htm
- *War is a Force That Gives Us Meaning*
  by Chris Hedges, Free Press, 2002

maintains strict neutrality and sends its report to the government involved, not to the public.

It is precisely because there are standards of civilized behavior beneath which no nation must fall that civil society demands an end to the abuse and torture of prisoners in Iraq, Afghanistan, and Guatanamo Bay. There must also be an end to the attacks on medical units and humanitarian organizations by all sides in conflicts. A country must maintain its integrity. If it doesn't, when the war is over it will have lost its soul.

Chris Hedges, who was a war correspondent for 15 years, has written a very troubling book, *War Is a Force That Gives Us Meaning*. He states that atrocities characterize all wars, without exception. "If we don't understand what war is, how it perverts us, how it corrupts us, how it dehumanizes us, how it ultimately invites us to our own self-annihilation, then we can become the victim of war itself."

Hedges describes times when he realized there was a force more powerful than war. That force is love. He writes of a Muslim man who fed milk to a Serb baby for 200 days while his neighbors heaped abuse on him. When he interviewed the Serb couple whose baby had been saved, they said they could never denigrate Muslims the way their Serb neighbors could because of that act.

He wrote, "What appear to be small acts of love — in those acts are the seeds of hope. That little child may grow up in the Serb part of Bosnia, where to this day there's terribly racist rhetoric against Muslims. And that child must know she is alive because of a poor Muslim farmer whom she may never meet."

When leaders do not obey the Geneva Conventions and order or permit the torture and abuse of prisoners, the responsibility for moral behavior falls to the individual soldier. Some refuse to participate in brutality and risk their own lives to oppose it. Their stories, like the story of the Muslim farmer, remind us that we have a choice to refuse to be complicit with evil.

We must ensure that the Geneva Conventions are upheld because war is a dehumanizing force and atrocities are so common. At the same time, we must be aware of how some individuals rise above such brutality and act with great compassion.

"Is There Such a Thing as a Just War?" Chris Hedges speaks at Salve Regina University, 2004.

96

Be a Bridge Across a Conflict

> Hope is not the conviction that something will turn out well, but the certainty that something makes sense regardless of how it turns out.
>
> — Vaclav Havel

Many nations have acted as bridges across conflicts for decades. The Scandinavian countries and Switzerland are well-known for bringing together antagonistic parties to meet in a neutral space where talks can take place in as relaxed an atmosphere as possible. Several American presidents hosted such meetings at Camp David and elsewhere, with success in either ending war (between Egypt and Israel) or in developing accords that advanced peace proposals (Israeli/Palestinian; Northern Ireland).

Talks that might not be possible in other settings are often productive when the host brings the prestige of the US presidency. There is considerably more pressure on the leaders to come to an agreement when the entire world is watching.

Civil society contacts that are developed through kinship, religious, and ethnic bonds can be useful in encouraging parties to negotiate. Many election monitors in Ukraine's Orange Revolution were Canadians of Ukrainian origin, a large number of whom were supported by the Canadian government. They were extremely moved to be present at the historic event, and their presence contributed to the restraint of government troops.

If third-party nations can offer economic benefits as an incentive for the antagonistic nations to conclude a peace agreement, it can be an important contribution. Such benefits can include trade concessions, the end of embargoes, or the supply of energy and food aid.

The UN can work as a friend of the peace process and bring expertise and benefits to the negotiating parties. Sometimes, after lengthy negotiations by third parties have advanced the process to the place where agreement is possible, highly respected leaders can step in to offer support for the final peace agreement. This gives prestige to the leaders who accept the agreement, and reduces loss of face. Jimmy Carter and Nelson Mandela have both played this role.

Many national governments support agencies and NGOs that provide expertise in making the transformation to democracy, establishing justice systems, developing independent media, training magistrates, supporting programs to prepare women for leadership, and providing public education in participatory democracy.

Support Civil Society in Building Bridges

NGOs that work to bring people together from both sides of a conflict rely on major grants from governments or foundations to carry out their projects. However, as governments turn for help to international NGOs working in conflict areas, they need to respect the autonomy and neutrality of the NGOs. When people believe that an NGO has become the arm of a government, its members can be targeted for assassination. This is what happened to Doctors Without Borders in Afghanistan when military forces began distributing humanitarian aid and

- Global Action to Prevent War: www.globalactionpw.org
- Tobin Tax Initiative: www.ceedweb.org/iirp
- World Federalists: www.wfm.org

blurred the line between neutral aid organizations and the army.

Draw Attention to Areas in Conflict

Members of government who travel on fact-finding missions to areas in conflict are able to focus media attention on the area and can propose credible policies if their government wishes to intervene as a third party. Such trips often result in a state stopping its human rights abuses because of the negative publicity.

Develop a New Approach for Failed States

Wealthy governments must also develop new approaches for failed states. Leaving them in chaos and misery does not fulfill the wealthy country's international responsibility to protect a population. Failed states also provide safe havens for terrorist organizations, and illegal traders in drugs and arms. When negotiations occur outside a failed state, such as Somalia, the third-party intervenors need to ensure women are included in the discussions if they are going to succeed.

Fund Peace Operations

Peace operations need an assured source of funding. There are several proposals that could provide a large amount of money without putting the burden on a single state. One proposal, known as the Tobin tax (named after James Tobin, the economist who suggested it), would place a small tax on international currency transactions. Another proposal is to add a small tax to airline tickets at the place where the flights originate. These taxes do not affect the poor, but spread the responsibility among those who benefit from global security.

On March 23, 1999, the Canadian House of Commons passed a motion "that, in the opinion of the House, the government should enact a tax on financial transactions in concert with the international community."[1]

First generation Canadian/Ukrainian Daniel Sikorskyi joined in the celebrations in Ukraine during the Orange Revolution, 2004.

97

Adopt the Hague Agenda for Peace

> My dear friends and fellow peacekeepers. Don't despair. Don't be discouraged. And above all, don't give up.
>
> — Kofi Annan, Hague Appeal for Peace, 1999

The first international peace conference was held in The Hague in 1899 to prevent war and curb its excesses. The active interaction of governments led to the development of several immediate initiatives and laid the groundwork for conventions on warfare, the World Court, and eventually the United Nations. A hundred years later, civil society organized a conference to mark the event, with nearly 10,000 activists, government representatives, international governmental organizations, and community leaders from over 100 countries.

The Hague Appeal for Peace, a four-day conference in May 1999, had over 400 panels, workshops, and round tables. Participants explored mechanisms for abolishing war and creating a culture of peace for the 21st century. The Hague conference demonstrated the new democratic diplomacy — the collaboration of civil society with governments and intergovernmental organizations. Many world leaders and Nobel Peace Prize winners spoke at the conference, including UN Secretary General Kofi Annan. When he arrived in the plenary hall to a standing ovation, a huge banner was unrolled over a balcony. It read "Kofi Annan We Trust You."

The agenda from 1899 had three themes:

- Armaments.
- The peaceful settlement of disputes.
- International law.

In 1999 the citizens' *Hague Agenda for Peace and Justice for the 21st Century* focused on:

- Root causes of war/Culture of peace.
- International humanitarian and human rights law and institutions.
- Prevention, resolution, and transformation of violent conflict.
- Disarmament and human security.

Shortly after the civil society conference, governments held two meetings to commemorate the 1899 Hague conference and discuss the original agenda items. In a historic move, a delegation from the Hague Appeal for Peace (1999) was invited to attend the meetings as an equal partner with equal rights — the first time a civil

ANNA SCHORI

Cora Weiss.

- 1000 Women for the Nobel Prize: www.1000peacewomen.org
- Cora Weiss: www.peace.ca/coraweissbio.htm
- Hague Appeal for Peace: www.haguepeace.org
- International Action Network on Small Arms: www.iansa.org
- International Peace Bureau: www.ipb.org

society delegation sat with and spoke to government delegates as equal partners.

Some of the components of the *Hague Agenda* have already come to fruition. One is the demand that the UN address humanitarian intervention in cases of genocide and war crimes. The principle of "Responsibility to Protect" addresses that issue and places a moral obligation on the international community to intervene on behalf of citizens when the state is unwilling or unable to protect them (see Solution 98). The *Hague Agenda* also called for nations to sign and ratify the treaty that established the International Criminal Court in 1998. The treaty could not come into force until the 60th ratification. Civil society pressure continued unabated until the court came into existence in 2002 (see Solution 78).

The Hague conference launched the International Action Network on Small Arms (IANSA), a global network of NGOs dedicated to preventing the proliferation and unlawful use of small arms and light weapons. IANSA has proven to be an influential and effective network, receiving excellent cooperation from governments.

The Global Campaign for Peace Education was also initiated and became the focus of the Hague Appeal's continuing work.

In 50 key points, the *Hague Agenda* addresses education, the adverse effects of economic globalization, the sustainable use of environmental resources, human rights, gender, role of religions, child soldiers, sanctions, and international law.

One point is relevant to the treatment of prisoners taken in Iraq and Afghanistan. It calls for the establishment of a universal and effective system of *habeas corpus* that would prevent the arrest of people on political, ethnic, or other illegal grounds unless they had legal representation. To add teeth to the system of *habeas corpus*, the *Hague Agenda* calls for the right of appeal to regional or supra-regional human rights commissions or courts.

The *Hague Agenda* calls on governments to make the decision to wage war subject to democratic controls. "Nothing is more subversive of democracy than allowing the power to take a country to war to reside exclusively in the hands of the executive or military branches of government." It suggests that legislative approval be required before a nation can initiate armed conflict, except in extreme cases that require immediate action for self-defense. If the legislative branch of government actually had to hold a debate and vote, the public would be able to have some input by putting pressure on their representatives.

The Hague Appeal for Peace has published a number of books, particularly on peace education. Cora Weiss, the president, is also president of the International Peace Bureau, the oldest peace organization in the world, founded in 1892. She has twice been nominated for the Nobel Peace Prize, most recently as one of those nominated in a highly original project to award the prize to 1,000 women (see Solution 11).

98

Implement Responsibility to Protect

If humanitarian intervention is, indeed, an unacceptable assault on sovereignty, how should we respond to a Rwanda, to a Srebrenica — to gross and systematic violations of human rights that affect every precept of our common humanity?
— Kofi Annan, UN Secretary General

Kofi Annan's question is one of the most vexing and controversial in international relations. When can the outside world interfere inside a nation-state? The world did not provide sufficient peacekeeping troops in Rwanda, and 800,000 people died in that genocide. NATO's military intervention in Kosovo remains controversial because although it was supposed to stop ethnic cleansing, it may have caused more suffering than it prevented.

Canada responded to the Secretary General by establishing the International Commission for Intervention and State Sovereignty. The commission produced its report, *Responsibility to Protect* (R2P) in 2001. The report is a groundbreaking document of principles that are as important as those in the Universal Declaration of Human Rights. It sets out criteria for when and how intervention can be implemented if a state is unwilling or unable to protect all of its citizens.

The document uses strong, clear language that turns sovereignty on its head. It says that state sovereignty implies the responsibility to protect all its citizens. If a state is unwilling or unable to protect all its citizens, state sovereignty yields to the international responsibility to protect. In other words, the outside world must be responsible for the citizens in the event of genocide, mass rape, or starvation.

The international community has three specific responsibilities:

- To prevent mass suffering by addressing root causes and the direct causes of internal conflict and other crises.

- To react to compelling human needs with measures that may include sanctions and international prosecution or, in extreme cases, military intervention.

- To rebuild by providing full assistance with recovery, reconstruction, and reconciliation, and to prevent recurrence by addressing the root causes of the crisis.

Prevention is the most important dimension, and all preventative measures must be exhausted before armed intervention is contemplated. In a requirement that sounds similar to one used in medicine, the least intrusive and coercive measures must be used before more coercive or intrusive ones are tried.

UN Secretary General Kofi Annan.

The commission is very specific in its insistence that the threshold for action must be high, and there must be clear evidence of large-scale loss of life, ethnic cleansing, or mass acts of terror or rape. There must be the right intention — saving lives and averting suffering. The intervention must not be for the purpose of regime change, but rather for the protection of civilians. This stipulation means that interventions that kill civilians cannot be used.

Armed intervention must be the last resort, after a wide range of nonviolent options have been used. If coercive measures are necessary, they must be the minimum necessary to achieve the protection objective, and there must be reasonable prospects of success.

The intervention must be multilateral and under the right authority — the UN. If the Security Council is unable to reach a decision in a reasonable time, the report calls for a "uniting for peace" procedure that can move the discussion to an Emergency Special Session of the General Assembly.

Finally, the intervention must have clear objectives and resources to match. There must be a common military approach with clear chain of command. The goal must be to protect the citizens, not defeat a state; it must comply with international humanitarian law; and it must be coordinated with humanitarian organizations.

There is a final stipulation that protection of the troops cannot become the principal objective.

Member states of the UN embraced the principles of *Responsibility to Protect* in the outcome document of the 2005 World Summit. Their statement focuses on the international body's commitment to prevent genocide, war crimes, ethnic cleansing, and crimes against humanity. It calls for further discussion by the General Assembly of the principles of Responsibility to Protect and its implications with respect to the UN Charter and international law.

The input of civil society is vital as this new approach to sovereignty and humanitarian intervention is discussed nationally and internationally. The World Federalists have established an excellent project to involve civil society in promoting and discussing *Responsibility to Protect*. Our voices are needed to ensure that the principles are not distorted to justify military actions. Join the discussion and let your government know that this is not a new way to sell war, but a new way to protect the innocent.

- *Responsibility to Protect*: www.iciss.ca/report-en.asp
- World Federalist Project to Support R2P: www.responsibilitytoprotect.org

99

Remember Your Humanity

We appeal as human beings to human beings: Remember your humanity, and forget the rest. If you can do so, the way lies open to a new Paradise; if you cannot there lies before you the risk of universal death.

— The Russell-Einstein Manifesto, July 9, 1955

Fortunately for the world, conscience is not limited to civil society. Many people working in government or the economic sector do so because they have committed their lives to serving the public good. I have been privileged to work with many of those people, and I am enormously grateful to them for their dedication and integrity.

Douglas Roche was a member of Parliament from Edmonton, Alberta, for 12 years, was the Canadian Ambassador for Disarmament, and finally was appointed to the Canadian Senate, where he served until mandatory retirement at the age of 75. This distinguished Canadian is well-known internationally for being a founder of Parliamentarians for Global Action and the Middle Powers Initiative (MPI).

The late US senator Alan Cranston was also a leader of the MPI, an organization that bridges between governments to bring about the elimination of nuclear weapons. Senator Cranston was an inspiring figure who was passionately concerned about nuclear disarmament. After serving 24 years in government, he continued his whirlwind speaking and lobbying until he died at age 86. I remember that he carried copies of the Mayors for Peace covenant in his briefcase

and gave them to everyone he met, asking them to enlist their own mayors.

The MPI works with middle powers because when the major powers are at a stalemate, it is often countries like Canada, Sweden, and others that are able to introduce resolutions and work together to advance disarmament. When senators Roche and Cranston called on governments, doors opened wide, and they were able to take influential delegations to meet at the highest levels in middle-power countries.

Senator Roche is a prolific author who brings both creativity and common sense to the proposals the MPI carries to government leaders. He has always recognized the importance of civil society working together with government. When he was Ambassador for Disarmament, he held annual three-day retreats of his 50-person Consultative Group, which was made up of equal numbers of senior officials from the departments of Defence and Foreign Affairs, and members of major NGO peace groups. The Cold War was in full swing, and those of us who attended anticipated stormy confrontations between government and NGOs.

Instead, highly skilled facilitators were able to bring out the common concerns of all participants in a way that produced agreement on key directions for Canadian foreign policy, with no blood shed in the process. The groundwork laid in those meetings has allowed the government to not only continue regular consultations with civil society representatives, but also to include two NGO representatives on the Canadian delegations to disarmament conferences.

- Acronym Institute for Disarmament Diplomacy: www.acronym.org.uk
- Global Security Institute: www.gsinstitute.org
- Middle Powers Initiative: www.middlepowers.org
- Parliamentarians for Global Action: www.pgaction.org

Sometimes governments make inspired choices when they name their diplomats to the UN or the secretaries of state they send to negotiate in intractable conflicts, such as the Middle East and Northern Ireland. The integrity and humanity of the diplomat can spell success or failure for an initiative, just as the chemistry between leaders can color the outcome of talks.

Sweden's ambassador Henrik Salander led the Swedish initiative to bring together a group of nations, the New Agenda Coalition, to advance proposals for the elimination of nuclear weapons. The coalition was influential in convincing the nuclear weapons states at the UN 2000 Non-Proliferation Treaty Review Conference to agree on the 13 steps to eliminate nuclear weapons (see Solution 80).

Salander chaired the preparatory committee (PrepCom) for the 2005 Non-Proliferation Treaty review, and although he was complimented for his adroit leadership, the delegates were disappointed that the meeting did not grapple with the serious issues facing them.

Salander is also a rock musician who recently reconstituted his old band and is recording again in his spare time. At the end of the PrepCom, he astonished the delegates and NGOs by producing his guitar from behind the platform and wistfully singing his own thoughts to the melody of the Beatle's song "Yesterday" (words below). The enthusiastic applause that followed was a mixture of thanks for his chairmanship and thanks for his giving voice to their disappointment in the outcome.[1]

Summary,

On only my responsibility
So full of endless possibility
Oh I believe in "Summary"

Suddenly

I'm not half the Chair I used to be
No more shadow hanging over me
Oh "Summary" came suddenly
Why did it have to be so correct and factual?
Why not try to say something bold and actua-a-al?

Summary

All my troubles seem so far away
Now I need a place to hide away
Oh I believe in "Summary"
Mmmm mmm mmm

Ambassador Henrik Salander.

BHASKAR MENON/UNDIPLOMATIC TIMES

100

Establish a Global Emergency Response Force

> Too many people are thinking of security instead of opportunity. They seem to be more afraid of life than death.
>
> — James F. Bymes

Healthy societies are supported by three pillars: government, the economy, and an engaged civil society, and all are dependent on a sustainable environment. The third pillar, civil society, is of equal importance to the other three because it brings the conscience of culture to the decisions of power. All three pillars must work together nationally and globally for the public good if we are to prevent violence, terror, and war.

How might the world work together, using the three pillars, to prevent armed conflict? The support provided by the three pillars could be strengthened if they were coordinated to form a sophisticated networking body with authority to respond to the stages of conflict:

- Rising tensions.
- Outbreak of violence.
- Ceasefire and peace agreements.
- Reconciliation and reconstruction.

The body, which I will call a Crisis Center, would receive information from governments, the UN, civil society, and the financial sector and distribute it to accredited parties. The information would include indicators that an area was at increased risk of armed conflict, as well as the field analyses from all sectors.

Each sector would independently implement a series of responses tailored to the particular dimensions of the crisis and would keep the Crisis Center apprised of their actions. Civil society would assess the peace capacity of the society in conflict and set into motion a series of interventions that might include the following:

- Visits by trusted outside dignitaries, specialists in conflict resolution and mediation, or delegations from respected religious organizations or institutes;
- Programs, developed by specialists, for using media to build peace;
- Collaboration by women's organizations inside and outside the area;
- Exchanges with societies that have peacefully resolved similar conflicts;
- Solutions designed to address environmental issues;
- Witnesses and accompaniers who could protect those working toward peace and justice.

All such activities would be developed carefully to avoid making a situation worse by favoring one party or unintentionally providing funds that allowed arms to be purchased.

Governments, regional organizations, and the UN would advance diplomatic measures to defuse the tensions and support initiatives to address injustices. They would stop the flow of arms into the region and provide incentives for the groups in conflict to try working together. Governments would also ensure that aid going to the region was building peace, not abetting the conflict. Outside governments would offer space and confidentiality where leaders could meet on neutral ground for negotiation and mediation.

The financial sector, working with international police, would track and stop money laundering, freeze outside bank accounts of the leaders of the conflict, block outside air travel for

- Forum for Early Warning and Response: www.alertnet.org
- Global Action to Prevent War: www.globalactionpw.org
- International Alert: www.international-alert.org
- International Crisis Group: www.crisisgroup.org
- Responsibility to Protect: www.iciss.ca/report-en.asp
- Safer World: www.Saferworld.org.uk

leaders, and stop the trade of conflict resources that provide the financial fuel for the conflict.

Advances in international law that end impunity for individuals responsible for war crimes and crimes against humanity will deter some unscrupulous leaders from actions that were previously unpunished. Already today, there are leaders who are reluctant to travel because they could face arrest in countries that have indicted them for war crimes.

Multinational corporations' role in promoting armed conflict must be ended by bringing corporations under the control of elected governments. There are many suggestions for how to do this, particularly in the United States. One is to pass legislation to clarify that corporations are not the equivalent of persons under the law. Another is to legislate that a corporation's responsibility to provide profits for its shareholders must not be at the expense of the public good. Corporations must be responsible for the full costs of production, including the environmental and social dimensions, as well as the financial outlay. If corporations' legal obligations were clearly defined, governments would have the option of removing the charter of a corporation that was not fulfilling its full responsibilities.

The Crisis Center, under orders from the UN Secretary General, would deploy a standing UN Emergency Peace Force. Sections of the multinational force would be located in various sites around the world so that it could respond within 48 hours. Its personnel would be trained in the diverse responses needed in a complex emergency. They would train together so that all members

would be familiar with equipment and materials. The group Global Action to Prevent War proposes that such a force would have 10,000 to 15,000 personnel including civilian, police, judicial, and military members prepared to conduct multiple functions. They would provide the first response to an emergency and be replaced by other UN peacekeeping or peacemaking forces as appropriate. This force could also be made available for emergency response to natural disasters such as hurricanes and earthquakes.

UN peacekeepers assisting an injured boy in Kenya.

101

Join the Second Superpower

So hope for a great sea change
On the far side of revenge
Believe that a further shore
Is reachable from here
Believe in miracles
And cures and healing wells

— Seamus Heaney, from *The Cure at Troy* .

Just before the tide turns, the sea appears deceptively quiet. Then rushing fingers of water appear on the shore, signaling that a massive change is already on its way.

The signs of change I see everywhere have convinced me that the tide has already begun to turn toward justice. When I began to follow the Internet reports of the millions of people who marched in 2003 against the Iraq war, I sensed a new global consciousness that each one of us has an obligation to the other, not only to resolve our differences nonviolently, but also to protect and restore our fragile planet. I know that behind the millions who marched, there were millions more working for justice in other ways.

People often ask me what they can do when they feel overwhelmed by despair about the world situation. The best advice I have ever been given is to "think like a plant and turn to the light." Follow the positive and take the small steps that lead toward the world we want, instead of watching the shadow. As truth and reconciliation commissions have shown, the highest qualities in humanity — generosity, compassion, and forgiveness — have the power to overcome the lowest.

A second bit of advice that I have found very helpful is to work within my own sphere of influence. Presidents and prime ministers may not be in my sphere of influence, but people elected in my district are available to me, and they pay attention to letters and phone calls from their constituents. I met with one elected official to discuss my concern about American nuclear submarines visiting our harbor. She was very surprised and said, "In two years, you are the first person to raise a question about nuclear weapons." I was as surprised as she was that no one else had raised this issue.

My family and friends are within my sphere of influence, as I am within theirs. If it is true that each of us is separated by only six degrees from any other person on Earth, then my influence on those closest to me may be spreading to the very people that I want most to influence.

We are all called upon to contribute to this huge, demanding task. The children today are asking us to do it. The children of the future are asking us to do it. And at last, the time is right.

When I think of the profound change that global civil society is helping to achieve, I think of the euphoric experience of being in Kazakhstan in 1990 when the Kazakhs held a massive demonstration in the desert, near the Soviet nuclear test range. The protests forced President Gorbachev to end underground testing. Hundreds of people came from the rest of the world to call for a halt to nuclear tests. Shoshone Indians came from Nevada, in solidarity with Kazakhs who were suffering the health effects of decades of nuclear tests in their region.

When the speeches and demonstration ended, we ate dinner sitting on low stools in yurts, the tents of the Kazakhs. There were 20 of us in each yurt, with a host and an interpreter who sat in the center of a circle of tables. We had a feast of vegetables and nuts, dried fruits and conserves, steaming dishes of spicy lamb, pungent horsemeat, and chicken. Horse milk and fragrant tea were passed along with vodka and cognac.

The host said, "I was raised to believe that there was an enemy lurking outside Kazakhstan, waiting to destroy us, and therefore, we had to test our nuclear bombs here. Now you are in my yurt, and you don't fit my images. Mary, you are not the enemy. Ulff, you are not, and Tom, you are not my enemy. Who then is my enemy?" He paused. "We are all one people. You are more than my friends, you are my family." He asked us to sing for them.

What song would he like? "We Shall Overcome."

It was nearly midnight. I could imagine the US and Soviet satellites faithfully recording the activities at the Soviet nuclear test range, looking down on a circle of white yurts lit up against the night sky. Inside were hundreds of people eating a traditional feast. They paused from their eating, and in a dozen different languages they sang together: We Shall Overcome.

The host asked me to propose a toast from my experience as a woman and a doctor. I said that I could only imagine how a doctor felt delivering a newborn in Karaul, into an uncertain future. Our responsibility is to all children. They have the right to health and peace no matter where they are born.

—Mary-Wynne Ashford

"You are more than my friends, you are my family." Kazakh tribesman hosts international demonstrators in a yurt on the Soviet nuclear test range, 1990.

Notes

Introduction

1.

1. Nicanor Perlas, *Shaping Globalization: Civil Society, Cultural Power and Threefolding* (Quezon City, Philippines: Center for Alternative Development Initiatives, 2000).
2. *Preventing Deadly Conflict* (New York: Carnegie Corporation, 1997).

3.

1. Carl Sagan, "Global Consequences of Multiple Nuclear Explosions" *Science* 222, no. (4630) 1283-1292 (1983).
2. Myron Allukian and Paul Atwood, "Public Health and the Vietnam War," *War and Public Health*, ed. Victor W. Sidel and Barry S. Levy (Washington: American Public Health Association, 2000).
3. Eric Hoskins, "Public Health and the Persian Gulf War," *War and Public Heath*, ed. Victor W. Sidel and Barry S. Levy (Washington: American Public Health Association, 2000).
4. Ruth Sivard, ed., *World Military and Social Expenditures*, 16th ed. (Washington: World Priorities, 1996).

4.

1. *Landmine Monitor Report 2005* [online]. [Cited February 17, 2006]. Annual report of the International Campaign to Ban Landmines, November 5, 2005. www.icbl.org/lm/2005.
2. Michael Renner, "Disarming Post War Societies" *State of the World 2005: Redefining Global Security* [online]. [Cited February 22, 2006]. Worldwatch Institute's flagship annual, January 2005. www.worldwatch.org/pubs/sow/2005/.
3. Les Roberts, et al., "Mortality Before and After the 2003 Invasion of Iraq: Cluster Sample Survey," *The Lancet* 364, no. 9,448 (2004).

4.

4. Eric Hoskins, "Public Health and the Persian Gulf War," *War and Public Heath*, ed. Victor W. Sidel and Barry S. Levy (Washington: American Public Health Association, 2000).
5. *Depleted Uranium* [online]. [Cited February 23, 2006]. World Health Organization Media Centre fact sheet 257, January 2003. www.who.int/mediacentre/factsheets/fs257/en.

5.

1. Will, Lester, "Poll: Most in US Oppose Nuclear Weapons," Associated Press, March 31, 2005 (posted on Truthout website, ww.truthout.org/).
2. Kenjiro Yokoro and Nanao Kamada, "The Public Health Effects of the Use of Nuclear Weapons" *War and Public Health*, ed. Victor W. Sidel and Barry S. Levy (Washington: American Public Health Association, 2000).
3. M.V. Ramana, *Bombing Bombay? Effects of Nuclear Weapons and a Case Study of a Hypothetical Explosion* (Boston: IPPNW, 1999).

7.

1. Ruth Sivard, ed., *World Military and Social Expenditures*, 16th ed. (Washington: World Priorities, 1996); Matthew White, *Historical Atlas of the 20th Century* [online]. [Cited October 3, 2005]. Death Tolls for the Man-made Megadeaths of the 20th Century, October 18, 1998; page last updated June 2005. users.erols.com/mwhite28/warstatx.htm#Rankings.

8.

1. John Perkins, *Confessions of an Economic Hit Man* (San Francisco: Berrett-Koehler, 2004).

9.

1. Sarah Anderson and John Cavanagh, *Top 200: The Rise of Corporate Global Power* [online]. [Cited October 4, 2005]. Report for Institute for

Policy Studies, December 4, 2000.
www.ips-dc.org/reports/top200text.htm.

10.

1. R. Bircham, *The Military and the Environment* (Worldwatch, 1992).

2. Gwynne Dyer, *Future Tense: The Coming World Order* (Toronto: McClelland & Stewart, 2004).

3. Linda McQuaig, "History Will Show U.S. Lusted after Oil," *Toronto Star*, December 26, 2004. Also see Ignotus, "Seizing Arab Oil," *Harper's Magazine*, March 1975 (Available online) www.harpers.org/SeizingArabOil.html. It is possible that Ignotus is a pseudonym for Henry Kissinger.

11.

1. Helmut Anheier, Marlies Glasius, and Mary Kaldor, eds., *Global Civil Society 2004/5* (London: Sage, 2004).

2. Scilla Elworthy and Gabrielle Rifkind, *Hearts and Minds: Human Security Approaches to Political Violence* (London: Demos, 2005), available from www.demos.co.uk/catalogue/heartsandminds.

12.

1. Myriam Miedzian, *Boys Will Be Boys: Breaking the Link between Masculinity and Violence* (New York: Doubleday, 1991).

14.

1. Gene Sharp, *The Politics of Nonviolent Action: Power and Struggle*, vol. 1 (Boston: Porter Sargent, 1984). Also see Sharp's *Waging Nonviolent Struggle: 20th Century Practice and 21st Century Potential* (Boston: Porter Sargent, 2005).

2. *Mahatma Gandhi Complete Information Website* [online]. [Cited September 16, 2005]. Bombay Sarvodaya Mandal. www.mkgandhi.org/.

3. Peter Ackerman and Jack Duvall, *A Force More Powerful: A Century of Nonviolent Conflict* (New York: St. Martin's Press, 2000).

15.

1. Thich Nhat Hanh, *Living Buddha, Living Christ* (New York: Riverhead Books, 1995).

2. Jose Martinez, "Hack Returns Jeweler's Lost Diamond Fortune," *New York Daily News*, August 6, 2005.

20.

1. Walter Wink, *Engaging the Powers: Discernment and Resistance in a World of Domination* (Minneapolis: Fortress Press, 1992).

SOLUTION 5

1. Mel Duncan and David Hartsough, *Draft Proposal for a Global Nonviolent Peace Force* [online]. [Cited January 29, 2006]. April 2000. www.peace.ca/globalnonviolentpeaceforce.htm.

2. Ibid.

SOLUTION 6

1. Lawrence Martin, "Another Case of Mass Deception?" *Globe and Mail*, September 2, 2004.

SOLUTION 8

1. E. Garcia, ed., *Pilgrim Voices: Citizens as Peacemakers* (Quezon City: Ateneo de Manila University Press, 1994).

2. Peter Ackerman and Jack Duvall, *A Force More Powerful: A Century of Nonviolent Conflict* (New York: St. Martin's Press, 2000).

3. "Chile: Defeat of a Dictator," written and produced by Steve York as one of the series *A Force More Powerful: A Century of Non-Violent Conflict*, York Zimmerman Inc. and WETA (Washington DC), 2000.

SOLUTION 9

1. Myriam Miedzian, *Boys Will Be Boys: Breaking the Link between Masculinity and Violence* (New York: Anchor Books, 1991).

SOLUTION 11

1. Michelle Guido, *Gender Split on War* [online]. [Cited October 2, 2005]. Article from *San Jose Mercury News* on United for Peace and Justice website, March 4, 2003. www.unitedforpeace.org/article.php?id=1296.

2. *JWA — Bella Abzug — Biography* [online]. [Cited October 2, 2005]. Jewish Women's Archive www.jwa.org/exhibits/wov/abzug/bio.html.

SOLUTION 13

1. Anne M. Pearson, *The Mahila Shanti Sena: New Women's Peace Movement in India* [online]. [Cited October 2, 2005]. Peace Magazine, Jan/Mar 2004. www.peacemagazine.org/archive/v20n1p15.htm.

2. Acharya Ramamurti, *Total Culture of Peace* [online]. [Cited October 2, 2005]. 2003 Mahatma Gandhi Lecture on Nonviolence, McMaster University Department of Humanities, October 2, 2003. www.humanities.mcmaster.ca/gandhi/Lectures/2003-Ramamaurti.htm.

3. Mariette Sineau, *Institutionalizing Parity: The French Experience* [online]. [Cited October 2, 2005]. International Institute for Democracy and Electoral Assistance, 2002. www.idea.int/publications/wip/upload/CS-French_Exp-sineau.pdf.

4. UNIFEM, *Gender Issues in the Cambodian 1993 General Election* [online]. [Cited October 2, 2005]. UNIFEM East and Southeast Asia Regional Office, October 20, 1997. www.unifem-eseasia.org/projects/cambodia/Camelec.htm.

SOLUTION 14

1. Sara Poehlman-Doumbouya and Felicity Hill, *Women and Peace in the United Nations* [online]. [Cited October 2, 2005]. Life & Peace Institute, *New Routes* 6, no. 3 (2001) 28–32. www.life-peace.org/sajt/filer/pdf/New_Routes/nr200103.pdf.

SOLUTION 15

1. Sarah Hipperson, *Greenham Common Women's Peace Camp 1981–2000* [online]. [Cited October 2, 2005]. A brief history of the peace camp. www.greenhamwpc.org.uk/.

2. *Greenham: A Common Inheritance* [online]. [Cited October 2, 2005]. West Berkshire District Council site on Greenham and Crookham Commons. www.greenham-common.org.uk.

SOLUTION 16

1. Ruth Rosen, *American Mums' Warning of Radiation Ignored* [online]. [Cited October 2, 2005]. Third World Network Features, January 1998. www.ratical.org/radiation/WSP1961.html.

2. Ibid.

3. Brenda J. Valance, "Russia's Mothers — Voices of Change — Committee of Soldiers' Mothers of Russia," *Minerva: Quarterly Report on Women and the Military,* Fall-Winter 2000.

SOLUTION 17

1. Matt Carney, *The Guerrilla Girls of the PKK* [online]. [Cited October 2, 2005]. Transcript from *Dateline* SBS TV, October 20, 2004. www.sbs.com.au/dateline.

SOLUTION 21

1. Dylan Mathews, *War Prevention Works: 50 Stories of People Resolving Conflict* (Oxford: Oxford Research Group, 2001).

SOLUTION 23

1. *Samantha Smith* [online]. [Cited October 3, 2005]. Website of the Samantha Smith Foundation, 2005. www.samanthasmith.info/History.htm.
2. *Soldiers of Peace* [online]. [Cited October 3, 2005]. Online companion to CNN's special coverage *The World's Children*, 1999. edition.cnn.com/SPECIALS/1999/children/stories/child.soldiers/.
3. Ibid.

SOLUTION 24

1. Nola-Kate Seymoar and Juan Ponce de Leon, eds., *Creating Common Unity* (Canada: Friends of the United Nations, 1997).

SOLUTION 26

1. *We Are All Related: A Celebration of Cultural Heritage* (Vancouver, BC: George T. Cunningham Elementary, 1996).
2. UNESCO, *Education for Peace and Reconciliation: Project Descriptions and Educational Materials — Lebanon* [online]. [Cited October 3, 2005]. Descriptions of peace camp program and educational materials, September 19, 2000. www.ginie.org/ginie-crises-links/pr/lebanon.html.

SOLUTION 27

1. C.E. Cunningham and L.J. Cunningham, "Reducing Playground Aggression: Student Mediated Conflict Resolution," *The ADHD Report* 3, no. 4 (1995).

SOLUTION 32

1. *Voices in the Wilderness: 9 Years* [online]. [Cited September 10, 2005]. History and purpose of the organization, March 18, 2005. vitw.org/archives/806.
2. Kathy Kelly, *Where You Stand Determines What You See* [online]. [Cited September 10, 2005].

Article on AntiWar.com website, June 25, 2005. antiwar.com/orig/kelly.php.
3. Ibid.
4. Mel Duncan and David Hartsough, *Draft Proposal for a Global Nonviolent Peace Force* [online]. [Cited January 29, 2006]. April 2000. www.peace.ca/globalnonviolentpeaceforce.htm.

SOLUTION 33

1. Jody Williams and Stephen Goose, "The International Campaign to Ban Landmines," *To Walk without Fear — The Global Movement to Ban Landmines*, ed. Maxwell A. Cameron, Brian W. Tomlin, and Bob Lawson (Oxford University Press, 1998); Jacqui Boulle and Debbie Newton, *Case Study: The International Campaign to Ban Landmines (ICBL)* [online]. [Cited October 7, 2005]. Chapter 2 *Campaigning Toolkit for Civil Society Organisations engaged in the Millenium Development Goals*, published by CIVICUS. www.civicus.org/mdg/2-cs.htm.

SOLUTION 34

1. Democracy Watch, *New Political Fundraising Rules Passed into Law* [online]. [Cited October 3, 2005]. Update on Money in Politics campaign, August 2003. www.dwatch.ca/camp/BillC24AnalysisAug03.html.
2. Micah Sifry, "Clean Elections — Making a Difference" [online]. [Cited October 3, 2005]. *Yes! A Journal of Positive Futures*, Fall 2003. www.yesmagazine.org/article.asp?id=656.
3. Transparency International, *Corruption Fighters' Tool Kit* [online]. [Cited October 3, 2005]. Teaching Integrity to Youth: Examples from 11 countries, December 2004. www.transparency.org/toolkits.

SOLUTION 37

1. Kinda Jayoush, "Passover Time to Celebrate Differences," *Montreal Gazette*, April 23, 2005.

SOLUTION 39

1. Maria Cristina Caballero, "Academic Turns City into a Social Experiment" [online]. [Cited October 3, 2005]. *Harvard University Gazette*, March 11, 2004. www.news.harvard.edu/gazette/2004/03.11/01-mockus.html.

SOLUTION 41

1. Azim Khamisa, *Tariq's Gift* [online]. [Cited September 12, 2005]. *Noetic Sciences Review* 50, December 1999–March 2000, Institute for Noetic Sciences. www.noetic.org/publications/review/issue50/r50_Khamisa.html.

2. Judea Pearl and Akbar Ahmed, "Across the Great Divide," *Washington Post* in *Guardian Weekly*, August 13–19, 2004.

3. Meinrad Scherer-Emunds, "No Forgiveness, No Future: An Interview with Archbishop Desmond Tutu," *U.S. Catholic*, August, 2000; Archbishop Desmond Tutu, *Reconciliation in Post-Apartheid South Africa: Experiences of the Truth Commission* [online]. [Cited October 3, 2005]. Speech given at the Nobel Peace Laureates Conference, University of Virginia and Institute for Asian Democracy, November 5–6, 1998. www.virginia.edu/nobel/transcript/tutu.html.

SOLUTION 43

1. Mark Malan, Phenyo Rakate, and Angela McIntyre, *Peace with Justice? The Special Court and the Truth and Reconciliation Commission* [online]. [Cited February 2, 2006]. Chapter 11, *Peacekeeping in Sierra Leone: UNAMSIL Hits the Home Straight,* Monograph 68 from Institute for Security Studies, January 2002. www.iss.co.za/Pubs/Monographs/No68/Chap11.html#Anchor-4158.

2. Scilla Elworthy and Paul Rogers, "The 'War on Terrorism': 12 Month Audit and Future Strategy Options" (Oxford: Oxford Research Group, 2002).

SOLUTION 44

1. Lawrence Smallman, *Palestinians Weigh Non-Violent Option* [online]. [Cited February 1, 2005]. Aljazeera.net, September 2, 2004. english.aljazeera.net/NR/exeres/65985F75-696E-44CB-B759-16A2320A1457.htm.

2. Martin Smedjeback, *Ecumenical Accompaniers Walk in Gandhi's Footsteps* [online]. [Cited February 2, 2006]. Accompanier's report from Ecumenical Accompaniment Programme in Palestine and Israel, August 30, 2004. www.eappi.org/.

3. Smallman, "Palestinians Weigh Non-Violent Option."

4. American Friends Service Committee, *Nonviolence and the Olive Harvest* [online]. [Cited September 12, 2005]. *Faces of Hope*, AFSC Middle East Resource series, Spring 2005. www.afsc.org/israel-palestine/activism/documents/Olive_Nonviolence.pdf.

5. Nadia Hajib, "The Olive Tree and Its Shadow of Hope", *International Herald Tribune*, November 22, 2004.

SOLUTION 48

1. Johan Galtung, *High Road, Low Road: Charting the Course for Peace Journalism* [online]. [Cited February 2, 2006]. Track Two 7, no. 4 (December 1998). ccrweb.ccr.uct.ac.za/archive/two/7_4/p07_highroad_lowroad.html.

SOLUTION 50

1. Toni Mehrain, *Radio Sahar Seeks Sustainability* [online]. [Cited February 2, 2006]. Institute for Media, Policy and Civil Society. www.impacs.org/media/mediapeacebuilding/ Aghanistan/AfghanistanStories/.

SOLUTION 53

1. Richard Falk, "Opening Speech" (paper presented at the World Tribunal on Iraq, Istanbul, June 24, 2005).
2. Ibid.
3. Arundhati Roy, "Statement of the Jury of Conscience" (paper presented at the World Tribunal on Iraq, Istanbul, June 27, 2005).

SOLUTION 57

1. Andrew Moravcsik, "Dream on America: For Years, Much of the World Did Aspire to the American Way of Life. But Today Countries Are Finding More Appealing Systems in Their Own Backyards," *Newsweek International Edition*, January 31, 2005.

SOLUTION 58

1. Paul Rogat Loeb, "Hope in a Time of Fear," *The Nation*, September 20, 2004.
2. Human Security Centre, University of British Columbia, *Human Security Report 2005: War and Peace in the 21st Century* (New York: Oxford University Press, 2005). Available online www.humansecurityreport.info.
3. Miriam Raftery, *Anatomy of a Peace Movement Part Two: Labor Unions Add Muscle to Anti-War Push* [online]. [Cited February 4, 2006]. Raw Story website, November 1, 2005. rawstory.com/news/2005/Anatomy_of_ peace_movement_part_two_1101.html.

4. Steve Early, "Unions are Joining Peace Parade," *Boston Globe*, March 1, 2003. Available online www.commondreams.org/views03/0301-01.htm.

SOLUTION 59

1. Elisabeth Skons, et al., "World Military Spending," *SIPRI Yearbook 2004: Armaments, Disarmament and International Security*, ed. Stockholm International Peace Research Institute (Oxford: Oxford University Press, 2004).

SOLUTION 60

1. *Forests — Introduction and Campaign Aim* [online]. [Cited September 14, 2005]. Global Witness report on its forest campaigns. www.globalwitness.org/campaigns/forests/.
2. *Crime Prevention and Criminal Justice* [online]. [Cited September 14, 2005]. UN Office on Drugs and Crime report. www.unodc.org/ unodc/en/crime_prevention.html.

SOLUTION 61

1. *Nuclear Free Kobe* [online]. [Cited September 14, 2005]. Report on Kobe resolution to ban nuclear ships from its harbour. www.prop1.org/prop1/jkobef.htm.
2. Metta Spencer, "Mayors Are for Peace," *Peace Magazine*, July/September 2005.

SOLUTION 63

1. The three nonprofit organizations are Life for Relief and Development, Canada Democracy and International Law, and the Canadian Association for International Society for Peace and Human Rights.

SOLUTION 64

1. Ashutosh Varshney, *Ethnic Conflict and Civic Life: Hindus and Muslims in India* (New Haven: Yale University, 2002).

2. Lisa Jones, "A Tale of Two Mayors," *Grist*, April 4, 2002. Available online www.grist.org/news/maindish/2002/04/04/of/.

3. *Leftist Legalizer Elected Mayor of Bogotá in Voter Rebuke of Colombian President* [online]. [Cited February 4, 2006]. Stop the Drug War.org *Drug War Chronicle* 307, October 31, 2003. www.stopthedrugwar.org/chronicle/309/lucho.shtml.

SOLUTION 66

1. *Human Development Report* [online]. [Cited September 14, 2005]. Prepared by the UN Development Programme, 2005. hdr.undp.org/reports/global/2005/.

2. Andrew Moravcsik, "Dream on America: For Years, Much of the World Did Aspire to the American Way of Life. But Today Countries Are Finding More Appealing Systems in Their Own Backyards," *Newsweek International Edition*, January 31, 2005.

3. Diana Barahona, *Return to Venezuela* [online]. [Cited September 14, 2005]. Counterpunch, August 1, 2005. www.counterpunch.org/barahona08012005.html.

SOLUTION 68

1. Andrew Moravcsik, "Dream on America: For Years, Much of the World Did Aspire to the American Way of Life. But Today Countries Are Finding More Appealing Systems in Their Own Backyards," *Newsweek International Edition*, January 31, 2005.

SOLUTION 69

1. Michael Renner, "Disarming Post War Societies," *State of the World 2005* (Worldwatch Institute, 2005).

2. Sarah Meek, *Buy or Barter: The History and Prospects of Voluntary Weapons Collection Programmes* [online]. [Cited February 4, 2006]. Monograph 22 from the Institute for Security Studies, March 1998. www.iss.co.za/Pubs/Monographs/No22/Contents.html.

3. Ibid.

4. "Brazil's Gun Ban Referendum Stirs up Opposing Views," *Terra Viva IPS UN Journal* 13, no. 167 (2005). Available online cosmicfantasia.com/content/view/581/88/.

5. Meek, *Buy or Barter*.

6. *New Statistics Canada Study Shows Decline in Firearms Homicide Rates Continues* [online]. [Cited February 4, 2006]. Press release from the Coalition for Gun Control, October 1, 2003. www.guncontrol.ca/Content/New/release%20on%20juristat.pdf.

SOLUTION 70

1. Elisabeth Skons, et al., "World Military Spending," *SIPRI Yearbook 2004: Armaments, Disarmament and International Security*, ed. Stockholm International Peace Research Institute (Oxford: Oxford University Press, 2004).

SOLUTION 71

1. Saul Landau, "Chile's Pinochet Indictment a Victory for International Law," *Miami Herald*, December 30, 2004.

2. Daniela Ponce, *After 30 Years on Hold, Chileans Make a Breakthrough* [online]. [Cited September 20, 2005]. Article from Pinochet Watch, 2005. www.tni.org/pin-watch/watch58.htm.

SOLUTION 73

1. Bill Moyers, *Keynote Address to the National Conference on Media Reform* [online]. [Cited October 3 2005]. Posted on Common Dreams News Center, November 12, 2003. www.commondreams.org/views03/1112-10.htm.

2. Geoff Mulgan, Omar Salem, and Tom Steinberg, *Wide Open: Open Source Methods and Their Future Potential* [online]. [Cited September 17, 2005]. Demos, 2005 www.demos.co.uk/catalogue/wideopen/.

SOLUTION 77

1. Hilary French, *Global Security Brief #7: Upcoming World Summit Offers Rare Opportunity to Redesign the U.N. For the Future* [online]. [Cited September 8, 2005]. Security brief from the Worldwatch Institute, September 2005. www.worldwatch.org/features/security/briefs/7.

2. Douglas Roche, "The Case for a United Nations Parliamentary Assembly," *A Reader on Second Assembly and Parliamentary Proposals*, edited by Saul H. Mendlovitz and Barbara Walker (New York: Center for UN Reform Education, 2003).

SOLUTION 78

1. *Insight on the International Criminal Court: Tenth Anniversary Special Edition* [online]. [Cited September 21, 2005]. Newsletter of the NGO Coalition for the ICC, 2005. www.iccnow.org/publications/insight/insight_anniv_en.pdf.

2. Jean-Marc De La Sablière, "Statement by the French Ambassador De La Sablière after the Vote of Resolution 1593" (Paper presented at the UN Security Council, 2005).

3. Ibid.

SOLUTION 81

1. *Chronology of State Use and Biological and Chemical Weapons Control* [online]. [Cited September 20, 2005]. Chemical and Biological Weapons Resource Page from the Monterey Institute's Center for Nonproliferation Studies, October 2001. cns.miis.edu/research/cbw/pastuse.htm.

SOLUTION 82

1. Steven C. Welsh, *Iraq Prisoner Abuse and the Geneva Conventions* [online].[Cited February 12, 2006]. From *CDI Defense Monitor*, Center for Defense Information, July 9, 2004. www.cdi.org/news/law/defense-monitor-prisoner-abuse.cfm.

SOLUTION 83

1. *Missile Defense: The Current Debate* [online]. [Cited January 12, 2006]. Congressional Research Service report for Congress, coordinated by Steven A. Hildreth, updated July 19, 2005. www.fas.org/sgp/crs/weapons/RL31111.pdf.

2. Ernie Regehr, *Reviewing BMD Options and Implications for Canada* [online]. [Cited September 21, 2005]. Project Ploughshares Briefing 05-1, February 2005. www.ploughshares.ca/libraries/Briefings/brf051.pdf.

SOLUTION 84

1. Quoted by Paul Meyer, "The Prevention of an Arms Race in Outer Space: Statement by Ambassador Paul Meyer" (paper presented at the Conference on Disarmament, Geneva, June 30, 2005).

2. Rebecca Johnson, *PAROS Discussions at the 2004 UN First Committee* [online]. [Cited September 21, 2005]. Report for the Acronym Institute for Disarmament Diplomacy, October 20, 2004. www.acronym.org.uk/un/2004paro.htm.

3. Ibid.

4. Ernie Regehr, *Reviewing BMD Options and Implications for Canada* [online]. [Cited September 21, 2005]. Project Ploughshares Briefing 05-1, February 2005. www.ploughshares.ca/libraries/Briefings/brf051.pdf.

5. *Address by Prime Minister Paul Martin at the United Nations* [online]. [Cited October 8, 2005]. Office of the Prime Minister of Canada, September 22, 2004. pm.gc.ca/eng/news.asp?id=266.

SOLUTION 85

1. Robert McMahon, *Central Asia: Treaty on Nuclear Weapon-Free Zone Advances* [online]. [Cited February 10, 2006]. *Central Asia in Focus*, July 29, 2005. www.rferl.org/featuresarticle/2005/07/dc0e71d0-79c1-4213-9b23-d86453c71778.html.

SOLUTION 86

1. *A Decade on the Front Lines: International Crisis Group 1995-2005* [online]. [Cited February 12, 2006]. The Crisis Group history, 2005. www.crisisgroup.org/library/documents/miscellaneous_docs/crisis_group_history_1995_2005.pdf.
2. Ibid.
3. Ibid.
4. Ibid.

SOLUTION 87

1. Doug Mellgren, "Editor sorry for Muslim cartoons," *The Star*, February 10, 2006.
2. James Brandon, "Koranic Duels Ease Terror," *Christian Science Monitor*, February 4, 2005.

SOLUTION 88

1. Martin Bright, *Leak Shows Blair Told of Iraq War Terror Link* [online]. [Cited February 11, 2006]. *The Observer (UK)*, August 28, 2005. observer.guardian.co.uk/politics/story/0,6903,1558066,00.html.

SOLUTION 89

1. "Majority of Israelis and Palestinians Support Geneva Initiative Content," *Haaretz*, January 18, 2005.

SOLUTION 90

1. Justus Leicht, *German Court Declares Iraq War Violated International Law* [online]. [Cited February 11, 2006]. World Socialist website, September 27, 2005. www.wsws.org/articles/2005/sep2005/iraq-s27.shtml.
2. Naomi Klein, "Baghdad Year Zero: Pillaging Iraq in Pursuit of a Neocon Utopia," *Harper's*, September 24, 2004.

SOLUTION 91

1. *The Continuation of the People's Power Revolution in the Philippines. A Pearl of Great Price* [online]. [Cited September 21, 2005]. People Building Peace: 35 Inspiring Stories from Around the World; a publication of the European Centre for Conflict Prevention in cooperation with International Fellowship of Reconciliation and the Coexistence Initiative of the State of the World Forum, May 1999. www.gppac.net/documents/pbp/2/4_contin.htm.
2. *Citizens Take the Initiative in Uraba, Colombia: Zones of Peace in the Heart of a Bitter War* [online]. [Cited September 20, 2005]. People Building Peace (see above), May 1999. www.gppac.net/documents/pbp/2/5_colomb.htm.

SOLUTION 92

1. Geoffrey Forden, Pavel Podvig, and Theodore A Postol, *Colonel Petrov's Good Judgment* [online]. [Cited September 21, 2005]. Peace Magazine 17, no. 2 (Apr-June 2001). www.peacemagazine.org/archive/v17n2p16.htm.
2. Alan Phillips and Steven Starr, *Eliminate Launch on Warning* [online]. [Cited February 12, 2006]. Physicians for Global Survival, 2005. www.pgs.ca/updir/Eliminate_LoW_059.cwk.htm.

SOLUTION 93

1. Thomas Nagy, *The Secret Behind the Sanctions: How the US Intentionally Destroyed Iraq's Water Supply* [online]. [Cited September 11, 2005]. Article from *The Progressive* posted on Common Dreams NewsCenter website, September 2001. www.commondreams.org/views01/0808-07.htm.

2. M.W. Ashford and U. Gottstein, "The Impact on Civilians of the Bombing of Kosovo and Serbia," *Medicine, Conflict and Survival* 16, no. 3 (2000).

SOLUTION 94

1. Carol Boss, *Peace Talks: The Nonviolent Peaceforce* [online]. [Cited February 12, 2006]. Excerpts from program broadcast on KUNM Radio, August 26, 2005. www.goodradioshows.org/peaceTalksL30.html.

2. "Children as Zones of Peace" in *The State of the World's Children 1996. Children in War* (UNICEF, 1996).

SOLUTION 96

1. *Tobin Tax Motion Passes in Canada's Parliament* [online]. [Cited February 12, 2006]. Press release from Blaise Salmon of RESULTS Canada, posted on Tobin Tax Initiative website, March 24, 1999. www.ceedweb.org/iirp/canadames.htm.

SOLUTION 99

1. Rebecca Johnson, *The 2002 Prepcom: Papering over the Cracks?* [online]. [Cited February 12, 2006]. Article from the Acronym Institute's *Disarmament Diplomacy* 64 (May-June 2002). www.acronym.org.uk/dd/dd64/64npt.htm.

Index

About the Authors

Mary-Wynne Ashford grew up in Edmonton, Alberta, and moved to Calgary to raise a family. At the age of 38, she returned to university to study medicine and graduated in 1981 from the University of

Calgary. While running a practice, Dr. Ashford became an activist and has spent more than 20 years writing, speaking, making films, and organizing against nuclear weapons. She also managed to take time out to earn a PhD from Simon Fraser University in response to her desire to understand more about the roots of violence. She subsequently taught at the University of Victoria (UVic) for five years as a tenured professor.

Missing the intensity of medical practice, she returned to work as a palliative care physician at Victoria Hospice until her retirement in 2003. She continues to serve as an adjunct professor at UVic.

Dr. Ashford is currently leading an initiative of Physicians for Global Survival to create a web-based resource called "Responsibility to Care: The Physicians' Call to End War" (see www.r2care.org).

Guy Dauncey is an author, speaker, and consultant who specializes in developing a positive vision of a post-industrial, environmentally sustainable future and translating that vision into action. He has been self-employed for 30 years, working in the fields of positive social, economic, and environmental change in Britain and Canada.

After completing a sociology degree at Nottingham, UK, he traveled overland to India to study Gandhian village life, then crossed the Sahara to experience life in a Senegalese village. Back in Britain, he worked as a college lecturer and was active in the peace movement while researching a book on the integration of consciousness into Darwin's theory of evolution. A bad car crash led to a spell of unemployment, which prompted him to write *The Unemployment Handbook* (1981). Following his involvement with various community economic initiatives, he wrote *After the Crash: The Emergence of the Rainbow Economy* (1987), championing the importance of local economies and socially responsible businesses. He is co-founder of the Victoria Car Share Cooperative; publisher of *EcoNews*, a monthly environmental newsletter; president of the BC Sustainable Energy Association; a director of Prevent Cancer Now!; and author of *Earthfuture: Stories from a Sustainable World* and *Stormy Weather: 101 Solutions to Global Climate Change*. His website is www.earthfuture.com.

If you have enjoyed *Enough Blood Shed* you might also enjoy other

BOOKS TO BUILD A NEW SOCIETY

Our books provide positive solutions for people
who want to make a difference. We specialize in:

**Environment and Justice • Conscientious Commerce • Sustainable Living
Ecological Design and Planning • Natural Building & Appropriate Technology
New Forestry • Educational and Parenting Resources • Nonviolence
Progressive Leadership • Resistance and Community**

New Society Publishers

ENVIRONMENTAL BENEFITS STATEMENT

New Society Publishers has chosen to produce this book on Enviro 100, recycled paper made with **100% post consumer waste**, processed chlorine free, and old growth free.

For every 5,000 books printed, New Society saves the following resources:[1]

38	Trees
3,421	Pounds of Solid Waste
3,764	Gallons of Water
4,910	Kilowatt Hours of Electricity
6,219	Pounds of Greenhouse Gases
27	Pounds of HAPs, VOCs, and AOX Combined
9	Cubic Yards of Landfill Space

---

[1]Environmental benefits are calculated based on research done by the Environmental Defense Fund and other members of the Paper Task Force who study the environmental impacts of the paper industry.
For more information on this environmental benefits statement, or to inquire about environmentally friendly papers, please contact New Leaf Paper – info@newleafpaper.com Tel: 888 • 989 • 5323.

For a full list of NSP's titles, please call **1-800-567-6772** *or check out our website at:*

www.newsociety.com

NEW SOCIETY PUBLISHERS